Intrusion Prevention Fundamentals

Earl Carter
Jonathan Hogue

Cisco Press

800 East 96th Street
Indianapolis, IN 46240 USA

Intrusion Prevention Fundamentals

Earl Carter and Jonathan Hogue

Copyright© 2006 Cisco Systems, Inc.

Published by:
Cisco Press
800 East 96th Street
Indianapolis, IN 46240 USA

Printed in the United States of America 1 2 3 4 5 6 7 8 9 0

First Printing   January 2006

Library of Congress Cataloging-in-Publication Number: 2005922371

ISBN: 1-58705-239-3

Warning and Disclaimer

This book is designed to provide an overview of intrusion prevention by examining Host-based Intrusion Prevention capabilities and Network-based Intrusion Prevention functionality. Every effort has been made to make this book as complete and as accurate as possible, but no warranty or fitness is implied.

The information is provided on an "as is" basis. The authors, Cisco Press, and Cisco Systems, Inc., shall have neither liability nor responsibility to any person or entity with respect to any loss or damages arising from the information contained in this book or from the use of the discs or programs that may accompany it.

The opinions expressed in this book belong to the author and are not necessarily those of Cisco Systems, Inc.

Corporate and Government Sales

Cisco Press offers excellent discounts on this book when ordered in quantity for bulk purchases or special sales. For more information, please contact: **U.S. Corporate and Government Sales**   1-800-382-3419   corpsales@pearsontechgroup.com

For sales outside of the U.S., please contact: **International Sales**   1-317-581-3793   international@pearsontechgroup.com

Trademark Acknowledgments

All terms mentioned in this book that are known to be trademarks or service marks have been appropriately capitalized. Cisco Press or Cisco Systems, Inc., cannot attest to the accuracy of this information. Use of a term in this book should not be regarded as affecting the validity of any trademark or service mark.

Feedback Information

At Cisco Press, our goal is to create in-depth technical books of the highest quality and value. Each book is crafted with care and precision, undergoing rigorous development that involves the unique expertise of members from the professional technical community.

Readers' feedback is a natural continuation of this process. If you have any comments about how we could improve the quality of this book, or otherwise alter it to better suit your needs, you can contact us through e-mail at feedback@ciscopress.com. Please make sure to include the book title and ISBN in your message.

We greatly appreciate your assistance.

Publisher	John Wait
Editor-in-Chief	John Kane
Executive Editor	Brett Bartow
Cisco Representative	Anthony Wolfenden
Cisco Press Program Manager	Jeff Brady
Production Manager	Patrick Kanouse
Development Editor	Deadline Driven Publishing
Senior Project Editor	San Dee Phillips
Copy Editor	Kevin Kent
Technical Editors	Greg Abelar, Gary Halleen, Shawn Merdinger
Editorial Assistant	Raina Han
Book and Cover Designer	Louisa Adair
Composition	Mark Shirar
Indexer	Tim Wright

CISCO SYSTEMS

Corporate Headquarters
Cisco Systems, Inc.
170 West Tasman Drive
San Jose, CA 95134-1706
USA
www.cisco.com
Tel: 408 526-4000
    800 553-NETS (6387)
Fax: 408 526-4100

European Headquarters
Cisco Systems International BV
Haarlerbergpark
Haarlerbergweg 13-19
1101 CH Amsterdam
The Netherlands
www-europe.cisco.com
Tel: 31 0 20 357 1000
Fax: 31 0 20 357 1100

Americas Headquarters
Cisco Systems, Inc.
170 West Tasman Drive
San Jose, CA 95134-1706
USA
www.cisco.com
Tel: 408 526-7660
Fax: 408 527-0883

Asia Pacific Headquarters
Cisco Systems, Inc.
Capital Tower
168 Robinson Road
#22-01 to #29-01
Singapore 068912
www.cisco.com
Tel: +65 6317 7777
Fax: +65 6317 7799

Cisco Systems has more than 200 offices in the following countries and regions. Addresses, phone numbers, and fax numbers are listed on the **Cisco.com Web site at www.cisco.com/go/offices.**

Argentina • Australia • Austria • Belgium • Brazil • Bulgaria • Canada • Chile • China PRC • Colombia • Costa Rica • Croatia • Czech Republic
Denmark • Dubai, UAE • Finland • France • Germany • Greece • Hong Kong SAR • Hungary • India • Indonesia • Ireland • Israel • Italy
Japan • Korea • Luxembourg • Malaysia • Mexico • The Netherlands • New Zealand • Norway • Peru • Philippines • Poland • Portugal
Puerto Rico • Romania • Russia • Saudi Arabia • Scotland • Singapore • Slovakia • Slovenia • South Africa • Spain • Sweden
Switzerland • Taiwan • Thailand • Turkey • Ukraine • United Kingdom • United States • Venezuela • Vietnam • Zimbabwe

About the Authors

Earl Carter, CCNA, is a consulting engineer and member of the Security Technologies Assessment Team (STAT) for Cisco Systems, Inc. He performs security evaluations on numerous Cisco products, including everything from the PIX Firewall and VPN solutions to Cisco CallManager and other VoIP products. He started with Cisco doing research for Cisco Secure Intrusion Detection System (formerly NetRanger) and Cisco Secure Scanner (formerly NetSonar).

Jonathan Hogue, CISSP, is a technical marketing engineer in Cisco Security Business Unit, where his primary focus is the Cisco Security Agent. He has been involved with host-based security products since 1999 when he joined Trend Micro. In 2001, he began working with one of the first host intrusion prevention products, StormWatch by Okena, Inc. Okena was subsequently acquired by Cisco Systems.

About the Technical Reviewers

Greg Abelar has been an employee of Cisco Systems since December 1996. He was an original member of the Cisco Technical Assistance Security team, helping to hire and train many of the engineers. He has held various positions in both the Security Architecture and Security Technical Marketing Engineering teams at Cisco. Greg is the primary founder and project manager of the Cisco written CCIE Security exam.

Gary Halleen has been an employee of Cisco Systems, Inc., since 2000, and is a consulting systems engineer for security products. Gary works closely with Cisco security product teams and has presented at Networkers and other security conferences. Before he worked at Cisco, Gary held security positions at a college and an Internet service provider. Working with local law enforcement, Gary helped to prosecute the first successful computer crimes conviction in his state.

Shawn Merdinger is a security researcher based in Austin, Texas, with seven years of experience in the network security industry. He currently works with TippingPoint (a security division of 3Com), analyzing VoIP security. Before Shawn joined TippingPoint, he worked as a Security Research Engineer with the Cisco Systems Security Technologies Assessment Team (STAT) and Security Evaluation Office (SEO), where he performed vulnerability assessments on a variety of devices, technologies, and implementations. Shawn holds a master's degree from the University of Texas at Austin. Shawn is also an avid supporter of the local non-profit group AustinFreeNet, which helps to bridge the Digital Divide.

Dedications

Earl's dedication: Without my loving family, I would not be where I am today. They always support all the projects that I undertake. Therefore, I dedicate this book to my wife Chris, my daughter Ariel, and my son Aidan.

Jonathan's dedication: To my wife Liz, for believing in me.

Acknowledgments

First, we want to say that many people helped us during the writing of this book (too many to be listed here). Everyone that we have dealt with has been very supportive and cooperative. The technical editors, Greg Abelar, Shawn Merdinger, and Gary Halleen, supplied us with their excellent insight and greatly improved the accuracy and clarity of the text.

This Book Is Safari Enabled

The Safari® Enabled icon on the cover of your favorite technology book means the book is available through Safari Bookshelf. When you buy this book, you get free access to the online edition for 45 days.

Safari Bookshelf is an electronic reference library that lets you easily search thousands of technical books, find code samples, download chapters, and access technical information whenever and wherever you need it.

To gain 45-day Safari Enabled access to this book:

- Go to http://www.ciscopress.com/safarienabled
- Enter the ISBN of this book (shown on the back cover, above the bar code)
- Log in or Sign up (site membership is required to register your book)
- Enter the coupon code 4NF1-NPSG-QN6H-3TGF-DYJP

If you have difficulty registering on Safari Bookshelf or accessing the online edition, please e-mail customer-service@safaribooksonline.com.

Contents at a Glance

Introduction   xxi

Part I   Intrusion Prevention Overview   3

Chapter 1   Intrusion Prevention Overview 5

Chapter 2   Signatures and Actions   33

Chapter 3   Operational Tasks   53

Chapter 4   Security in Depth   71

Part II   Host Intrusion Prevention   87

Chapter 5   Host Intrusion Prevention Overview   89

Chapter 6   HIPS Components   101

Part III   Network Intrusion Prevention   133

Chapter 7   Network Intrusion Prevention Overview   135

Chapter 8   NIPS Components   149

Part IV   Deployment Solutions   175

Chapter 9   Cisco Security Agent Deployment   177

Chapter 10   Deploying Cisco Network IPS   203

Chapter 11   Deployment Scenarios   229

Part V   Appendix   259

Appendix A   261

Glossary   271

Index   278

Contents

Introduction   xxi

Part I   Intrusion Prevention Overview   3

Chapter 1   Intrusion Prevention Overview 5

Evolution of Computer Security Threats 5

Technology Adoption 7

Client-Server Computing 7

The Internet 9

Wireless Connectivity   10

Mobile Computing   10

Target Value   11

Information Theft   12

Zombie Systems   12

Attack Characteristics   12

Attack Delivery Mechanism   13

Attack Complexity   14

Attack Target   15

Attack Impact   16

Attack Examples   17

Replacement Login   17

The Morris Worm   17

CIH Virus   19

Loveletter Virus   19

Nimda   20

SQL Slammer   21

Evolution of Attack Mitigation   22

Host   23

Antivirus   23

Personal Firewalls   24

Host-Based Intrusion Detection   25

Network   25

System Log Analysis   25

Promiscuous Monitoring   25

Inline Prevention   26

IPS Capabilities   27

Attack Prevention   27

Regulatory Compliance   27

Summary   28

Technology Adoption   28

Target Value   29

Attack Characteristics   30

Chapter 2   Signatures and Actions   33

Signature Types   34

Atomic Signatures   34

Atomic Signature Considerations   34

Host-Based Examples   35

Network-Based Examples   35

Stateful Signatures   36

Stateful Signature Considerations   36

Host-Based Examples   36

Network-Based Examples   37

Signature Triggers   37

Pattern Detection   40

Pattern Matching Considerations   41

Host-Based Examples   41

Network-Based Examples   41

Anomaly-Based Detection   42

Anomaly-Based Detection Considerations   42

Host-Based Examples   43

Network-Based Examples   43

Behavior-Based Detection   44

Behavior-Based Detection Considerations   44

Host-Based Examples   44

Network-Based Examples   44

Signature Actions   45

Alert Signature Action   45

Atomic Alerts   45

Summary Alerts   46

Drop Signature Action   46

Log Signature Action   47

Block Signature Action   47

TCP Reset Signature Action   47

Allow Signature Action   47

Summary   48

Chapter 3   Operational Tasks   53

Deploying IPS Devices and Applications   53

Deploying Host IPS   53

Threat Posed by Known Exploits   54

Criticality of the Systems   54

Accessibility of the Systems   54

Security Policy Requirements   55

Identifying Unprotected Systems   55

Deploying Network IPS   55

Security Policy Requirements   56

Maximum Traffic Volume   56

Number and Placement of Sensors   57

Business Partner Links   58

Remote Access   58

Identifying Unprotected Segments   58

Configuring IPS Devices and Applications   59

Signature Tuning   59

Event Response   60

Deny   61

Alert   61

Block   61

Log   61

Software Updates   61

Configuration Updates   62

Device Failure   62

Inline Sensor Failure   62

Management Console Failure   63

Monitoring IPS Activities   64

Management Method   65

Event Correlation   65

Security Staff   66

Incident Response Plan   66

Securing IPS Communications   66

Management Communication   66

Out-of-Band Management   67

Secure Protocols   67

Device-to-Device Communication   68

Summary   68

Chapter 4   Security in Depth   71

Defense-in-Depth Examples   72

External Attack Against a Corporate Database   72

Layer 1: The Internet Perimeter Router   73

Layer 2: The Internet Perimeter Firewall   74

Layer 3: The DMZ Firewall   75

Layer 4: Network IPS   75

Layer 5: NetFlow   76

Layer 6: Antivirus   76

Layer 7: Host IPS   77

Internal Attack Against a Management Server   77

Layer 1: The Switch   78

Layer 2: Network IPS   78

Layer 3: Encryption   78

Layer 4: Strong Authentication   79

Layer 5: Host IPS   79

The Security Policy   79

The Future of IPS   80

    Intrinsic IPS   80

    Collaboration Between Layers   81

        Enhanced Accuracy   81

        Better Detection Capability   82

        Automated Configuration and Response   82

Summary   83

Part II   Host Intrusion Prevention   87

Chapter 5   Host Intrusion Prevention Overview   89

Host Intrusion Prevention Capabilities   90

    Blocking Malicious Code Activities   90

    Not Disrupting Normal Operations   90

    Distinguishing Between Attacks and Normal Events   91

    Stopping New and Unknown Attacks   91

    Protecting Against Flaws in Permitted Applications   91

Host Intrusion Prevention Benefits   92

    Attack Prevention   92

    Patch Relief   92

    Internal Attack Propagation Prevention   93

    Policy Enforcement   94

    Acceptable Use Policy Enforcement   95

    Regulatory Requirements   96

Host Intrusion Prevention Limitations   96

    Subject to End User Tampering   96

    Lack of Complete Coverage   97

    Attacks That Do Not Target Hosts   97

Summary   97

References in This Chapter   98

Chapter 6   HIPS Components   101

Endpoint Agents   101

    Identifying the Resource Being Accessed   102

        Network   104

        Memory   105

        Application Execution   107

        Files   108

        System Configuration   108

        Additional Resource Categories   109

    Gathering Data About the Operation   110

        How Data Is Gathered   110

        What Data Is Gathered   115

    Determining the State   115

        Location State   116

        User State   117

        System State   118

Consulting the Security Policy   119
   Anomaly-Based   120
   Atomic Rule-Based   121
   Pattern-Based   122
   Behavioral   122
   Access Control Matrix   124
Taking Action   124
Management Infrastructure   125
   Management Center   125
    Database   126
    Event and Alert Handler   127
    Policy Management   128
   Management Interface   129
Summary   130

Part III   Network Intrusion Prevention   133

Chapter 7   Network Intrusion Prevention Overview   135

Network Intrusion Prevention Capabilities   135
   Dropping a Single Packet   136
   Dropping All Packets for a Connection   137
   Dropping All Traffic from a Source IP   137
Network Intrusion Prevention Benefits   137
   Traffic Normalization   138
   Security Policy Enforcement   138
Network Intrusion Prevention Limitations   138
Hybrid IPS/IDS Systems   140
Shared IDS/IPS Capabilities   141
   Generating Alerts   141
   Initiating IP Logging   142
    Logging Attacker Traffic   142
    Logging Victim Traffic   142
    Logging Traffic Between Attacker and Victim   143
   Resetting TCP Connections   143
   Initiating IP Blocking   143
Summary   145

Chapter 8   NIPS Components   149

Sensor Capabilities   150
   Sensor Processing Capacity   150
   Sensor Interfaces   151
   Sensor Form Factor   152
    Standalone Appliance Sensors   153
    Blade-Based Sensors   153
    IPS Software Integrated into the OS on Infrastructure Devices   154

Capturing Network Traffic   154
    Capturing Traffic for In-line Mode   155
    Capturing Traffic for Promiscuous Mode   157
        Traffic Capture Devices   158
        Cisco Switch Capture Mechanisms   161
Analyzing Network Traffic   164
    Atomic Operations   164
    Stateful Operations   164
    Protocol Decode Operations   165
    Anomaly Operations   165
    Normalizing Operations   165
Responding to Network Traffic   166
    Alerting Actions   166
    Logging Actions   167
    Blocking Actions   167
    Dropping Actions   167
Sensor Management and Monitoring   168
    Small Sensor Deployments   168
    Large Sensor Deployments   169
Summary   170

Part IV Deployment Solutions   175

Chapter 9   Cisco Security Agent Deployment   177
Step1: Understand the Product   178
    Components   178
        Cisco Security Agents   178
        CSA Management   179
    Capabilities   179
Step 2: Predeployment Planning   180
    Review the Security Policy   180
    Define Project Goals   181
        Balance   181
        Problems to Solve   183
    Select and Classify Target Hosts   184
        Select Target Hosts   184
        Classify Selected Hosts   185
    Plan for Ongoing Management   187
    Choose the Appropriate Management Architecture   187
Step 3: Implement Management   189
    Install and Secure the CSA MC   189
    Understand the MC   190
    Configure Groups   191
        Policy Groups   191
        Secondary Groups   192
    Configure Policies   194

Step 4: Pilot   194

Scope   195

Objectives   195

Step 5: Tuning   196

Step 6: Full Deployment   197

Step 7: Finalize the Project   198

Summary   199

Understand the Product   199

Predeployment Planning   199

Implement Management   200

Pilot   200

Tuning   200

Full Deployment   200

Finalize the Project   200

Chapter 10   Deploying Cisco Network IPS   203

Step 1: Understand the Product   205

Sensors Available   205

Cisco IPS 4200 Series Appliance Sensors   206

Cisco Catalyst 6500 Series IDS Module   206

Cisco IDS Network Module   207

Cisco IOS IPS Sensors   208

In-line Support   208

Management and Monitoring Options   209

Command-Line Interface   209

IPS Device Manager   209

CiscoWorks Management Center for IPS Sensors   209

CS-MARS   210

NIPS Capabilities   211

Signature Database and Update Schedule   212

Step 2: Predeployment Planning   212

Review the Security Policy   212

Define Deployment Goals   213

Security Posture   213

Problems to Solve   215

Select and Classify Sensor Deployment Locations   216

Austin Headquarters Site   216

Large Sales Office Sites   217

Manufacturing Sites   218

Small Sales Office Sites   218

Plan for Ongoing Management   218

Choose the Appropriate Management Architecture   218

Step 3: Sensor Deployment   221

Understand Sensor CLI and IDM   221

Install Sensors   221
  Configuring the Sensor   221
  Cabling the Sensor   222
Install and Secure the IPS MC and Understand the Management Center   222

Step 4: Tuning   222
  Identify False Positives   223
  Configure Signature Filters   224
  Configure Signature Actions   224

Step 5: Finalize the Project   225

Summary   225
  Understand the Product   226
  Predeployment Planning   226
  Sensor Deployment   226
  Tuning   226
  Finalize the Project   227

Chapter 11   Deployment Scenarios   229

Large Enterprise   229
  Limiting Factors   231
  Security Policy Goals   231
  HIPS Implementation   231
    Target Hosts   232
    Management Architecture   232
    Agent Configuration   233
  NIPS Implementation   233
    Sensor Deployment   234
    NIPS Management   235

Branch Office   236
  Limiting Factors   237
  Security Policy Goals   237
  HIPS Implementation   238
    Target Hosts   238
    Management Architecture   238
    Agent Configuration   238
  NIPS Implementation   239
    Sensor Deployment   239
    NIPS Management   239

Medium Financial Enterprise   240
  Limiting Factors   241
  Security Policy Goals   241
  HIPS Implementation   241
    Target Hosts   242
    Management Architecture   242
    Agent Configuration   242

NIPS Implementation 242
   Sensor Deployment 242
   NIPS Management 243
Medium Educational Institution 243
Limiting Factors 244
Security Policy Goals 245
HIPS Implementation 245
   Target Hosts 245
   Management Architecture 245
   Agent Configuration 246
NIPS Implementation 246
   Sensor Deployment 246
   NIPS Management 247
Small Office 247
Limiting Factors 248
Security Policy Goals 248
HIPS Implementation 248
   Target Hosts 249
   Management Architecture 249
   Agent Configuration 249
NIPS Implementation 250
Home Office 250
Limiting Factors 251
Security Policy Goals 251
HIPS Implementation 251
   Management Architecture 251
   Agent Configuration 251
NIPS Implementation 252
Summary 252
Large Enterprise 253
Branch Office 253
Medium Financial Enterprise 254
Medium Educational Institution 254
Small Office 255
Home Office 255

Part V Appendix 259

Appendix A 261

Glossary 271

Index 278

Icons Used in This Book

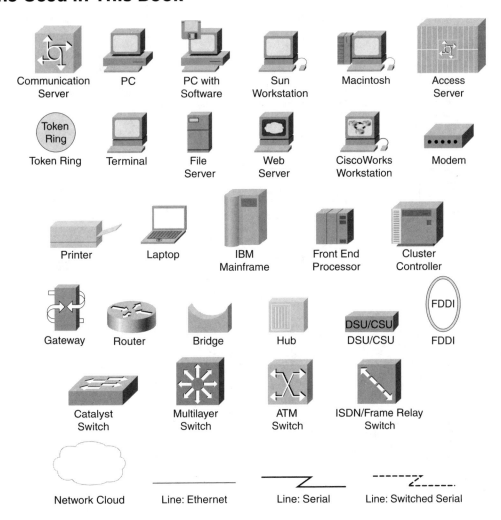

Command Syntax Conventions

The conventions used to present command syntax in this book are the same conventions used in the IOS Command Reference. The Command Reference describes these conventions as follows:

- **Boldface** indicates commands and keywords that are entered literally as shown. In actual configuration examples and output (not general command syntax), boldface indicates commands that are manually input by the user (such as a **show** command).

- *Italics* indicate arguments for which you supply actual values.

- Vertical bars (|) separate alternative, mutually exclusive elements.

- Square brackets [ ] indicate optional elements.

- Braces { } indicate a required choice.

- Braces within brackets [{ }] indicate a required choice within an optional element.

Introduction

Intrusion Prevention is a fairly new technology that you can deploy to protect your network from attack and help enforce your security policy guidelines. Understanding this technology is vital to successfully deploying this technology on your network. This book is designed to provide an overview of Intrusion Prevention that enables technology analysts and architects, especially those in charge of corporate security, to determine how Intrusion Prevention can be deployed on their networks. Furthermore, the information provided assists the reader to assess the benefits of Intrusion Prevention.

Goals and Methods

The goal of this book is to provide an introduction and in-depth overview of Intrusion Prevention as a technology, rather than a technical configuration guide. It uses real-world scenarios and fictitious case studies to walk readers through the lifecycle of an IPS project from needs definition to deployment considerations. Cisco IPS products are used as examples to help readers learn how IPS works, make decisions about how and when to use the technology, and what "flavors" of IPS are available. However, the intent of the material is to provide information on Intrusion Prevention as a technology, not just Cisco Intrusion Prevention products. The book answers questions such as the following:

- Where did IPS come from? How has it evolved?
- How does IPS work? What components does it have?
- What security needs can IPS address? How?
- Does IPS work with other security products? What is the "big picture?"
- Are there best practices related to IPS? What are they?
- How is IPS deployed, and what should be considered before a deployment?

Intrusion Prevention can be applied to your network at both the host level and at the network level. Each of these levels has specific capabilities that complement each other to provide a stronger overall level of security protection. This book explains the benefits of each of these areas of protection, and it walks the reader through detailed deployment examples to help you understand the steps you need to perform to deploy Intrusion Prevention on your network.

This Book's Audience

The primary audience for this book comprises information technology analysts and architects, especially those in charge of corporate security, networks, and business needs. These people should have an intermediate level of experience. The secondary audience includes network and security engineers with advanced experience as well as general technology analysts and journalists with experience at a beginner's level.

This book assumes that the reader has a basic understanding of common security technologies such as antivirus, Intrusion Detection Systems, and firewalls. Readers should also have a basic understanding of security threat and security regulations.

How This Book Is Organized

This book is organized into five major parts with subsections for each part. Part I introduces Intrusion Prevention technology as a whole, with subsections that detail the history and evolution of Intrusion Prevention System (IPS), the reason for its evolution, and continuing technology trends. Part II focuses on Host Intrusion Prevention specifically, how it works technically, an in-depth technical look at its components, what problems it can solve, purchase decisions, and so on. Part III examines Network Intrusion Prevention in a similar manner. Part IV delves into deployment of both technologies. Part V provides a sample Request for Information (RFI) document as well as a glossary of some key terms associated with Intrusion Prevention.

- **Part I: Intrusion Prevention Overview**

  The initial part provides a high-level overview of intrusion prevention. This overview provides the reader with a strong background understanding of Intrusion Prevention that is expanded in the Host Intrusion Prevention and Network Intrusion Prevention parts.

  — **Chapter 1, "Intrusion Prevention Overview"**—This chapter examines the factors that led to the existence of IPS, the evolution of security threats, the evolution of attack mitigation, and basic IPS capabilities.

  — **Chapter 2, "Signature and Actions"**—This chapter discusses the types, triggers, and actions of IPS signatures.

  — **Chapter 3, "Operational Tasks"**—This chapter reviews the high-level tasks related to using IPS. These include deployment, configuration, monitor IPS activities, and secure IPS communications.

  — **Chapter 4, "Security in Depth"**—This chapter demonstrates the importance of security in depth. It gives examples, explains the role of the security policy, and describes future IPS developments that re-enforce the concept.

- **Part II: Host Intrusion Prevention**

  This part provides detailed information about Host Intrusion Prevention and uses Cisco Security Agent (CSA) as a realistic example. The information provided, however, is not detailed step-by-step configuration examples. Instead, it explains in detail how the products can be used to provide Intrusion Prevention. Throughout each chapter, specific information is provided as to how CSA handles specific Host Intrusion Prevention problems that you might experience on your network.

  — **Chapter 5, "Host Intrusion Prevention Overview"**—This chapter looks at the capabilities, benefits, and limitations of HIPS.

  — **Chapter 6, "HIPS Components"**—This chapter examines the inner workings of HIPS agents and management infrastructures.

- **Part III: Network Intrusion Prevention**

  This part provides detailed information about Network Intrusion Prevention, along with realistic information to use Cisco Network Intrusion Prevention products. The information provided, however, is not detailed step-by-step configuration examples. Instead, it explains in detail how the products can be used to provide Intrusion Prevention. Each chapter provides detailed information on Cisco Network Intrusion product capabilities and how those capabilities can protect your network.

    — **Chapter 7, "Network Intrusion Prevention Overview"**—This chapter explains the capabilities that Network Intrusion Prevention Systems (NIPS) can add to a network to enhance its security posture.

    — **Chapter 8, "NIPS Components"**—This chapter analyzes and explains the various components that comprise a NIPS, including various sensor types and management options.

- **Part IV: Deployment Solutions**

  This section walks you through the deployment of Intrusion Prevention in different network configurations.

    — **Chapter 9, "Cisco Security Agent Deployment"**—This chapter describes the tasks and decisions you need to make during the implementation of a real-world HIPS product, the Cisco Security Agent (CSA).

    — **Chapter 10, "Deploying Cisco Network IPS"**—This chapter describes the tasks and decisions you need to make during the implementation of a real-world NIPS deployment, using the Cisco Network Intrusion Prevention System products as an example.

    — **Chapter 11, "Deployment Scenarios"**—This chapter covers an assortment of IPS deployment scenarios where each scenario uses a different type of company as an example.

- **Part V: Appendix**

    — **Appendix A, "Sample Request for Information (RFI) Questions"**—This appendix provides a sample RFI to help the reader understand some of the issues that need to be considered when defining your IPS deployment requirements.

- **Glossary**—The glossary provides the definitions for various terms related to Intrusion Prevention along with definitions of other terms related to the book that the reader might need to understand.

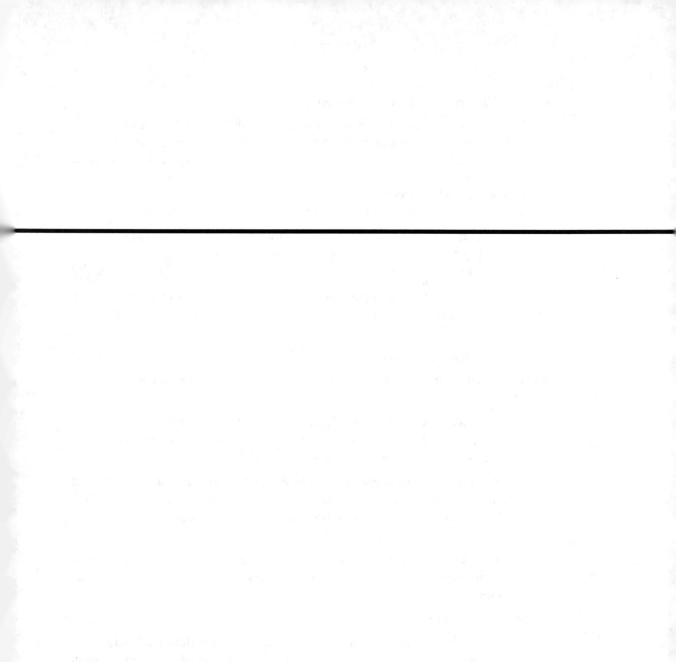

Part I: Intrusion Prevention Overview

Chapter 1   Intrusion Prevention Overview

Chapter 2   Signatures and Actions

Chapter 3   Operational Tasks

Chapter 4   Security in Depth

Intrusion Prevention Overview

Computer and network security products evolve. Like living things, they change, grow, and adapt to reflect the conditions around them. Specifically, new threats to security force conditions in which security products adapt by implementing countermeasures that can handle the new threats. Examining the birth of a product and its evolution helps you understand why the product exists, what it can do, and how it might change in the future.

Intrusion Prevention Systems (IPS) are security protection devices or applications that can prevent attacks against your network devices. These systems began life as an adjunct feature of contemporary products, such as firewalls and antivirus products, and evolved into an independent and full-featured set of products in their own right. You find two types of IPSs: Network and Host. This chapter examines the factors that led to the existence of IPSs. It describes the evolution of computer security threats, the evolution of attack mitigation, and some of the IPSs' capabilities.

Evolution of Computer Security Threats

Security threats have always been around. Anything of value makes a viable target for a thief. Traditionally, theft required physical access to the object being stolen, limiting the number of attackers and increasing the chances of the perpetrator's being caught. This model applied to initial personal computer systems in which the computer was treated like another piece of expensive electronic equipment worth stealing.

Initially, mainframes and minicomputers allowed access to a limited number of directly connected dumb terminals. Gradually, the need for extended connectivity became more important. This need for connectivity led to dialup access to mainframes and minicomputers. Adding dialup connectivity increased the scope of attackers by enabling anyone across the world (with access to a telephone and a computer with a modem) to attempt to access the systems. This access, however, was still fairly limited in that attackers had to determine the phone number to use to connect to the computer system and pay the long distance charges if they were not in the same physical vicinity as the system being accessed. Furthermore, because mainframes and minicomputers were very expensive, attackers had difficulty gaining access to a system to try to find security vulnerabilities (except on the limited number of operational systems).

The development of the Internet has created an environment in which millions of computers across the world are all connected to each other. Furthermore, access to this network is fairly ubiquitous and cheap, enabling any thieves in the world to target your computer, regardless of their physical location. Personal computers are now also cheap. Attackers can easily (and cost effectively) set up various computers with different operating systems and search for exploitable vulnerabilities. Searching for vulnerabilities on systems that they control enables attackers to refine their exploit code before using it on actual systems. After they find a new vulnerability and develop an exploit, they can attack similar systems across the world. Therefore, the way you protect your computer assets has to change to match this new threat landscape. In addition, the international and distributed nature of the Internet makes it very difficult to regulate and control attacks against computer systems.

To protect access to internal networks, most companies deploy a firewall at their network perimeter to limit external access. The development of wireless network access (another technological enhancement) has enabled attackers to bypass these perimeter protection mechanisms. With wireless access, users do not need to be physically connected to gain access to the network. The problem is that wireless connectivity does not stop at the walls of your building. In many deployments, attackers can sit in the parking lot in front of your business and potentially gain access to your wireless network. Without proper protection, this wireless access gives attackers direct connectivity to your internal network.

FIREWALL

A *firewall* is a software or hardware application that limits network access to a private network from external networks. By limiting access, a firewall protects computer resources on the private (or internal) network. Firewalls can control which external systems can access which private systems, as well as limit the systems and applications to which private systems are allowed to connect.

The threats computer security professionals faced two-and-a-half decades ago are comparatively rudimentary and trivial by today's standards. They had no need for IPSs at that time. Unfortunately, threats have matured rapidly since then and are now sophisticated enough to warrant an advanced countermeasure like an IPS.

Many factors impact the security threats to which a computer system is vulnerable. Naturally, some threats are more severe than others, so when trying to understand why an IPS is necessary in today's networks, you need to consider the following factors:

■ Technology adoption

■ Target value

■ Attack characteristics

Technology Adoption

It is sometimes easy to forget that, at 75 years of age, the digital computer industry as a whole is fairly young. You still find plenty of room for innovation, and new innovations in computing occur regularly. Inventions such as the personal computer and the Internet force businesses to change the way they operate.

The operational change might take some time because businesses don't usually adopt new technologies quickly. New technology comes with a set of risks, such as poor return on investment, security concerns, training costs, and so on. However, most technologies reach a point at which the rewards for adoption outweigh the risks. At that point, the technology is widely adopted, and the potential security risks become a reality. Even when these technologies are adopted, however, the objective many times is to simply get the technology working, with security being left as a future add on.

Four widely adopted technologies stand out as having had a tremendous impact on the evolution of security threats and thus the evolution of IPSs:

- Client-server computing
- The Internet
- Wireless connectivity
- Mobile computing

Client-Server Computing

Before the client-server architecture became commonplace in the 1990s, most businesses relied solely on mainframes for their computing needs. Users gained access to the mainframe using dumb terminals that were physically connected to the mainframe (but not each other), had a computer screen and a keyboard, but had almost no processing capability. All processing occurred on the mainframe.

MAINFRAMES

Mainframes are large and powerful computers that support thousands of simultaneous users. Early mainframes operated in timesharing mode, where all users shared processor time, or batch mode, where user programs were sequentially executed on the computer.

Client-server is a computing architecture that has largely replaced mainframes because of its lower cost of ownership. In client-server processing, power is not centralized. Instead, it is distributed across many networked computers, each acting as either a client or server. Clients are expected to provide a great deal of processing power so that the servers can be free to handle intensive computational operations.

CLIENT-SERVER ARCHITECTURE

Servers are passive because they wait for a request from a client, fulfill the request, and send it back. Clients actively send requests and wait for a reply from the server. In either case, both computers must be networked together and have processing capability.

Attacks against dumb terminals were limited because the attacker needed physical access to the system. One common attack against these systems was for one user to use the dumb terminal and then run a program that mimicked the normal login program in an attempt to steal login credentials from other users who tried to use the dumb terminal. A terminal, however, that cannot store data and has no processor is usually not an attractive target. Furthermore, dumb terminals cannot be used as a client or a server because they have no processing capability and are not connected together.

Dumb terminals were replaced by personal computers or workstations that could meet the requirements of the client-server architecture. This resulted in a dramatic increase in the number of target hosts and networks available to an attacker. Figure 1-1 illustrates this increase. Large businesses can have hundreds of thousands of networked computers, all of which are potential targets for an attack.

Figure 1-1 *Mainframe Versus Client-Server*

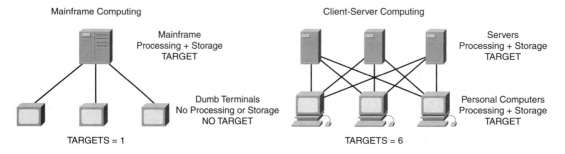

A client-server architecture not only has more targets for an attacker, but it is also all networked together. If an attacker is able to compromise one computer, any computer connected to the compromised system is now a secondary target. Peer-to-peer networking contributed greatly to this problem by increasing the number of potential pathways between the systems. Furthermore, because the networked computers have high-speed connections and fast processors, they are very valuable and powerful targets.

PEER-TO-PEER NETWORKING

A peer-to-peer network differs from client-server because unlike the client-server model, each node on the peer-to-peer network functions as both a client and server and any system can communicate with any other system on the network. Figure 1-2 diagrams the difference between these architectures.

Figure 1-2 *Client-Server Versus Peer-to-Peer Networking*

Client-Server

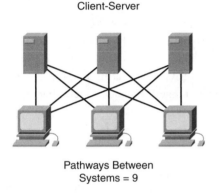

Pathways Between
Systems = 9

Peer-to-Peer

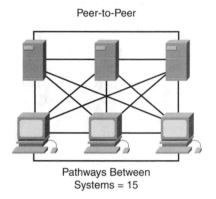

Pathways Between
Systems = 15

The Internet

Client-server and peer-to-peer architectures multiplied the number of the potential targets. Even so, attackers needed to have a way to connect to a network or computer to attack it.

Enter the Internet, which allows attackers to rapidly reach millions of targets all over the globe. Any Internet-connected host or network is reachable by any attacker from practically anywhere. Despite the risks, the Internet is a powerful business tool, and almost every business uses it in one way or another.

INTERNET

The Internet is a global communications network that connects networks across the world, enabling millions of computer systems to interact with each. The Internet originated from the ARPANET network in 1969. ARPANET was a Department of Defense research testbed that interconnected various universities and other research organizations. A common misconception is that the Internet refers only to traffic to web servers. The Internet actually supports numerous protocols and applications in addition to web traffic (such as FTP, VoIP, SMTP, and instant messaging protocols).

A by-product of ubiquitous Internet use is that the communications protocol it uses, TCP/IP, has also grown in popularity. TCP/IP was designed to connect different types of systems together; it wasn't designed to be secure. Using the basic TCP/IP transport protocols presents a number of security risks, but these transport protocols are so commonly used to communicate between systems that virtually every computer is forced to use TCP/IP to some degree to access the network.

TCP/IP SECURITY RISKS

TCP/IP supports various transport protocols. The two most popular are Transport Control Protocol (TCP) and User Datagram Protocol (UDP). By default, both of these protocols send information across the network unencrypted. Because UDP is connectionless, spoofing the source address (pretending to be someone else's computer) is a trivial task, as are flooding and sending malformed packets. TCP connections are also subject to numerous attacks, including malformed packets, resource starvation, and hijacking.

Wireless Connectivity

Traditionally, you accessed a network by plugging a network cable into a switch port on the network. Therefore, to gain access to the network, you had to have some sort of physical access to your facility. Wireless connectivity removed the physical restriction for access to your network.

Wireless connectivity enables an increase in productivity because it enables your users to easily remain connected as they travel from their desk to a meeting in a conference, or from one meeting to another. Furthermore, wireless connectivity is cheaper because you do not have to install switch ports throughout your entire facility.

However, unlike switch ports, the signals from your wireless access points do not stop at the walls of your facility. Without effective security measures installed, an attacker can easily gain access to your wireless network without ever entering your building.

Mobile Computing

Mobile computing refers to the collection of technologies that makes it possible for employees to remotely perform the same duties they could while at the office. Portable computers, mobile phones, and personal digital assistants (PDAs) are becoming just as powerful as similar non-mobile equipment. Still, many of the computing resources a mobile worker needs are stored in the office, so the mobile devices have to be able to access them remotely.

Corporations commonly make these resources available to their remote workers through dialup or Internet virtual private network (VPN) connections. Typically, once a user has made an authorized connection to the corporate network, the user's device acts like an ordinary network participant. It has virtually unfettered access (with maybe only minimal restrictions because of traversing through a firewall).

Having a mobile workforce is tremendously beneficial, but to realize the benefit companies must accept an equal amount of risk. Mobile workers use many powerful and potentially vulnerable devices that are frequently outside of the office. While not in the office, these devices are far more vulnerable because they are not protected by the countermeasures that would guard them ordinarily. At the same time, they are able to access the corporate network at will.

The upshot is that huge numbers of mobile devices are very vulnerable and tempting targets for attackers. Especially considering that once a device is compromised, the attacker can sometimes use the device's remote access to attack the corporate network.

Another aspect of mobile computing is the increased use of wireless network connectivity. Wireless connectivity enables laptops and PDAs to remain connected as users move from their desks to meetings in various conference rooms.

NOTE   Wireless mobile computing also refers to remaining connected while moving from one network or zone to another (such as when switching between different cell phone towers).

Remaining connected increases the worker's productivity, but the wireless access increases the security risks because access to the wireless network does not necessarily end at the walls of the building. This analogy also applies to various wireless devices connected to your computer, cell phone, or PDA, such as wireless headsets, mice, and keyboards. An attacker might place calls on your cell phone by attacking the Bluetooth protocol that enables your wireless headset to communicate with your cell phone.

Target Value

Initially, personal computers were lucrative targets for their actual hardware. Currently, computer hardware is relatively cheap; however, personal computers are still lucrative targets because of the following factors:

- Information theft
- Zombie systems acquisition

Information Theft

Originally, many computer systems were used for local applications, such as word processing and playing games. Over time, especially after Internet usage became popular, the information stored on personal computers (both business and personal) has become much more valuable. Today, it is common for millions of people to access their banks and other financial institutions using their personal computers. Business computers frequently house sensitive information such as source code, locally stored e-mail archives, and business roadmaps. The information stored on computers has become more valuable than the actual systems themselves. Furthermore, these business systems (usually laptops) are frequently used away from the office (when working at home and when traveling).

Zombie Systems

Originally, people had PCs that were connected to the Internet via a dialup modem. These systems, therefore, were connected to the Internet only for a short period of time (limiting the attack window timeframe). With the deployment of high-speed Internet connections, many people have systems directly connected to the Internet 24 hours a day (dramatically increasing the attack window timeframe). Many of these always connected machines are running vulnerable software. By compromising these vulnerable systems, attackers can build a network of machines (known as *zombies*) that they can use to perform various kinds of attacks. Furthermore, these attacks do not directly originate from the attackers, so tracing the attack back to the real attackers becomes more difficult.

Attack Characteristics

The threats resulting from technology adoption are not, by themselves, enough to compel the creation of a new countermeasure such as an IPS. Combine new technology threats with increasingly sophisticated and formidable attacks and you have circumstances dangerous enough to warrant IPSs. This section defines a loose model called *attack characteristics* to categorize the level of threat an attack poses.

The model uses a consistent set of attributes called attack characteristics to characterize attacks. Breaking down attacks into these attack characteristics enables you to compare various attacks using consistent factors. When an attack has one or more characteristics that are dramatically more dangerous than the same characteristic(s) in previous attacks, you have an indication that existing security countermeasures might not be enough to stop it. This section explores four attack characteristics:

- Delivery mechanism

- Complexity

- Target

- Impact

Attack Delivery Mechanism

Delivery mechanism is the method by which an attack is disseminated. When considering the attack delivery mechanism, you need to consider the following two aspects:

- Reach of the attacker

- Protection from discovery

Before media and networks were commonplace, the prevailing delivery mechanism was to deliver the attack in person. The replacement login attack (see the "Attack Examples" section later in the chapter) is a classic example of physical delivery. Of all the delivery mechanisms, physical has the shortest reach. The only targets in reach are the ones that an attacker can touch.

The next best approach is to distribute an attack using media of some kind. The most traditional media are floppy disks, although they are not in much use today because removable Universal Serial Bus (USB) storage devices are smaller and store far more data. Media distribution via floppy disks is more efficient and grants a longer reach than physical access; however, floppy disks change hands fairly slowly, and the reach of this sort of attack is still limited.

Modems, which have been commercially available since 1962, are another option. Attackers created tools they could use to find unsecured modems. Still, finding unsecured modems is a lengthy process, and modem connections are relatively slow. Modems give attackers a longer reach. To improve the efficiency of modem-based attacks, attackers developed tools known as war-dialers to more effectively identify modem connections.

WAR-DIALER

A *war-dialer* is a tool that dials a specified range of phones numbers looking for modem connections. An attacker can start a war-dialer on his computer and let it run for days, attempting to locate potential modem connections. Later, the attacker attempts to connect to the phone numbers identified, looking for modem connections with weak authentication.

The furthest reach currently available is granted by the Internet. Internet access has also become very fast because of high-speed connectivity via cable and digital subscriber line (DSL) modems. Attackers use Internet access to distribute attacks virtually anywhere they want at great speed, with low cost, and with great convenience. Further, the Internet grants a certain amount of anonymity, providing protection from discovery.

Protection from discovery is the second factor that determines the delivery mechanism threat level. It has to do with the risk that the attacker will be identified before, after, or during attack delivery. Naturally, most attackers would rather not be identified.

Physical dissemination is the least protective delivery mechanism because attacker stands a good chance of being spotted. Even with no eyewitnesses, the attacker might leave clues such as fingerprints behind. Remote delivery mechanisms make it easier for the attacker to remain anonymous.

Media, modems, and the Internet are more anonymous delivery mechanisms and thus have a higher threat level. Even so, none of the three are completely anonymous. It might be difficult, but it is quite possible to track an attack back to its point of origin, and thus the attacker, even if it was delivered via the Internet.

Several delivery mechanisms significantly increase the protection from discovery. One method is to use obfuscation techniques, and one such technique uses zombies to deliver attacks instead of the attacker's own machines, thus hiding the attacker from whoever might be looking. Tracking the attack back to the original attacker through one or more zombie systems is definitely difficult but not necessarily impossible.

Another way to avoid discovery is to deliver the attack wirelessly. An attacker can get within range of an unsecured wireless access point with access to the Internet, use it to deliver an attack, and leave. The chances of discovery are slim. An added advantage of using wireless is that it reaches mobile targets like phones and PDAs. Attacks that use the wireless delivery method can easily have a very high threat level. A simple (but effective) wireless attack is called *drive-by spamming*.

DRIVE-BY SPAMMING

Spam involves sending large volumes of unsolicited e-mail. With drive-by spamming, an attacker drives around searching for unsecured wireless networks. Whenever an unsecured wireless network is located, the attacker uses the network to send a large amount of spam e-mail traffic (legitimately from the wireless network). Detecting the true source of this spam can be very difficult.

Attack Complexity

Attack complexity is a measurement of the attack based on the following two factors:

■   Complexity to launch the attack

■   Complexity to detect the attack

The complexity to launch the attack helps you assess how easy it is for an attacker to use a specific attack. The more difficult an attack is to launch, the fewer the number of attackers that can successfully execute the attack. The Internet connects millions of computers together, potentially giving a large number of attackers access to your computer resources. Therefore, it is important to determine how likely it is an attack will be used against your network.

The number of operations an attack performs on the target usually determines its complexity at being detected. An attack that compromises the target and spreads to others performs only two operations and has a fairly low threat level. By contrast, an attack that compromises the target, spreads, deletes files, makes the machine into a zombie, and initiates a denial-of-service (DoS) attack is very complex and should be assigned a high threat level. Nimda and Slammer (see the "Attack Examples" section) are perfect examples of contrasting complexity.

Attack Target

The following two factors determine the threat level in the target category:

- Total number of potential targets

- Value of the potential targets (impact if compromised)

A vulnerability in a rarely used application provides fewer opportunities for an attacker than a vulnerability in an operating system that is used on millions of computers. The larger the potential number of targets is, the more usual it is that a higher threat level is assigned to a given attack.

In general, you have fewer servers than you have clients. Therefore, an attack that targets clients usually has more targets than an attack that targets servers. However, servers are usually more important to an organization than client systems. Servers typically contain more important data and provide important business functions. If a server is made unavailable by an attack, that impacts many users, as opposed to just one if a client is unavailable. Furthermore, a compromised server can be used to attack the client systems that attempt to connect to services on the server (exploiting vulnerabilities in the client systems).

Attacks that target one small category of servers might be assigned a low level of threat. If the target servers provide critical business functions such as web pages and database servers, the threat level is high. Likewise, if both servers and personal computers are targeted, the threat level should be high.

Attack Impact

The final attack characteristic is the impact that the attack generates. Many times, the impact is related to the intent of the attacker. Some common goals of an attacker include the following:

- Curiosity

- DoS

- Theft of confidential information

- Revenge

- Construction of a network of compromised machines

The intent attribute has to do with the objective of the attack. Not all attacks have an evil intent. The Morris worm (see the "Attack Examples" section), for example, was an accident. The author, Robert Morris, meant for the worm to do nothing more than count the number of hosts connected to the Internet. The damage it did was because of a bug in the worm's programming and not intentional at all. Nevertheless, the impact was still a major DoS on numerous systems. The impact threat level, however, was only medium because of the limited use of the Internet at the time.

Since the Morris worm, attacks have become increasingly malicious. Some delete data, steal confidential information, and/or intentionally deny service. Some of the most insidious are written by criminal organizations for the purpose of financial gain. For example, some criminal organizations maintain vast collections of zombies, which they rent to other organizations. Other criminals extort users by encrypting their data and then demanding money to decrypt it. Attacks with these types of intent have a threat level of high.

In other situations, someone with potentially good intentions might try to use a "benevolent" worm to try to remove or counter the effects of a malicious worm. A good example is creating a worm to patch systems that are vulnerable to a specific exploit. Similar to the Morris worm, however, these "benevolent" worms usually end up causing more harm than benefit.

The intent of attackers, as well as the impact of the attack, is very important. If attackers have access to a specific exploit, then they can search out systems that are vulnerable to the exploit, gaining control of a large number of systems to use as zombie systems. On the other hand, if attackers are trying to steal information from a specific company, then they seek out vulnerabilities specific to that company's network and use it to obtain the needed information.

Attack Examples

Now that you know what the attack characteristics are, you can apply them to any attack to evaluate the threat levels. This section uses several real-world attacks to illustrate the process. Also, each of the attack examples demonstrates an increase in one or more threat levels in comparison to prior attacks.

Replacement Login

The intent of this attack is to capture user login credentials. It requires that attackers have physical access to mainframe terminals. Attackers use the terminal to replace the login procedure for the computer with their own.

The attackers' program masquerades as a standard username and password prompt, but when users enters their credentials, it displays an "Invalid Username or Password" message. Users think that they simply mistyped something, but the program actually captures the login credentials and stores them somewhere for later retrieval. After the attackers' fake login program runs, the real login prompt appears, and users can log in.

Table 1-1 outlines the attack characteristics for the "Replacement Login" attack. There was no real discovery year for this technique. The delivery mechanism can be categorized as physical because you had to physically log into a dumb terminal connected to the mainframe and run your fake login program. The fake login program, however, was usually not very complex because most of the dumb terminals supported only textual displays (unlike the highly graphical nature of current displays). The target was the mainframe, but most accounts had limited privileges; therefore, the target threat level was low because the effect to the actual mainframe operation was limited. The impact was theft of login credentials, but the accounts usually had limited privileges (and the victim had to log in at the same terminal where your fake login program was running). So, the impact was considered only in the medium range.

Table 1-1   *Replacement Login Attack Characteristics*

Discovery Year	Delivery Mechanism	Complexity	Target	Impact
None	Physical (Threat level low)	Simple (Threat level low)	Mainframe computers (Threat level low)	Theft of information (Threat level medium)

The Morris Worm

In 1988, a Cornell University graduate student wrote and released a worm that propagated using the Internet. Between 6000 and 9000 UNIX-based computers were infected. The worm was not written to cause damage, but to spread to as many systems as possible. Unfortunately, a bug in the worm caused it to infect individual computers many times, resulting in widespread system slowdowns and crashes.

Prior to this worm and for a time after, the most common way to distribute attacks was using media that limited the attack's propagation and reach. The interesting thing about this worm is that it was one of the first distributed using the Internet. It infected systems by exploiting known operating system and application vulnerabilities. After the system was infected, the worm would infect other systems connected to the Internet, which demonstrated how the Internet is a powerful way to propagate attacks.

Table 1-2 outlines the attack characteristics for the Morris worm. This worm was launched in 1988 by Robert T. Morris. The delivery mechanism was via the nascent Internet. Because of the small size of the early Internet, using the Internet as the delivery mechanism was only a medium threat level. The attack was relatively simple (because the early Internet had virtually no security measures in place), and it targeted UNIX servers that were not extremely critical (compared to servers of today), resulting in low threat levels for both of these categories. Even though Morris had no malicious intent, his worm actually took down the Internet at the time. This impact, however, was only a medium threat level because, at the time, not that much work was being accomplished via the Internet. A similar disruption today would have a huge economic impact.

Table 1-2   *Morris Worm Attack Characteristics*

Discovery Year	Delivery Mechanism	Complexity	Target	Impact
1988	Internet (Threat level medium)	Simple (Threat level low)	UNIX computers (Threat level low)	Spread rapidly and caused network outages (Threat level medium)

VIRUSES, WORMS, AND TROJANS

Viruses, worms, and Trojan horses are all examples of malicious code and sometimes the terms are used interchangeably. However, there are differences between them. Most of the differences revolve around the infection mechanism.

A *virus* attaches itself to a legitimate program so that when the program is executed, it infects other programs on the system. Usually, it is attached to an executable, although, in the 1990s, viruses would sometimes attach themselves to documents. Viruses propagate manually when an infected program or document is exchanged.

A *worm* is a subcategory of virus. The primary difference is that it is able to travel from machine to machine without help from a person; it is self-replicating.

Trojan horses appear to be useful programs but are actually malicious. Unlike viruses and worms, Trojan horses do not infect other files or self-replicate.

CIH Virus

CIH, also known as Chernobyl or Spacefiller, was one of the most damaging widely circulated viruses ever. It did not have the capability to self-propagate, but it infected some widely distributed files, such as a firmware update from Yamaha and a game demo from Activision. The payload activated on April 26, 1999. CIH severely damaged a large number of computers by destroying all data on the hard drive and, in some cases, damaging the system BIOS so that the computer could not even be turned on.

The CIH virus is notable because it demonstrated malicious code's damage potential. Few viruses, worms, or Trojans since CIH have done as much permanent and intentional damage, but the possibility of a future threat that does is still very real. An attack that deletes data and uses the Internet to propagate could be terribly damaging.

Table 1-3 outlines the attack characteristics of the CIH virus. This virus was discovered in 1998. It spread via floppy disks, which is not a very efficient or fast delivery mechanism, so the delivery mechanism is considered a relatively low threat level. CIH targeted personal computers that were beginning to be used for creating important documents and other applications, so the target threat was medium. The impact of the virus was the deletion of system information making the impact threat level high.

Table 1-3   *CIH Virus Attack Characteristics*

Discovery Year	Delivery Mechanism	Complexity	Target	Impact
1998	Media (Threat level low)	Simple (Threat level low)	Personal computers (Threat level medium)	Delete data (Threat level high)

Loveletter Virus

By 2000, e-mail had become a commonplace application. The Loveletter virus, released that year, took advantage of the widespread adoption of e-mail. It consisted of an e-mail message with the worm as an attachment that masqueraded as a loveletter. Recipients were encouraged to open the attachment (and invoke the virus) by the subject of the message, which was "ILOVEYOU" and the fact that the sender address was usually one that the recipient recognized.

> **NOTE**   Researching the Loveletter virus, you will find that some people call it a worm and other people call it a virus. Because the user had to open the attachment to infect his machine (and launch the Loveletter program), we stick to calling it a virus because it is not truly self-replicating.

After a system was infected, the virus sent itself to everyone in the infected system's e-mail contact list. It also initiated a DoS attack on the official White House website's IP address, damaged important multimedia files on the system, and caused widespread e-mail outages. Loveletter caused an estimated $10 billion in economic damages.

Table 1-4 outlines the attack characteristics of the Loveletter virus. Loveletter was discovered in 2000 and is an ideal example of a drastic leap in threat level. Loveletter used Microsoft Outlook Visual Basic commands to perform its operations and incorporated social engineering to trick the user into continuing its spread, giving the complexity a medium threat level. It was delivered using e-mail and the Internet. The target systems were personal computers that were still only moderately important to business operation, so the target threat level can be considered a medium level. At the time, e-mail use was becoming widespread, but it had not achieved the business reliance that it has today. So, the delivery mechanism of e-mail is considered only a medium threat (especially because the user had to actually open the attachment). The impact of the virus, however, was a threat level of high. Not only did the virus impact the operation of personal computers, but it also slowed down entire networks and severely impacted the operation of the mail servers themselves, making Loveletter multifaceted and very dangerous.

Table 1-4   *Loveletter Worm Attack Characteristics*

Discovery Year	Delivery Mechanism	Complexity	Target	Impact
2000	E-mail (Threat level medium)	Somewhat (Threat level medium)	Personal computers (Threat level medium)	Spread, delete data, deny service (Threat level high)

Nimda

Prior to the Nimda worm, most malicious code traveled from system to system using just one or two methods. Loveletter, for example, propagated using only e-mail and file infection. Nimda, which is *admin* spelled backwards, used many propagation vectors. It infected local files, infected files via peer-to-peer file shares, attached itself to e-mails, and used a vulnerability to infect Microsoft web servers.

Although it didn't delete data, Nimda's complexity and variety of delivery mechanisms made it very difficult to stop. Also, it compromised the security settings of any infected host by giving anyone with network access full access to the hard drive. It was one of the first worms to rate a high threat level in every category.

Table 1-5 outlines the attack characteristics of the Nimda worm. Nimda was discovered in 2001 and incorporated multiple delivery mechanisms, giving it a high delivery threat level. Nimda was also fairly complex. It was the first virus/worm to actually infect other files (as opposed to just making multiple copies of itself), making removal more complicated, giving it a high complexity threat level. Nimda targeted personal computers and server systems. By 2001, personal computers and network connectivity had become a much more vital component to enhance the productivity of workers. Causing computers to crash or preventing network access now had significant business impact, giving Nimda the target threat level of high.

Table 1-5   *Nimda Attack Characteristics*

Discovery Year	Delivery Mechanism	Complexity	Target	Impact
2001	Internet, e-mail, peer-to-peer (Threat level high)	Complex (Threat level high)	Personal computers, web servers (Threat level high)	Spread, theft of information (Threat level high)

SQL Slammer

Slammer propagated with unprecedented speed. It attacked Microsoft database servers and was delivered via the Internet. After a server was infected, it didn't take long for the worm to infect all the other servers it could reach. In fact, it infected most of its estimated 75,000 victims within the first 10 minutes. Another important characteristic of the Slammer worm is that it targeted a service that, for many companies, is mission critical. Databases oftentimes store the most valuable and frequently used data a company has. If they are not available for any reason and access to the data is lost, the company can lose a tremendous amount of money.

When Slammer hit, its propagation could have been halted by "turning off" all the databases it targeted. Because of the mission critical nature of the service, most organizations could not afford to do that. Any time an attack targets required services, such as databases or network authentication, it is very difficult for organizations to arrest its propagation because doing so would deprive the users of a service they must have to do their jobs.

> **NOTE** Not being able to prevent the spread of SQL Slammer is a classic example of how business needs often override security concerns in many situations. In this situation, blocking SQL traffic at network routers would have had a much more damaging impact on the network than allowing the SQL Slammer worm to spread until all the systems could be patched.

Table 1-6 outlines the attack characteristics for the SQL Slammer worm. This worm, discovered in 2003, was delivered using the Internet but targeted a buffer overflow in Microsoft SQL servers. Exploiting a buffer overflow is not very complicated, so the SQL Slammer's complexity is in the low threat range. The delivery used the Internet, but because most SQL servers are protected from direct Internet access, the delivery threat level is only medium. The target of SQL Slammer was database servers. These systems are critical to business operations so the target threat level is high. Finally, the impact of the SQL Slammer worm is also a high threat level because of a couple of factors. First, the attacker gained control of critical database systems. Another side effect was that thousands and thousands of client systems were compromised because these systems had a simple SQL server program (Microsoft SQL Server 2000 Desktop Engine [MSDE]) running on them by default (unknown to most users of the client systems). Compromise of the clients systems also led to the compromise of more server systems because the client system had access to the internal SQL servers (which were protected from direct Internet access).

BUFFER OVERFLOW VULNERABILITY

A *buffer overflow vulnerability* results when an application does not perform sufficient bounds checking on input data. If a program tries to place too much data into a memory buffer, the program will usually try to access an illegal memory location, causing the program to crash. By carefully crafting the input data, an attacker can sometimes cause the unchecked input data to overwrite the program stack so that code of his choosing is executed on the targeted system (allowing the attacker to gain control of the system).

Table 1-6   *SQL Slammer Attack Characteristics*

Discovery Year	Delivery Mechanism	Complexity	Target	Impact
2003	Internet (Threat level medium)	Simple (Threat level low)	Database servers (Threat level high)	Spread (Threat level high)

Evolution of Attack Mitigation

The attack examples in the previous section and Figure 1-3 show how, over the last two decades, attacks have become more dangerous and difficult to defeat. They have more effective delivery mechanisms, are more complex, hit more targets, and do more damage. Furthermore, today's attacks are developed very rapidly and take advantage of vulnerabilities in commonly used communication mechanisms and required services.

Figure 1-3 *Attack Timeline*

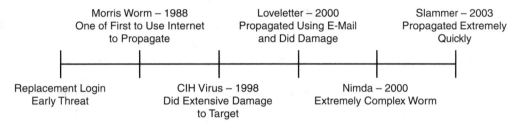

This rapid evolution had the attack mitigation tools that existed prior to IPS straining to keep up. They were not evolving as quickly as the attacks they were expected to handle. The gaps between their capabilities and the capabilities of attacks were growing. IPS was designed to fill these gaps.

You have essentially two types of IPSs: Network and Host. Network IPS analyzes network activity. Host IPS examines activities on each individual computer. This section illustrates the deficiencies of the host- and network-based technologies that prompted the development of IPSs.

Host

A wide variety of technologies can mitigate attacks at a host level. Each of the following technologies has weaknesses for which Host IPS was designed to compensate:

- Antivirus

- Personal firewalls

- Host-based Intrusion Detection

Antivirus

Antivirus is the most widely deployed security technology in the world. It identifies and eliminates viruses by scrutinizing the content of files and comparing what it finds with a database of known virus patterns (see the Chapter 2 section, "Signature Types" for more information about pattern matching). When the antivirus identifies a virus in a file, it is usually able to clean, delete, or quarantine the file.

This approach works well for viruses that are known and exist in the pattern database. It's practically useless if the virus isn't in the database or the target's database is out-of-date. Anti-virus administrators must depend on the product vendor to add virus patterns to the database quickly. After the database has been updated by the vendor, administrators must obtain the update and distribute it to all of their hosts.

The update process often takes a long time. The vendor has to obtain and analyze a sample of the virus, update the virus database, make it available to customers, and then the customers have to download and distribute it to all of their hosts. Each step adds minutes, hours, or days to the process.

Unfortunately, today's attacks propagate so quickly that the signature database cannot be updated in time. Slammer, for example, took 10 minutes to infect 75,000 hosts. You have almost no way to protect a host with a new virus signature in less than 10 minutes. Slammer demonstrated that technologies that rely on updates to protect a system from attack are not sufficient.

Personal Firewalls

Personal firewalls also use pattern-matching except that they match the signatures with data arriving via the network rather than files. If content in the data stream matches an attack in the signature database, the data is discarded. In that sense, personal firewalls rely on updates just like antivirus. They cannot stop an attack for which they do not have a signature, and the signature update process sometimes takes too long to be effective.

Personal firewalls combine the signature approach with the ability to block unauthorized network connections. If an attack relies on a network connection to propagate, the firewall can block its connection. Network connection blocking is also able to prevent an infected host from infecting other hosts by blocking the infection's outbound connection attempts.

The trouble with connection blocking is made clear by worms like Nimda, Loveletter, and Slammer. Nimda and Loveletter used e-mail as a delivery mechanism. You could configure your personal firewall to block e-mail connections, but then your e-mail would be useless. The same goes for the Microsoft database connections that Slammer used to propagate. The propagation of the Slammer worm could have been limited by blocking all database connections, but then you would have killed regular access to your database servers as well.

When attacks propagate using *authorized* network connections, security professionals are faced with a very tough decision. Do I use my personal firewall to block the connection and lose money by denying service to the database or e-mail, or do I allow the machine to be infected? Neither decision is particularly palatable.

Host-Based Intrusion Detection

Host-based Intrusion Detection System (HIDS) products monitor system and network resources to detect when they are being used inappropriately. It is a useful counterpart to port blocking firewalls because it is able to detect malicious activity even after an authorized connection has been permitted by the firewall. When malicious activity is detected, the HIDS notifies the appropriate IT personnel.

Knowing what malicious activity has occurred is certainly valuable. However, if the attack the HIDS detected damaged the system, the damage is done and now must be undone. That can be expensive. Worms like CIH and Nimda are capable of doing so much damage that many IT security staff came to the conclusion that *detecting* an attack is nice but *preventing* it from doing damage is critical.

Network

Analyzing the operation of your network is important for optimum performance as well as for detecting attacks against your network. Detecting attacks on your network evolved through the following stages:

- System log analysis
- Promiscuous monitoring
- Inline prevention

System Log Analysis

The simplest way to monitor your network is by analyzing the log files generated by the devices on your network. The problem with analyzing log file information is that it provides a limited view of the attacks being launched against your network. Analyzing logs (to produce useful information) is also a very time-consuming task. Furthermore, by the time that you analyze the logs, the attack has already been conducted.

Promiscuous Monitoring

Instead of relying on log file information, early Intrusion Detection Systems (IDSs) started to promiscuously monitor the traffic on your network. By examining the actual traffic on the network, these IDSs could identify a wide range of attacks against your network. To respond to attacks, these systems provided various response mechanisms, including the following response mechanisms:

- Generating alarms
- Resetting TCP connections

■ IP blocking

■ Logging traffic

AUTOMATED RESPONSE

Although IDSs have always provided some form of automated response to various attacks, many deployments used that functionality only sparingly. Instead of an automated response, many deployments chose to require human intervention. The IDS monitored the network, generating alarms when attacks were detected. It was then up to the operator to take the appropriate response.

Although Intrusion Detection could react to intrusive traffic, the actions that it provided were still reactive and allowed the initial attack traffic to reach the target system.

Inline Prevention

IPSs expanded on the functionality provided by Intrusion Detection by enabling you to prevent attacks against your network. Attack prevention is possible with IPSs because the IPS device acts a Layer 2 forwarding device. This enables the IPS device to drop traffic that is considered intrusive before it reaches the target system.

OPEN SYSTEMS INTERCONNECTION MODEL

Computer systems communicate with each other across the network using protocols. The Open Systems Interconnection (OSI) model divides the functions of a protocol into a series of layers, with each layer only directly communicating with the layer above and below it. The OSI model establishes the following layers:

■ **Layer 1**—Physical layer (an example is the physical cables)

■ **Layer 2**—Data link layer (an example is Ethernet)

■ **Layer 3**—Network layer (an example is IP)

■ **Layer 4**—Transport layer (an example is TCP)

■ **Layer 5**—Session layer (an example is SMB)

■ **Layer 6**—Presentation layer (an example is ASCII)

■ **Layer 7**—Application layer (an example is HTTP)

IPS Capabilities

Intrusion Prevention provides numerous capabilities at both the host level and the network level, but from a high-level perspective, the capabilities provided by Intrusion Prevention fall into the following two major categories:

■ Attack prevention

■ Regulatory compliance

Attack Prevention

The main capability provided by Network Intrusion Prevention is the ability to prevent malicious traffic from reaching the target system. Detection systems have been used for years, but each of them always allowed a certain amount of malicious traffic to reach the target systems (because they were reactive in nature). With the introduction of Intrusion Prevention, you have the ability to proactively defend your network against attack.

Besides preventing attacks, Intrusion Prevention also enables you to enforce RFC compliance. For example, many peer-to-peer applications take advantage of the fact the outbound traffic to a destination port of TCP port 80 is usually allowed by the perimeter firewall to communicate using TCP port 80 as well. By enforcing RFC compliance, your IPS can ensure that traffic using the TCP port actually matches the HTTP definition (RFC 2616).

> **NOTE**   For a more detailed explanation of Host IPS capabilities, refer to Chapter 5, "Host Intrusion Prevention Overview," and Chapter 6, "HIPS Components." Similarly, Chapter 7, "Network Intrusion Prevention Overview," and Chapter 8, "NIPS Components," provide detailed explanations of the Network IPS capabilities.

Regulatory Compliance

Regulations force many network operators to guarantee that certain security restrictions are enforced on your network. These requirements are especially robust with the respect to networks that handle medical information on patients. Deploying both NIPS and HIPS can assist in being compliant with many of these requirements.

> **NOTE**   For more information on regulatory compliance issues, refer to Chapter 5.

Summary

Security threats have always been around. Anything of value makes a viable target for a thief. Traditionally, theft required physical access to the object being stolen, limiting the number of attackers and increasing the chances of the perpetrator's being caught.

Mainframes and minicomputers allowed access to a limited number of directly connected dumb terminals. Gradually, the need for extended connectivity became more important. This need for connectivity led to dialup access to mainframes and minicomputers. Adding dialup connectivity increased the scope of attackers by enabling anyone across the world (with access to a telephone and a computer with a modem) to attempt to access the systems.

The development of the Internet has created an environment in which millions of computers across the world are all connected to each other. Furthermore, access to this network is fairly ubiquitous and cheap, enabling any thieves in the world to target your computer, regardless of their physical location.

Many factors impact the security threats that a computer system is vulnerable to. Some threats are more severe than others. When trying to understand why an IPS is necessary in today's networks, you need to consider the following factors:

■   Technology adoption

■   Target value

■   Attack characteristics

Technology Adoption

Businesses don't usually adopt new technologies quickly, because new technology comes with a set of risks, such as poor return on investment, security concerns, training costs, and so on. New technologies are eventually implemented (even though security on these technologies might not be initially incorporated into the solution).

Four widely adopted technologies stand out as having had a tremendous impact on the evolution of security threats and thus the evolution of IPSs:

■   Client-server computing

■   The Internet

■   Wireless connectivity

■   Mobile computing

Client-server is a computing architecture that has largely replaced mainframes because of its lower cost of ownership. In client-server processing, power is not centralized. Instead, it is distributed across many networked computers, each acting as either a client or server. If attackers are able to compromise one computer, any computer connected to the compromised system is now a secondary target. Peer-to-peer networking contributed greatly to this problem by increasing the number of potential pathways between the systems.

Client-server and peer-to-peer architectures multiplied the number of the potential targets. Even so, attackers need to have a way to connect to a network or computer to attack it. The Internet provided an interconnected network of millions of potential targets for attackers to choose from.

Wireless connectivity enables an increase in productivity because it enables users to easily remain connected as they travel from their desk to a meeting in a conference room or from one meeting to another. Furthermore, wireless connectivity is cheaper because you do not have to install switch ports throughout your entire facility. However, without effective security measures installed, it is easy for an attacker to access your wireless network without ever entering your building.

Mobile computing refers to the collection of technologies that makes it possible for employees to remotely perform the same duties they could while at the office. Portable computers, mobile phones, and PDAs are becoming just as powerful as similar non-mobile equipment. Still, many of the computing resources a mobile worker needs are stored in the office so the mobile devices have to be able to access them remotely.

Target Value

Initially, personal computers were lucrative targets for their actual hardware. Currently, computer hardware is relatively cheap; however, personal computers are still lucrative targets because of the following factors:

- Information theft

- Zombie systems acquisition

The information stored on personal computers (both business and personal) has become much more valuable. Today, it is common for millions of people to access their banks and other financial institutions using their personal computers. Business computers frequently house sensitive information such as source code and business roadmaps. The information stored on computers has become more valuable than the actual systems themselves.

With the deployment of high-speed Internet connections, many people have systems directly connected to the Internet 24 hours a day (dramatically increasing the attack window timeframe). By compromising these vulnerable systems, attackers can build a network of machines (known as *zombies*) that they can use to perform various kinds of attacks. Furthermore, these attacks do not directly originate from the attackers, so tracing the attack back to the real attackers becomes more difficult.

Attack Characteristics

When an attack has one or more characteristics that are dramatically more dangerous than the same characteristic(s) in previous attacks, it is an indication that existing security countermeasures might not be enough to stop it. Four major attack characteristics are as follows:

- Delivery mechanism

- Complexity

- Target

- Impact

Delivery mechanism is the method by which an attack is disseminated. When considering the attack delivery mechanism, you need to consider the following two aspects:

- Reach of the attacker

- Protection from discovery

Attack complexity is a measurement of the attack based on the following two factors:

- Complexity to launch the attack

- Complexity to detect the attack

The following two factors determine the threat level in the target category:

- Total number of potential targets

- Value of the potential targets (impact if compromised)

The final attack characteristic is the impact that the attack generates. Many times, the impact is related to the intent of the attacker. Some common goals of an attacker include the following:

- Curiosity

- DoS

- Theft of confidential information

- Revenge

- Construction of a network of compromised machines

Over the last two decades, attacks have become more dangerous and difficult to defeat. They have more effective delivery mechanisms, are more complex, hit more targets, and do more damage. Furthermore, today's attacks are developed very rapidly and take advantage of vulnerabilities in commonly used communication mechanisms and required services.

You have essentially two types of IPSs: Network and Host. A Network IPS analyzes network activity. A Host IPS examines activities on each individual computer. Deficiencies in both Network- and Host-based Intrusion Detection led to the development of the current IPS product offerings.

Intrusion Prevention provides numerous capabilities at both the host level and the network level, but from a high-level perspective, the capabilities provided by Intrusion Prevention fall into the following two major categories:

- Attack prevention

- Regulatory compliance

CHAPTER 2

Signatures and Actions

Before you decide to buy a product of any kind, you usually want to know exactly what it is you're buying. That way, you don't get something you don't want. This seems like a reasonable goal, but achieving this goal isn't always easy. What's challenging is the vocabulary used to describe what the product does and how it works. Two different products might have a feature with the same name, but the feature in each product might actually be completely unrelated. Without an industry agreed-upon set of definitions, product marketing can use terminology to make each product appealing to customers, even if this usage makes it difficult for customers to compare the functionality between different IPS products.

Take the purchase of a new vehicle, for example. Three different automobiles claim to have drive stabilization systems. That sounds great, but does the system work in the same way for each car? Is one more suitable for your needs than the other? How is the system implemented? Close examination might show how the system in one car reduces vibration when driving over bumpy roads whereas in another car it helps control the vehicle's balance during sharp turns. The name for the feature is exactly the same, but what it actually does is very different.

Seeing through the fog of feature names and marketing buzzwords is especially difficult when the product of interest is in a new technology, such as Intrusion Prevention. Intrusion Prevention System (IPS) product data sheets and websites tend to use vague product descriptors like deep packet inspection, anomaly detection, innate defense models, signatures, and behavior-based and advanced network intelligence. The descriptors might be accurate, but the functionality behind the words is often not consistent from product to product.

The way to see through the words and discern the product functionality is to create clear definitions for commonly used feature names. One feature commonly associated with IPS is signatures. Attack signatures have been around for long enough that the definition should be universally understood, but that's not the case. Simply put, an IPS signature is any distinctive characteristic that identifies something. Using this definition, all IPS products use signatures of some kind, regardless of what the product descriptions claim. To find something and stop it, you must be able to identify it, and for you to identify it, it must display a distinct characteristic. Signatures are distinguished by the following characteristics:

- Signature types

- Signature trigger

- Signature actions

Signature Types

Signatures fall into one of the following two basic categories depending on their functionality:

- Atomic signatures

- Stateful signatures

This section examines these signature types in further detail. Furthermore, the triggering mechanisms explained later in this chapter can be used with both of these base signature types. The major distinction between these two base signature types is whether or not the inspection process requires the IPS device to maintain state about previous actions that have been observed.

Atomic Signatures

Atomic signatures represent the simplest signature type. For an atomic signature, a single packet, activity, or event is examined to determine if the signature should trigger a signature action. Because these signatures trigger on a single event, they do not require your intrusion system to maintain state. The entire inspection can be accomplished in an atomic operation that does not require any knowledge of past or future activities.

STATE

State refers to situations in which you need to analyze multiple pieces of information that are not available at the same time. It also refers to tracking established TCP connections (connections that have gone through the initial three-way handshake). Valid TCP traffic also refers to traffic that has the correct sequence numbers for an established connection. For Network IPSs, state signatures usually refer to signatures that require analyzing traffic from multiple packets.

Atomic Signature Considerations

One drawback with atomic signatures is that you have to know all the atomic events that you want to look for. For each of these events, you then have to create the appropriate signature. As the number of atomic signatures increases, just managing the different signatures can become overwhelming.

Another drawback is that these signatures can be applied only to situations in which the context of the event is not important. For example, assume that you have a simple string match signature that triggers an alert action whenever the traffic that it is analyzing contains **/etc/passwd**. If you apply this simple string signature to monitor TCP traffic, an attacker can generate alerts by sending a flood of TCP packets with the **/etc/passwd** string in payload. The alerts are generated even if the connection is not part of a valid TCP connection (because it is an atomic signature). Furthermore, analyzing the alerts can minimize the time that your security staff spends identifying more serious attacks that represent valid attacks against your network. Generating a large number of bogus alerts can also impact the performance of your monitoring applications and devices.

Nevertheless, atomic signatures have their advantages. First, these signatures consume minimal resources (such as memory) on the IPS/IDS device. These signatures are also easy to understand because they search only for a specific event. Finally, traffic analysis for these atomic signatures can usually be performed very quickly and efficiently.

Host-Based Examples

Host-based IPS examines many operations on the system, including function calls, files accessed, and so on. One common method for detecting anomalous user behavior is to establish a baseline of the operations that a user normally performs on the system. Then by monitoring deviations from the baseline, you can detect potentially malicious activity. For example, if a function call is never invoked normally (except in connection with malicious activity), then triggering a signature action whenever it is called is a simple example of a host-based atomic signature. Another example of this is an application that you consider a problem. For example, you might want to trigger a signature action whenever a command shell is invoked on the local system.

> **NOTE**   Command shells are used to access the command-line interface on most operating systems. Accessing the command-line interface is a common mechanism to launch attacks against the system. On any operating system, such as Windows, which relies heavily on a graphical user interface, utilizing the command shell to configure the system can be indicative of uncommon behavior.

Network-Based Examples

A good example of a network-based atomic signature is the *LAND* attack. By inspecting a single packet, your Network-based (or Host-based) IPS can identify this attack. Because everything is contained in a single packet, no state information is needed to identify this attack.

LAND ATTACK

The LAND attack is a denial-of-service (DoS) attack in which an attacker sends a TCP packet (with the SYN bit set) to a system in which the source and destination IP address (along with the source and destination port) are the same. When it was first discovered, many IP stacks crashed the system when they received a LAND attack.

Stateful Signatures

Unlike atomic signatures, stateful signatures trigger on a sequence of specific events that requires the IPS device to maintain state. The length of time that the signatures must maintain state is known as the *event horizon*. Configuring the length of the event horizon is a tradeoff between consuming system resources and being able to detect an attack that occurs over a long period of time.

EVENT HORIZON

Stateful signatures usually require several pieces of data to match an attack signature. The maximum amount of time over which an attack signature can successfully be detected (from the initial data piece to the final data piece needed to complete the attack signature) is known as the *event horizon*. The intrusion system must maintain state information for the duration of the event horizon. The length of event horizon varies from one signature to another. The important point to consider is that an IPS cannot maintain state information indefinitely without eventually running out of resources. Therefore, an IPS uses a configured event horizon to determine how long it looks for a specific attack signature once an initial signature component is detected.

Stateful Signature Considerations

The main limitation to stateful signatures is that maintaining state consumes memory resources on your IPS/IDS device. Usually, however, this is not a significant problem if the IPS product is designed to efficiently use its resources. If your IPS does not efficiently manage resources when maintaining state, then the large consumption of resources (such as memory and CPU) can lead to a slow response time, dropped packets, missed signatures, and so on, which adversely impacts the effectiveness of your IPS.

Requiring a specific event to be detected in a known context increases the likelihood that the activity represents legitimate attack traffic. This minimizes the false positives generated by the stateful signatures.

Host-Based Examples

For a host-based example, we are going to use a commonly used Windows command shell called **cmd.exe**. As opposed to our atomic host-based example earlier in this chapter, in this situation, we do not want to trigger a signature action whenever **cmd.exe** is invoked (because our users use this program frequently). Our examination, however, reveals that many attacks invoke **cmd.exe** remotely. To remotely execute **cmd.exe**, the attacker must make a network connection to the host. This information can be used to refine our atomic signature by adding state. The stateful signature triggers a signature action when **cmd.exe** is invoked, but only if the application invoking **cmd.exe** first accepted a network connection.

The Host-based IPS must remember which applications have accepted network connections. This state information can then be examined whenever **cmd.exe** is invoked.

Network-Based Examples

Often, Network-based IPS signatures are stateful signatures because the information needed can usually be distributed across multiple packets. Even a simple string match signature is usually stateful because the string can occur across multiple packets (because the IPS must examine the data from all the packets until the successful match is made). For example, if you want to search for the string **/etc/password** in an HTTP URL, you might have to check multiple packets because the string can be distributed across more than one packet (although it can occur in a single packet as well).

Other examples of stateful signatures are the signatures used to monitor TCP traffic. To minimize the ability of an attacker to generate a large number of bogus alarms, most TCP attack signatures are valid only if the signature trigger is observed on a valid TCP connection. For example, suppose your signature triggers on the string **/etc/password** in a Telnet connection. Telnet uses TCP port 23, so the first thing that the IPS needs to track is established connections to TCP port 23. Then it also needs to track the sequence numbers for the established Telnet connections. Finally, whenever the string **/etc/password** is observed on an established TCP connection with the correct sequence numbers, then the signature triggers. Without maintaining this state, an attacker can generate a flood of invalid alarms by sending a flood of TCP packets to port 23 containing the string **/etc/password** (without ever actually establishing any valid TCP connections to port 23).

Signature Triggers

The heart of any IPS signature is the mechanism that causes it to trigger. These triggering mechanisms can be simple or complex, and every IPS incorporates signatures that use one or more of these basic *triggering mechanisms* to trigger signature actions. These triggering mechanisms can be applied to both atomic and stateful signatures. Current IPSs incorporate various triggering mechanisms when developing signatures, including the following:

■   Pattern detection

■   Anomaly-based detection

■   Behavior-based detection

TRIGGERING MECHANISM

Triggering mechanisms refer to the conditions that cause an intrusion system to generate a signature action. For example, the triggering mechanism for a burglar alarm might be a motion detector that detects the movement of an individual entering the alarmed room. A Network IPS might trigger a signature action if it detects a packet with a payload containing a specific string going to a specific port. A Host-based IPS might trigger a signature action when a specific function call is invoked. Anything that can reliably signal an intrusion or security policy violation can be used as a triggering mechanism.

PROTOCOL DECODES

Another common triggering mechanism is called *protocol decodes*. Instead of simply looking for a pattern anywhere in a packet, protocol decodes involve breaking down a packet into the fields of a protocol and then searching for specific patterns in a specific protocol field or some other malformed aspect of the protocol fields. The advantage of protocol decodes is that it enables a more granular inspection of traffic and reduces false positives.

Table 2-1 shows the relationship between the various signature types and triggering mechanisms.

Table 2-1   *Signature Type Versus Signature Trigger*

Signature Trigger	Signature Type	
	Atomic Signature	**Stateful Signature**
Pattern detection	No state required to examine pattern to determine if signature action should be applied	Must maintain state or examine multiple items to determine if signature action should be applied
Anomaly detection	No state required to identify activity that deviates from normal profile	State required to identify activity that deviates from normal profile
Behavior detection	No state required to identify undesirable behavior	Previous activity (state) required to identify undesirable behavior

The following sections explain the signature triggering mechanisms in detail. Table 2-2 and Table 2-3 provide example signatures that illustrate the various combinations of signature types and triggering mechanisms to help clarify how the different signature types and triggers combine to create useful signatures.

Table 2-2 *Host-Based Signature Examples*

Signature Trigger	Signature Type	
	Atomic Signature	**Stateful Signature**
Pattern detection	Searching for the string **confidential** in a data file	Searching for the string **SELECT FROM** in a URI
Anomaly detection	Detecting a function call that is not part of the normal profile	Two function calls that are part of the normal profile, but have never been called within 1 second of each other
Behavior detection	Searching for any invocation of **cmd.exe**	Searching for an e-mail application (program that has previously generated or received e-mail traffic) invoking command.com

Table 2-3 *Network-Based Signature Examples*

Signature Trigger	Signature Type	
	Atomic Signature	**Stateful Signature**
Pattern detection	Detecting for an Address Resolution Protocol (ARP) request that has a source Ethernet address of FF:FF:FF:FF:FF:FF	Searching for the string *confidential* across multiple packets in a TCP session
Anomaly detection	Detecting traffic that is going to a destination port that is not in the normal profile	Verifying protocol compliance for HTTP traffic
Behavior detection	Detecting abnormally large fragmented packets by examining only the last fragment	Searching for RPC requests that do not initially utilize the PortMapper

Each of these triggering mechanisms has its benefits and drawbacks. Using the correct triggering mechanism in the appropriate situation greatly improves its efficiency. IPS devices that support multiple triggering mechanisms can more adequately support efficient signatures for a wide variety of activities without significantly impacting the performance of the IPS device.

By understanding the mechanisms that a signature can use to identify an activity, you can more efficiently determine a product's true capabilities.

Pattern Detection

The simplest triggering mechanism is identifying a specific pattern. This pattern can represent a textual or binary string or it can be other patterns, such as a sequence of function calls. Besides simple string patterns, most systems provide enhanced pattern detection using the following mechanisms:

■ Regular expression (regex) patterns

■ Deobfuscation techniques

Specifying string patterns using *regex* provides the ability to efficiently search for textual patterns (using a single regular expression) while making it harder to bypass the pattern without detection.

REGULAR EXPRESSION

A *regex* is a pattern-matching language that enables you to define a flexible search pattern. Using *regex*, you can easily define complex search patterns. Many different programs use *regex* to enable you to define custom search strings. In the UNIX world, for example, the **grep** command is a common program that utilizes *regex* to search for text inside of files (or other output). For example, to perform a case-insensitive search for the word **attack** in the file named **output.results**, you can use the following command:

```
grep [Aa][Tt][Tt][Aa][Cc][Kk] output.results
```

This command finds various permutations of the word attack, such as ATTAck, attack, AttaCk, and so on.

Besides searching using flexible string patterns, many protocols (such as HTTP) accept multiple encoding mechanisms for input data. Some of the common encoding mechanisms include the following:

■ American Standard Code for Information Interchange (ASCII)

■ Hexadecimal

■ Unicode

NOTE Hackers often combine these encoding methods in an effort to trick IPS devices and other monitoring applications. In the past, various web servers could be tricked into accessing data and applications from other directories in what is known as a directory traversal attack.

Unless your IPS can decode the input data correctly (before performing a pattern search), it will miss valid strings that have been obfuscated. For example, the following patterns each request the same web page:

- **http://10.10.10.10/index.html/../etc/password**

- **http://10.10.10.10/index.html/%2e%2e/etc/password**

- **http://10.10.10.10/index.html/%c0%ae%c0%ae/etc/password**

In each of these requests, the **..** is being represented differently. If your IPS correctly deobfuscates these requests (before performing a pattern search), then it can correctly detect the attempt to request a web page outside of the root of the web server's directory tree in each of these web requests (which all request the same web page).

Pattern Matching Considerations

Depending on the fidelity of the patterns that your signatures use, one of the problems with pattern matching can be the rate of false positives generated, especially with atomic signatures.

One of the benefits of pattern matching is that the signature clearly correlates to a specific attack. When the signature triggers, you know which attack it is detecting. This is different from anomaly detection in which the signature indicates only that something outside of the configured normal parameters has been detected.

Host-Based Examples

A Host-based IPS product might have the capability to examine the data inside a file on the hard disk. An example of a pattern-based signature trigger is the word **confidential** being detected in any data file. A stateful signature with the same triggering mechanism might look for the word **confidential** in inbound network traffic. The pattern is the same, but can be matched only if multiple packets have been re-assembled.

Network-Based Examples

Most Network-based IPS devices include a robust pattern-matching capability because many of the attack signatures involve searching for patterns in different network protocols. Most of these pattern-matching signatures are also stateful signatures because the information being examined can occur across multiple packets.

> **NOTE**   Examining network traffic using pattern matching does not work when the traffic stream is encrypted. However, Host-based IPS might be able to examine the traffic depending on where it is examining the traffic (before or after the decryption).

The following regex string searches for an attempt to change the working directory to the root directory during an FTP session:

```
[ \t]*[Cc][Ww][Dd][ \t]+[~]root
```

Examining traffic with a destination port of 21 (the default FTP server port) detects FTP sessions in which the user attempts to change the working directory to **root**.

> **NOTE**   If you have FTP servers listening on ports other than TCP port 21, then you need to configure your IPS to monitor these non-standard ports to have the IPS identify FTP attacks to these other ports.

Anomaly-Based Detection

Anomaly-based (also known as profile-based detection) signatures are not based on a specific event. Instead these signatures trigger when a certain activities deviate from what is considered normal. To utilize an anomaly-based signature, you must first determine what normal activity means for your network or host. This is usually accomplished by monitoring your network (or specific applications on your host) for a specific period of time to observe what is considered normal activity. Once you define normal activity, then you can configure your anomaly-based signature to trigger whenever activity on the network or a specific host deviates from your defined normal profile by a certain amount.

Anomaly-Based Detection Considerations

One of the biggest limitations of anomaly-based signatures is that you need to learn (or define) what is considered normal. As your network evolves, your definition of normal might also have to change. Furthermore, you need to guarantee that during your learning phase, your network is free of the attack traffic that you are going to detect (otherwise, this activity will be considered normal traffic). Furthermore, just defining normal can sometimes be difficult because most networks comprise a heterogeneous mixture of systems, devices, and applications that continually change.

Another potential drawback to anomaly-based systems is that when a signature generates an alert, it might be very difficult to correlate that alert back to a specific attack, because the alert indicates only that non-normal traffic has been detected. More analysis is required to determine whether the traffic represents an actual attack and what the attack actually accomplished. Furthermore, if the attack traffic happens to be similar to normal traffic, the attack might go undetected.

Because anomaly-based signatures do not look for specific attacks, they can be used to detect previously unpublished attacks. This is a major advantage for anomaly-based detection. Instead of having to define a large number of signatures for various attack scenarios, you simply define a profile for normal activity. Any activity that deviates from this profile is then abnormal and triggers a signature action. The drawback is that an alert from an anomaly signature does not necessarily indicate an attack. It indicates only a deviation from the defined normal, which can sometimes occur from valid user traffic.

Host-Based Examples

A good example of anomaly detection is using the Profiler utility from the Cisco Security Agent (CSA) software. This tool allows you to monitor an application over a period of time. During this time, it records all of the functions calls that the application uses. You can then use this information to build a profile for the application that can then be used to identify when the application makes anomalous function calls (any function call that is not in the profile).

> **NOTE**   The Profiler utility is useful to analyze custom applications that are unique to your network. Most common applications (for a specific operating system) have already been incorporated into CSA's predefined rules. As of CSA version 4.5, the Profiler utility is now referred to as Application Behavior Investigation.

Sophisticated Host-based IPS tools might be able to apply stateful conditions to function calls recorded during the learning process. If two function calls that are a part of the normal profile occur within 1 second of each other and this has never happened before, this could trigger a signature. This is an example of a stateful signature with an anomaly-based triggering mechanism.

Network-Based Examples

A Network-based IPS can have various anomaly-based signatures. Some simple examples of anomaly signatures with the Cisco IPS solution are its flood signatures. These signatures detect floods of various types of traffic on your network. For example, you might want to monitor the amount of Internet Control Message Protocol (ICMP) traffic on your network. First, you need to measure the amount of ICMP traffic that appears on your network during normal operation. Then the flood signature triggers a signature action whenever the ICMP traffic on the network exceeds the configured maximum threshold for a specific length of time.

Other anomaly-based signatures involve ensuring that traffic to a set of ports matches a defined protocol specification. In this situation, the protocol specification defines what is considered normal. Any traffic that does not conform to this protocol specification is abnormal and triggers a signature action.

> **NOTE**   The Cisco application inspection and control (AIC) signatures provide signatures that provide you with anomaly detection signatures for both HTTP and the FTP by verifying protocol compliance.

Behavior-Based Detection

Behavior-based detection is similar to pattern detection, but instead of trying to define specific patterns, you are defining behaviors that are suspicious based on historical analysis. The behaviors define classes of activity that are known to be suspicious. For example, an e-mail client running shell commands using the Windows **cmd.exe** program normally indicates something unusual such as a virus attempting to do something to your system.

Behavior-Based Detection Considerations

Similar to pattern matching, behavior-based signatures must be defined before you can use them. It takes a lot of research to determine behaviors that do not occur normally and can accurately indicate suspicious behavior.

The use of behaviors enables a single signature to cover an entire class of activities without having to specify each individual situation. For example, having a signature that triggers a signature action when an e-mail client invokes **cmd.exe** enables you to apply the signature to any application whose behavior mimics the basic characteristics of an e-mail client without having to apply the signature to each e-mail client application individually. Therefore, if a user installs a new e-mail application, the signature still applies.

Host-Based Examples

Behavior-based signatures are easy to visualize at the host level. A simple example involves the **cmd.exe** program. This program is frequently used by malicious programs to execute commands and scripts on the system. It is also frequently used by users during their normal day-to-day operations. Using a behavior-based signature, you can detect suspicious invocations of **cmd.exe** while ignoring the normal uses of this program. For example, an e-mail client that invokes **cmd.exe** is performing suspicious activity (because the e-mail client does not need to run **cmd.exe** to operate). Incorporating a signature that triggers a signature action whenever **cmd.exe** is invoked by any e-mail client application is an excellent example of a behavior-based signature.

Network-Based Examples

At the network level, you might find it a little more difficult to identify the behavior-based signatures. For example, a signature that identifies attempts to directly access RPC applications is behavior-based, because the normal behavior is to first communicate with the PortMapper.

RPC PROTOCOL

The Sun Remote Procedure Call (RPC) protocol enables one system to run applications on another system across the network. These RPC applications are not bound to well-known ports. Instead, a program called the PortMapper keeps track of which RPC application is operating on which port. When a system wants to communicate with an RPC application on a remote system, it first contacts the PortMapper to find the port that the RPC application is operating. Then the system can communicate directly with the application through that port.

Signature Actions

Whenever a signature observes the activity that it is configured to detect, the signature triggers one or more actions. These actions fall into various categories, such as the following:

- Generating an alert

- Dropping or preventing the activity

- Logging the activity

- Resetting a TCP connection

- Blocking future activity

- Allowing the activity

Alert Signature Action

Monitoring the alerts generated by your Network-based and Host-based IPS systems is vital to understanding the attacks being launched against your network. If an attacker causes a flood of bogus alerts, examining them can overload your security analysts. Therefore, both network and host IPS solutions incorporate the following types of alerts to enable you to efficiently monitor the operation of your network:

- Atomic alerts

- Summary alerts

Understanding each of these types of alerts is vital to providing the most effective protection for your network.

Atomic Alerts

Atomic alerts (like atomic signatures) are generated every time a signature triggers. In some situations, this behavior is useful and indicates all occurrences of a specific attack. Other times, an attacker might be able to flood your monitor console with alerts if he can generate thousands of bogus alerts against your IPS devices or applications.

> **NOTE**   As a hybrid between atomic alerts and summary alerts, some IPS solutions also enable you to generate a single atomic alert and then disable alerts (for that signature and source address) for a specific period of time. This prevents you from getting overwhelmed with alerts while still giving you an indication that a specific system is doing something suspicious.

Summary Alerts

Instead of generating alerts for each instance of a signature, some IPS solutions enable you to generate summary alerts. A summary alert is a single alert that indicates multiple occurrences of the same signature from the same source address and or port.

Alarm summary modes limit the number of alerts generated and make it difficult for an attacker to consume resources on your sensor. With the summarization modes, however, you also receive information on the number of times that the activity that matches a signature's characteristics was observed during a specific period of time.

When using alarm summarization, the first instance of intrusive activity usually triggers a normal alert. Then, other instances of the same activity (duplicate alarms) are counted until the end of the signature's summary interval. When the length of time specified by the summary interval has elapsed, a summary alarm is sent, indicating the number of alarms that occurred during the time interval specified by the summary interval parameter.

AUTOMATIC SUMMARIZATION

Besides configuring a signature to generate summary alerts, some IPS solutions also enable you to cause summarization to occur automatically (even though the default behavior is to generate atomic alerts). In this situation, if the number of atomic alerts exceeds a configured threshold in a specified amount of time, the signature automatically switches to generating summary alerts (instead of atomic alerts). Then, after a defined period of time, the signature reverts to its original configuration. Automatic summarization enables you to automatically regulate the amount of alerts being generated.

Drop Signature Action

One of the most powerful actions for an IPS device is the capability to drop packets or prevent an activity from occurring. This action enables the device to stop an attack before it has the chance to perform malicious activity. Unlike a traditional IDS device, the IPS device actively forwards packets across two of its interfaces. Therefore, the analysis engine has the option to decide which packets should be forwarded and which packets should be dropped.

Besides dropping individual packets, the drop action can be expanded to drop all packets for a specific session or even all packets from a specific host for a certain amount of time. By dropping traffic for a connection or host, the IPS conserves resources by efficiently dropping traffic without having to analyze each packet separately.

Log Signature Action

In some situations, you do not necessarily have enough information to stop an activity, but you want to log the actions or packets that are seen so that you can analyze this information in more detail. By performing a detailed analysis, you can identify exactly what is taking place and make a decision as to whether it should be allowed or denied in the future.

Suppose you have a signature that looks for the string **/etc/password** and you configure the string with the logging action (based on the attacker IP address). Whenever the signature triggers, the IPS devices begins logging the traffic from the attacker's IP address for a specified period of time (or specified number of bytes). This log information is usually stored on the IPS device in a specific file. Because the signature also generates an alert, you observe the alert on your management console. Then you can retrieve the log data from the IPS device and analyze the activity that the attacker performed on the network after triggering the initial alarm.

Block Signature Action

Most IPS devices have the capability to block future traffic by having the IPS device update the access control lists (ACLs) on one of your infrastructure devices. This ACL stops traffic from an attacking system without requiring the IDS to consume resources analyzing the traffic. After a configured period of time, the IDS device removes the ACL. Network IPS devices usually provide this blocking functionality along with the other actions such as dropping unwanted packets. One advantage of utilizing the blocking action is that a single IPS device can stop traffic at multiple locations throughout your network, regardless of the location of the IPS device itself. For example, an IPS device located deep within the network can apply ACLs at your perimeter router or firewall.

TCP Reset Signature Action

A basic action that can be used to terminate TCP connections is generating a packet for the connection with the TCP RST flag set. Many IPS devices use the TCP reset action to abruptly end a TCP connection that is performing unwanted operations.

Allow Signature Action

The final action might seem a little confusing, because most IPS devices are designed to stop or prevent unwanted traffic on your network. The allow action is necessary so that you can define exceptions to your configured signatures. When you configure your IPS device to disallow certain activities, you sometimes need to allow a few systems or users to be exceptions to the configured rule. Configuring exceptions enables you to take a more restrictive approach to security because you first deny everything and then allow only the activities that are needed.

For example, suppose that the IT department routinely scans your network using a common vulnerability scanner. This scanning causes your IPS to trigger various alerts. These are the same alerts that the IPS generates if an attacker scans your network. By allowing the alerts from the approved IT scanning host, you can protect your network from intrusive scans while eliminating the false positives generated by the routine IT approved scanning.

> **NOTE**   Some IPS devices provide the allow action indirectly through other mechanisms, such as signature filters. If an IPS does not provide the allow action directly (through an action such as permit or allow), you need to search the product's documentation to find the mechanism you can use to enable exceptions to signatures.

Summary

Different products use different terminology to describe their product's functionality. For explanation purposes, our definition of a signature is any distinctive characteristic that identifies something. Based on this definition, all IPS devices use signatures to identify activity in your network traffic and on hosts on your network. Signatures are distinguished by the following characteristics:

- Signature type

- Signature trigger

- Signature actions

Signature types fall into the following two base categories:

- Atomic

- Stateful

The major distinction between these two base signature types is that atomic signatures do not require the IPS device to maintain state information about previous activity.

In conjunction with the base signature types, a signature needs to trigger one or more actions depending on one of the following triggering mechanisms:

- Pattern detection

- Anomaly-based detection

- Behavior-based detection

Table 2-4 outlines the relationship between the base signature types and the triggering mechanisms.

Table 2-4 *Signature Type Versus Signature Trigger*

Signature Trigger	Signature Type	
	Atomic Signature	**Stateful Signature**
Pattern detection	No state required to examine pattern to determine if signature action should be applied	Must maintain state or examine multiple items to determine if signature action should be applied
Anomaly detection	No state required to identify activity that deviates from normal profile	State required to identify activity that deviates from normal profile
Behavior detection	No state required to identify undesirable behavior	Previous activity (state) required to identify undesirable behavior

Pattern detection is the simplest triggering because it involves searching for a specific predefined pattern. This pattern might be textual, binary, or even a series of function calls.

Anomaly-based detection involves first defining a profile of what is considered normal. This normal profile can be learned by monitoring activity over a period of time. It can also be based on a defined specification (such as an RFC). Whenever activity is observed that is not included in the normal profile, the signature triggers some action. Correlating the signature to a specific attack, however, can be complicated.

Behavior-based detection is similar to pattern detection, but it detects classes of activities based on known unacceptable behavior. Therefore, instead of many signatures for each unwanted activity, a single signature can watch for a specific behavior. Once the behavior has been detected, the appropriate signature actions are applied.

Detecting unwanted activity is only the initial step in protecting your network. Once a signature triggers, your IDS device must take certain configured actions to mitigate the activity identified. Signature actions fall into the following categories:

- Generating an alert

- Dropping or preventing the activity

- Logging the activity

- Resetting a TCP connection

- Blocking future activity

- Allowing the activity

The alerts (or alarms) generated by your IPS device enable you to monitor the attacks being launched against your network. To efficiently monitor alerts, IPS devices incorporate the following types of alerts:

- Atomic alerts

- Summary alerts

CHAPTER 3

Operational Tasks

Intrusion Prevention technology can provide a key component to the overall protection of your network. Initially deploying an Intrusion Prevention System (IPS) on your network does require careful consideration to match the capabilities of your IPS with your unique network configuration. Furthermore, configuring your IPS and monitoring the alerts generated by your IPS devices requires dedicated personnel. This chapter provides a high-level view of the following operational tasks related to using IPS on your network:

- Deploying IPS devices and applications

- Configuring IPS devices and applications

- Monitoring IPS activities

- Securing IPS communications

Deploying IPS Devices and Applications

Each IPS deployment is fairly unique depending on your network configuration. Regardless of your network configuration, topology, and traffic patterns, you need to analyze your deployment from the following two perspectives:

- Deploying Host IPS

- Deploying Network IPS

Besides the initial deployment, you also need to continually evaluate your IPS and modify your deployment based on network threats and your ever-changing network.

Deploying Host IPS

The most optimum Host IPS deployment involves deploying Host IPS on every host on your network. In many situations, however, you are not able to deploy Host IPS on every system. Sometimes, you cannot cover all of your systems because your Host IPS product does not support certain operating systems that you use on your network. Most of the time, however, the limiting factor is cost. If your budget does not allow you to protect all of your systems with Host IPS, then you need to decide which systems to protect and which systems are left unprotected.

Deciding which systems to protect can be a tricky task. For example, you must decide whether it is better to protect end user laptops (a more accessible target when on unprotected networks) or focus on servers, which are more critical to the operation of your network. Some of the factors to consider when conducting a partial Host IPS deployment include the following:

■ Threat posed by known exploits

■ Criticality of the systems

■ Accessibility of the systems

■ Security policy requirements

After your initial deployment, you also need to identify unprotected systems. If your Host IPS deployment does not include every system, then identifying unprotected systems becomes even more difficult. Chapter 9, "Cisco Security Agent Deployment," provides a detailed analysis of the issues that you must consider when deploying Host IPS using the Cisco products as an example.

Threat Posed by Known Exploits

One of the factors to consider when deciding on whether or not to deploy Host IPS on a system is the number of known exploits for the operating system and applications used on the system. For example, if the operating system or applications used have a large number of known exploits, protecting the system with a Host IPS becomes more critical because a large number of exploits increases the ways in which an attacker can compromise the system. Furthermore, a large number of exploits might indicate a higher likelihood that new exploits for the system will be discovered in the future.

Criticality of the Systems

If a system is vital to the operation of your network, then protecting it with a Host IPS is paramount. By protecting the system, you decrease the chances that the system can become compromised. More importantly, the vital components of your network remain operational, reliably providing service to the various client systems on your network.

Accessibility of the Systems

Another factor that increases the chances that a system will be attacked is the accessibility of the system. A server that is in a fixed location protected by a firewall and Network IPS has limited accessibility. A laptop that moves from the company network to the user's home broadband network (as well as various broadband networks utilized for remote access when traveling, like public wireless networks) is very accessible to many different attackers. If this laptop is compromised while off the company network, it can wreak havoc when the system is again connected to the internal company network.

Security Policy Requirements

The underlining framework for all of your security decisions is your security policy. It defines requirements that must be met by systems on your network. Before considering other factors that impact your IPS deployment, you need to carefully analyze your security policy to identify requirements that must be met or add requirements to accommodate IPS. These requirements can then be used as a foundation upon which you can consider the other deployment factors.

Identifying Unprotected Systems

An ongoing task in any Host IPS deployment is the verification that all the targeted systems have your Host IPS software installed and operating on them. You need a mechanism to identify systems that you want to protect, but are not protected. You can then compare this list of unprotected systems to your policy on which systems should be protected to verify if you have systems that need to have the Host IPS software installed on them.

Deploying Network IPS

As is the case with Host IPS, the most optimum protection is provided by deploying Network IPS across your network to inspect all of your network traffic. Complete protection with Network IPS, however, is difficult to ensure. One of the main factors impacting Network IPS deployment is the traffic volume on your network. Figure 3-1 illustrates a sample Network IPS deployment for a small network. In this example, the maximum traffic volume is 100 Mbps so a single IPS sensor can monitor all the traffic entering the network at a single location. Because the IPS sensor bridges all traffic into and out of the protected network, it can examine that traffic for attacks and other traffic that violates the defined security policy.

Figure 3-1 *Small IPS Network Deployment*

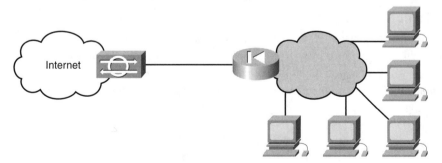

Even in the small deployment, you must decide whether to deploy the sensor outside your firewall (as shown in Figure 3-1) or behind your perimeter firewall. Placing the sensor outside the firewall enables you to observe all the attacks that are being launched against the network. Analyzing these attacks, however, can be manpower intensive because all traffic can reach the sensor. Furthermore, many of these attacks are going to be blocked by your firewall anyway before they reach the internal network. By deploying the sensor behind the firewall, you observe only attacks that make it through your firewall or attacks that originate from the internal network.

When deploying Network IPS on a large network, such as an enterprise network, you have to consider many factors. Some of the more important considerations include the following:

■   Security policy requirements

■   Maximum traffic volume

■   Number and placement of sensors

■   Business partner links (extranet connections)

■   Remote access

■   Identification of unprotected segments

You must consider these factors not only during your initial Network IPS deployment, but also as your network grows and changes. On an ongoing basis, you must reevaluate these factors to determine if your Network IPS deployment needs to be enhanced or revised to maintain optimum protection.

Security Policy Requirements

Your security policy might require that an IPS be in place to protect your network. The security policy might also contain other policies that your IPS sensors can be used to enforce. Identifying the security policy requirements that your Network IPS can enforce is one of the first steps that you should perform when planning your Network IPS deployment.

Maximum Traffic Volume

Whenever deploying an IPS sensor at a location in your network, you must consider the maximum bandwidth, the volume of new connections, and maximum concurrent connections that the sensor can support. At first, you might think that you would never deploy a sensor that could not handle the amount of traffic on the network. The traffic volume becomes an issue mainly because of the following two factors:

■   Network segments are not fully utilized.

■   Sensors can be costly.

If you have three 100 Mbps network segments that you want to monitor, you can guarantee that all the traffic is processed by using one or more sensors that are capable of handling 300 Mbps. With Cisco IPS sensors, you can use a single Cisco IPS 4255 that supports 600 Mbps. The Cisco IPS 4255 can easily process the 300 Mbps with extra processing power for future network growth. (For more information on specific Cisco IPS devices and capabilities, refer to Chapter 8, "NIDS Components.")

The cost of an IPS sensor usually varies based on the amount of traffic that it can process. So to save costs, you might want to deploy sensors that support the typical traffic volume on your network, because most network segments are not usually fully utilized. For example, suppose that we examine our three networks segments and discover that their maximum bandwidth almost never exceeds 80 percent of their capacity. Now the maximum amount of traffic that we need to examine is 240 Mbps. Instead of using a Cisco IPS 4255, we can now use a Cisco IPS 4240, because it can examine up to 250 Mbps.

Deploying your sensors based on the typical traffic volume enables you to save money on your IPS deployment. However, it does have a couple of drawbacks. First, you do not have any excess capacity to handle network growth. Secondly, you need to make sure that you verify that the actual amount of traffic on your network is not exceeding the sensor's capacity. If the traffic does exceed the sensor's capacity, some of the network traffic will not be analyzed by your sensor.

Number and Placement of Sensors

The maximum traffic volume is one of the factors that impact the number of sensors that you need to deploy. Besides deciding on the number of sensors and where you want to deploy them on your network, you also need to plan how you can manage the devices.

Most IPS products enable you to deploy IPS functionality in various locations throughout your network. Some of these locations include the following:

- Standalone appliances

- Specialized hardware blades

- Integrated into the operating system on infrastructure devices such as routers and switches

Examining the unique characteristics of your network helps you decide which of these options works best for your network topology. Chapter 10, "Deploying Cisco Network IPS," provides a detailed analysis of the issues that you must consider when deploying Network IPS using the Cisco products as an example.

Business Partner Links

Any link between your network and your business partners (known as extranets) needs to be monitored. Your business partner usually has a different security policy than you. Furthermore, you might run into legal liability issues if your business partner is attacked from a compromised system on your network. Therefore, deploying Network IPS to protect all of your extranets is very important.

> **NOTE**   It is also beneficial to have a high degree of coordination between the technical security team for your company and the technical security teams of your business partners. Through coordination, each team can proactively keep the other informed of potential attacks and other security concerns.

Remote Access

Most networks provide some type of remote access functionality to enable workers to access the corporate network from home and while traveling. Because this capability enables remote access into your network, it is also a prime target for attack. Monitoring any remote network access is vital to deploying an effective Network IPS solution.

Identifying Unprotected Segments

As your network grows, you need to continually verify that all the network segments are being monitored by your Network IPS sensors. Again, your security policy might help define your requirements. For example, deploying Network IPS at the edge of your network identifies attacks launched against your network from the Internet as well as attacks launched against hosts on the Internet from your network. But if you only examine the edge of your network, however, you are not able to identify attacks from one host on your network to another host on your network.

When you try to identify unprotected segments, identifying the source and destination for intrusive traffic that you are trying to monitor is beneficial. Table 3-1 shows some common source and destination segments.

Table 3-1   *Common Attack Sources and Targets*

Attack Source	Attack Target
Internet	Any internal system
Any internal system	Internet
Internal data network	Internal data network
Internal data network	Internal voice network
Internal voice network	Internal voice network

Table 3-1   *Common Attack Sources and Targets (Continued)*

Attack Source	Attack Target
Internal data network	External voice network
Internal voice network	External voice network
Server network	Any internal system
Any internal system	Server network

Configuring IPS Devices and Applications

For both Network and Host IPS, the configuration of your IPS is crucial for providing a strong defense against attack. Some of the major factors to consider with respect to IPS configuration include the following:

- Signature tuning

- Event response

- Software updates

- Configuration updates

- Device failure

Signature Tuning

Most IPS devices and applications provide a single default configuration or multiple default configurations. Using one of these default configurations is an ideal starting point for your IPS deployment. As you use your IPS, you need to tune specific signatures that generate false positives on your network.

FALSE POSITIVE

A false positive is a situation in which an intrusion system generates an alert or alarm after processing normal user traffic. Analyzing false positives limits the time that your security analyst have to examine actual intrusive activity on your network.

FALSE NEGATIVE

A false negative is a situation in which an intrusion system fails to generate an alert or alarm after processing attack traffic that it is configured to detect. Your intrusion system should not generate false negatives, because it means that known attacks being launched against your network are not being detected.

Besides false positives and false negatives, many people describe alarms using the terms true negatives and true positives. Table 3-2 highlights the differences between these different terms.

Table 3-2   *Common Alarm Terminology*

Network Activity	IPS Activity	Alarm Type
Normal user traffic	No alarm generated	True negative
Attack traffic	Alarm generated	True positive
Attack traffic	No alarm generated	False negative
Normal user traffic	Alarm generated	False positive

TRUE POSITIVE

A true positive is a situation in which an intrusion system generates an alarm in response to attack traffic that it is configured to detect. A true positive is effectively the opposite of a false negative.

TRUE NEGATIVE

A true negative is a situation in which normal network traffic does not generate an alarm. A true negative is effectively the opposite of a false positive.

Event Response

Whenever your Network IPS sensor identifies potentially malicious traffic, it must respond to the traffic by performing some type of action. You can usually configure each signature to generate one or more of the following actions:

- Deny
- Alert
- Block
- Log

> **NOTE**   Many intrusion systems provide filtering capabilities that enable you to limit the hosts or conditions in which signatures actually trigger (perform their configured actions). For example, if a signature is prone to false positives, you might configure the signature to trigger only on traffic that involves at least one external system, thus preventing false positives on traffic between two internal systems.

Deny

If a signature identifies a serious threat against your network, you might want your IPS sensor to stop the traffic. Operating in inline mode, your IPS sensor can selectively drop any traffic that it analyzes, thus preventing intrusive traffic from reaching the target system.

Alert

An alert or alarm is an indication that an attack has been detected by your IPS. Your security operators use the alerts generated by your IPS devices to understand the attacks and other traffic that traverse your network.

Block

Besides denying traffic with inline IPS devices, most IPS devices also enable you to initiate access control lists (ACLs) on other infrastructure devices to block network traffic. These ACLs, however, are applied only after initially detecting malicious traffic.

Log

The final IPS response is to log traffic. Logging traffic enables your security operators to analyze the traffic that an attacker sent to the network. By analyzing the captured traffic, the security operator can more effectively understand what an attacker is doing against your network.

Logging is usually initiated when a signature triggers and continues for a specified amount of time. Either all traffic from the attacking system (or the target system) is logged.

Software Updates

Every IPS is continually being enhanced to identify new attacks against your network. Furthermore, many existing signatures (see Chapter 2, "Signatures and Actions") are revised to make them more effective. Applying software updates to your IPS devices and applications is vital to maintain the optimum operation of your IPS. By keeping your IPS software current, you ensure that your network is being protected as effectively as possible.

Applying IPS software updates involves the following tasks:

- Checking for updates

- Deploying new updates

- Configuring new signatures

- Verifying the update

Configuration Updates

Besides software updates, you also need to identify the process by which you plan to deploy configuration updates to your IPS devices. Configuration updates refer to the changes that you make to the configuration of the IPS software to match the unique characteristics of your network. This information involves settings such as which signatures are enabled and which signatures actions are configured for each signature. As your network grows and changes or when your security policy changes, you need to update the configurations on your IPS devices.

SOFTWARE UPDATE

Software updates refer to installing new versions of the IPS software. This updated software usually provides enhanced functionality, but it can also fix known bugs with the IPS software. The enhanced functionality can include new software features and/or IPS signatures.

Device Failure

When your IPS devices have problems, you need to understand what the impact is going to be to your security posture. You need to know how your IPS reacts to the following two failure situations:

- Inline sensor failure
- Management console failure

Inline Sensor Failure

If the software on your IPS sensor fails, you need to understand how the sensor handles network traffic. If the sensor software is not functioning, you need to know whether the network traffic is passed without inspection or whether all traffic is dropped while the analysis software is not operating.

INLINE SENSOR

An inline sensor is a sensor that processes traffic, by acting as a Layer 2 forwarding device. Before forwarding traffic, the sensor analyzes the traffic searching for attacks and other security policy violations. The inline sensor actively forwards network traffic, as opposed to a traditional IDS sensor that passively monitors network traffic.

With Cisco IPS, you have the following three options with respect to software bypass:

- Auto
- On
- Off

Software bypass is the configuration that defines how the sensor processes network traffic when the sensor's analysis software is not operating. In *Auto* mode (also known as *Fail Open* mode), a sensor running in inline mode continues to forward traffic even if the sensor's analysis engine stops processing traffic. Although this traffic is not inspected by the sensor, the network is still operational. Auto mode is useful on networks where operation of the network takes the highest priority.

In *Off* mode (also known as *Fail Close* mode), a sensor running in inline mode stops forwarding traffic if the sensor's analysis engine software fails or stops. Because the sensor stops forwarding traffic, none of the traffic is allowed to pass the sensor without inspection. Off mode is useful on networks where the security of the network takes the highest priority.

In *On* mode, a sensor running in inline mode always forwards traffic without inspecting it. This mode is useful in debugging situations when you want to configure the sensor to forward traffic without performing any inspection on the traffic.

> **NOTE**   With Cisco IPS devices, you can also configure multiple sensors using an EtherChannel group. In this configuration, if any of the individual sensors loses power or stops operating, the traffic is automatically load balanced between the remaining sensors that are members of the EtherChannel group.

ETHERCHANNEL

EtherChannel is a functionality provided by Cisco switches that enables you to configure multiple trunk lines to be members of the same VLAN. Traffic for the VLAN is then load balanced between all trunk lines that are members of the EtherChannel group. The Cisco EtherChannel functionality provides fault-tolerant, high-speed links between switches, routers, and servers (see http://www.cisco.com/en/US/tech/tk389/tk213/technologies_white_paper 09186a0080092944.shtml).

Management Console Failure

Your management console provides a mechanism for your security operators to view the events that are occurring on your network. The management console needs to retrieve alerts or alarms from your IPS devices or applications (such as the Cisco Security Agent [CSA]). Your management software uses one of the following models to retrieve events from your IPS devices:

- Push model

- Pull model

> **NOTE** When managing the devices on your network, you will find it beneficial to have a separate management VLAN or out-of-band management network. Besides minimizing management access to your crucial network devices and thus enhancing your network's security, a separate management network (or VLAN) also prevents you from losing connectivity to your devices if an IPS sensor protecting those devices fails closed.

In the Push model, the IPS devices push events to your management console as they happen. If the management console is unreachable, you can lose events. Therefore, a failure of the management console can impact the security of your network.

In the *Pull* model, the management console itself retrieves events from the IPS devices when it is ready to receive them. The IPS devices basically buffer a certain amount of alert information, waiting for the management console to retrieve them. Short failures of your management console do not cause any alerts to be lost, as long as your management console retrieves the buffered events before the event buffer on the sensor is exceeded.

> **NOTE** The Cisco IPS solution uses the Pull model for both its network and host products. Therefore, a temporary failure of the management console should not result in a loss of event information, because the sensor stores the events in a local circular buffer until they are retrieved by the management console. If the management console fails to retrieve the event information before the buffer starts overwriting events, event information can be lost during a management console failure. On a normal network, however, the circular buffer can easily hold a couple of days' worth of events before the buffer starts overwriting unread events.

Monitoring IPS Activities

Monitoring the security related events happening on your network is also a crucial aspect of protecting your network from attack. Although your IPS can prevent numerous attacks against your network, understanding which attacks are being launched against your network enables you to assess how strong your current protections are and how you might need to enhance them as your network grows. Only by monitoring the security events on your network can you accurately identify the attacks and security policy violations that are occurring on your network.

When planning your monitoring strategy, you need to consider the following factors:

- Management method
- Event correlation
- Security staff
- Incident response plan

Management Method

You usually can choose from one of the following two management methods:

■   Individual

■   Centralized

Configuring each of your IPS devices individually is the easiest process if you have only a couple of sensors. As the number of sensors grows, managing the sensors individually becomes unmanageable. If you deploy a large number of sensors on your network, you need to also deploy a centralized management system that enables you to configure and manage all of your IPS devices from a single central system. Using the centralized management approach for large sensor deployments reduces the manpower required and enables greater visibility to all the events occurring on your network.

> **NOTE**   Although you can use an individual or centralized approach to configure your IPS device(s), you probably want to always use centralized reporting to enable more accurate event correlation.

Event Correlation

Event correlation refers to the process of correlating attacks and other events that are happening at different points across your network as well as multiple attacks happening at the same time. Using Network Time Protocol (NTP) and having your devices derive their time from an NTP server enables all the alerts generated by your IPS to be accurately time stamped. A correlation tool can then correlate the alerts based on their time stamps.

NETWORK TIME PROTOCOL

NTP (refer to RFC 1305) defines a network protocol that enables client systems to synchronize their system clocks by contacting a server system. Running NTP on your network devices enables each of them to time stamp events with a common system time. These time stamps can then be used to accurately access when specific events happened in relation to the actual time and other events on the network, regardless of which device observed an event.

Besides ensuring that all events are marked with a consistent time stamp, another factor that facilitates event correlation is deploying a centralized monitoring facility on your network. By monitoring all of your IPS events at a single location, you greatly improve the accuracy of your event correlation.

> **NOTE** Another factor to consider when performing event correlation is deploying a product that enables you to correlate not only IPS events but also other events on your network (such as syslog messages and NetFlow input). One product that provides this level of correlation is the Cisco Security Monitoring, Analysis and Response System (Cisco Security MARS) product (see http://www.cisco.com/en/US/products/ps6241/products_data_sheet0900aecd80272e64.html).

Security Staff

Your IPS generates numerous alerts and other events during the processing of your network traffic. Someone needs to analyze this activity and determine how well your IPS is protecting your network. Examining these alerts also enables your security operators to tune your IPS and optimize its operation for your unique network requirements.

Incident Response Plan

If a system is compromised on your network, you need to have a plan as to how you can respond. The compromised system needs to be restored to the clean state that it was in before it was attacked. Furthermore, you need to determine if the compromised system led to a loss of intellectual property or the compromise of other systems on your network. You might decide that after any compromise, you replace the hard drive on the effected system and rebuild it to its pre-attack state. Then you might analyze the compromised hard drive to perform a thorough forensic analysis on it.

Securing IPS Communications

You deploy IPS to help secure your network. If you do not use secure communications protocols to access your IPS devices, however, your IPS devices can become another avenue of attack.

IPS communications fall into the following two categories:

- Management communication
- Device-to-device communication

Management Communication

You need to configure and manage your IPS devices and applications. Doing this management and configuration directly on each device is very time consuming. Therefore, you usually perform many management and configuration tasks across the network. The network protocols that you use to communicate to your IPS devices need to be secure. Your options to perform secure management access are as follows:

■   Out-of-band management

■   Secure protocols

Out-of-Band Management

Out-of-band management involves using a network that is dedicated solely to management access. This network connects your IPS devices with a limited number of management systems, which makes it more difficult to attack. Because the network is solely for management, you can use protocols for management that you would not ordinarily use.

For example, an insecure management protocol such as Simple Network Management Protocol (SNMP) version 1 does not provide encrypted communication. Anyone who passively monitors that network can capture sensitive authentication credentials. Therefore, the use of SNMP version 1 is not recommended. However, some management systems do not support secured protocols. An out-of-band network is one way to mitigate the risk of using them because you are physically limiting access to only trusted systems.

NOTE   For an example of how to deploy an out-of-band management network, refer to the Cisco SAFE Enterprise white paper on the Cisco website.

Secure Protocols

Providing a totally separate management network is costly. A more common management solution involves using secure protocols such as Secure Shell (SSH). SSH encrypts the traffic going across the network, making it impossible for an attacker to easily capture authentication credentials by simply sniffing network traffic. Some of the secure protocols commonly used for management include the following:

■   SSH

■   Secure Hypertext Transfer Protocol (HTTPS)

■   SNMP version 3

NOTE   Even when using secure management protocols, however, you should implement Layer 2 security best practices to protect your network. Without implementing Layer 2 protections, an attacker can spoof traffic on your network and potentially compromise some of your secure management protocols.

Device-to-Device Communication

In many situations, your IPS devices communicate with each other or with other infrastructure devices. Some common examples of this communication with Cisco IPS devices include the following:

■ Sensor communication with a master blocking sensor

■ Sensor communications with a managed device

A managed device is an infrastructure device (such as a router, firewall, or switch) that your IPS device uses to deploy ACLs in response to attacks against the network. Only one IPS device can control the ACL on a specific managed device. When you configure your IPS device as a master blocking device, another IPS device can initiate an ACL on the managed device by communicating with the controlling IPS device (master blocking sensor).

Summary

Intrusion Prevention technology can provide a key component to the overall protection of your network. Initially deploying an IPS on your network does require careful consideration to match the capabilities of your IPS with your unique network configuration. Furthermore, configuring your IPS and monitoring the alerts generated by your IPS devices requires dedicated personnel.

Each IPS deployment is fairly unique depending on your network configuration. Regardless of your network configuration, however, you need to analyze your deployment from the following two perspectives:

■ Deploying Host IPS

■ Deploying Network IPS

The most effective Host IPS deployment involves deploying Host IPS on every host on your network. Some of the factors to consider when conducting a partial Host IPS deployment include the following:

■ Security policy requirements

■ Number of known exploits

■ Criticality of the systems

■ Accessibility of the systems

When deploying Network IPS on a large network, such as an enterprise network, you have to consider many factors. Some of the more important considerations include the following:

■   Security policy requirements

■   Maximum traffic volume

■   Number and placement of sensors

■   Business partner links (extranet connections)

■   Remote access

■   Identifying unprotected segments

Both Network and Host IPS configuration of your IPS is crucial to providing strong defense against attack. Some of the major factors to consider with respect to IPS configuration include the following:

■   Signature tuning

■   Event response

■   Software updates

■   Configuration updates

■   Device failure

Monitoring the security related events happening on your network is also a crucial aspect of protecting your network from attack. When planning your monitoring strategy, you need to consider the following factors:

■   Management method

■   Event correlation

■   Security manpower

■   Incident response plan

You deploy IPS to help secure your network. If you do not use secure communications protocols (such as SSH, HTTPS, and SNMPv3) and implement secure Layer 2 best practices to access your IPS devices, your IPS devices can become another avenue of attack. IPS communications fall into the following two categories:

■   Management communication

■   Device-to-device communication

CHAPTER 4

Security in Depth

No single security countermeasure can always stop all attacks. Effective security requires multiple layers of countermeasure, so that if one is bypassed, the attack still has to get through the next layer, the layer after that, and so on. This concept is called *defense-in-depth*, and is illustrated by Figure 4-1.

Figure 4-1 *Layered Defenses*

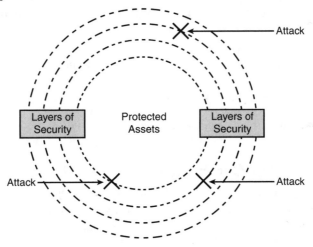

For example, a fence by itself is not enough to secure your home. The fence stops some attackers, but others climb over it. Some people might even knock your fence down. That is why you have doors and windows with locks on them, perhaps an alarm system, and even a safe for your valuables. Each layer makes it more difficult for the attacker to succeed.

Effective computer security should also be based on a defense-in-depth. An Intrusion Prevention System (IPS) is only one of many layers you employ to defend your computing resources. This chapter demonstrates the importance of computer security in depth. It will

- Give examples of effective defense-in-depth
- Explain the role of security policy
- Envision the likely future of IPS and how collaboration between layers greatly enhances defensive capabilities

Defense-in-Depth Examples

Defense-in-depth assumes that every countermeasure can potentially be bypassed by an attacker. However, if you put many countermeasures together, the odds of bypassing all of them without being detected becomes much more unlikely. However, because of operational concerns, the most secure solution cannot always be implemented and is not always practical.

Consider securing houses. The strongest walls are thick concrete walls with no windows. These walls are also more expensive than normal wooden framed walls. Furthermore, people prefer to have natural lighting, so most houses have numerous windows made of glass. The glass lets light in and enables people to view things happening outside their house. Although the glass windows are a weak link (because they are breakable), you can improve on them using the defense-in-depth strategy. By adding a clear plastic laminate to the inside of the window, you can ensure that when the window breaks, the pieces stay together. This laminate then prevents attackers from easily getting through the window even if they break the glass. In conjunction with the laminate, you probably want to add an alarm mechanism that triggers when the window is opened or the glass is broken. Both of these measures make it more difficult for robbers to get into your house through the window without being detected.

This section walks through two examples that show the strength of a defense-in-depth approach:

- External attack against a corporate database

- Internal attack against a management server

External Attack Against a Corporate Database

A prime target on your network is your corporate database. Hopefully, this database is housed on your internal network and protected by various security measures. These security measures should make it difficult for an attacker to launch a successful attack against your corporate database.

Many people might think that an external attack needs to come directly from your network Internet connection. However, external attackers can attack your corporate database in various ways. Some of the attack paths and mechanisms include the following:

- Accessing the database server from Internet

- Accessing the database server from a compromised internal system

- Accessing the database server from compromised DMZ web server

- Accessing the database server from a worm attack

Protecting against these external attacks falls into the following areas or layers:

- Layer 1: The Internet perimeter router

- Layer 2: The Internet perimeter firewall

- Layer 3: The DMZ firewall

- Layer 4: Network IPS

- Layer 5: NetFlow

- Layer 6: Antivirus

- Layer 7: Host IPS

Layer 1: The Internet Perimeter Router

The first layer of protection from an attack is your external router. A router, if properly configured, can prevent traffic from entering your network while spoofing your internal address space. A commonly used and effective method for preventing spoofed traffic is to enable unicast reverse path forwarding (uRPF). uRPF uses the router's routing table to examine incoming traffic on an interface. This means that when traffic arrives on an interface with a source IP address of 10.10.10.1, for example, the router examines its routing table to see which interfaces it would send traffic that had 10.10.10.1 as a destination address. If these two interfaces aren't the same, the spoofed traffic is dropped. Routers can also use access control lists (ACLs). ACLs are rules that permit, deny, or simply identify traffic based on the following parameters:

- Source IP address

- Destination IP address

- Source port

- Destination port

- IP protocol

A weakness of traditional router ACLs is that they must trust information contained within the network traffic. The router does not maintain state information on traffic and instead relies on whether or not bits are set in a packet to determine whether or not the traffic is valid. For example, a crafted attack packet could potentially set the ACK bit to 1, and a router might believe this traffic is response traffic to a session that originated inside the network.

VALID TCP CONNECTION

A valid TCP connection is one that has been initiated with a complete three-way handshake that starts with a SYN packet from the client, followed by a SYN-ACK packet from the server, followed by an ACK from the client. Valid TCP traffic also has sequence and acknowledgment numbers that match the current values for the TCP connection. For more information on the TCP protocol, refer to RFC 793.

For example, suppose ACME's corporate databases run on Microsoft's SQL Server, which defaults to using User Datagram Protocol (UDP) port 1434 for access to the database. Most companies already block this port, but ACME should verify that the ACLs on the router do not allow this port to pass, especially to the SQL Server. Because this traffic is UDP-based, this ACL should block all external traffic to this port. Simply limiting external connections, however, via ACLs is usually not effective because an attacker can spoof UDP traffic fairly easily.

Layer 2: The Internet Perimeter Firewall

Most companies want their default protection to prevent traffic from the Internet to the internal network, although they allow internal systems to easily access the Internet. A perimeter firewall can implement rules to enforce these protections. The firewall, however, also has additional functionality such as the following:

- Application inspection processing

- Stateful connection processing

- Network Address Translation (NAT)

Your perimeter firewall should be configured to prevent an external computer from making connections to your internal database server.

In the example, the perimeter firewall prevents any inbound connections to the internal network. At the same time, this firewall allows internal systems to make outbound connections (allowing return traffic only for connections initiated from the internal network).

The application inspection processing enables your firewall to perform a detailed analysis of network traffic at the application layer. This analysis can automatically alter packet contents (such as performing NAT on IP fields in the application data). It can also open up pinhole connections through the firewall based on application data (such as opening up voice audio streams).

Layer 3: The DMZ Firewall

External users need to access many systems (such as your corporate web server). These systems, therefore, are a prime attack target. By placing these systems in a demilitarized zone (DMZ), you limit the ability of an attacker to impact other areas of your network if they happen to be compromised (see Figure 4-2). If a DMZ server is compromised by an attacker, the only other systems an attacker can attempt to attack from the compromised server are other systems on the same DMZ. Any connectivity to other DMZs or the internal network must be explicitly defined on the firewall.

> **NOTE**   You should also limit the ability of your DMZ servers to initiate connections to other systems on the Internet. This prevents your public servers from attacking other systems on the Internet should they be compromised.

Figure 4-2   *DMZ Zone*

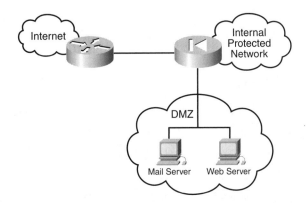

The firewall provides access to your web server and mail server; however, it can also provide some protection against many flooding attacks (such as a SYN flood). For example, the Cisco PIX firewall software version 7.0 and the Adaptive Security Appliance (ASA) provide various measures to protect against SYN flood attacks.

In the example, placing the public servers on a DMZ network prevents them from being used to attack the database server because they have no access to the internal network and the firewall is not configured to allow it. All connections to these public servers are initiated from the internal network.

Layer 4: Network IPS

Your Network IPS is continually analyzing the traffic passing through key points in your network. Using a large database of known attack signatures (a combination of patterns, protocol decodes, anomaly and behavioral analysis) your IPS sensors can prevent many attacks from reaching systems on your network.

If an attacker manages to pass attack traffic through your firewall, your Network IPS should detect it and take action. Actions are usually predefined and can include setting off an alarm or stopping the attack. You can also configure your Network IPS to alarm if it detects unauthorized traffic, such as connections originating from the database server destined to systems on the Internet.

Layer 5: NetFlow

NetFlow enables you to analyze the connections that occur on your network. Looking at the following connection parameters, you can identify patterns and other potentially anomalous activity:

- Source IP address

- Destination IP address

- Source port

- Destination port

- IP protocol

- Amount of data transmitted

In the example, NetFlow is used for anomaly identification. A baseline of connections patterns is established. Then using NetFlow, any connections that deviate from the established baseline are investigated.

In fact, Cisco Security Monitoring, Analysis and Response System (CS-MARS) accepts NetFlow data from routers and Layer 3 switches and then automates the security analysis of the NetFlow information. By learning what normal traffic is on the network, CS-MARS is able to alert on sudden changes in behavior.

Layer 6: Antivirus

Antivirus software protects systems on your network from a wide variety of viruses, Trojans, and worms. Antivirus software runs on the actual system that it protects. Therefore, the protection moves with the system. This is especially beneficial for highly mobile systems, such as laptops. Your business network might have a wide variety of security measures in place, but when your users take their corporate laptops home, those same protections are usually not in place (except for those that run on the laptops themselves).

In the example, antivirus software protects user systems from becoming compromised by known viruses. Protecting user systems prevents the user computers from being used as a launching point for attacks against the network.

Layer 7: Host IPS

Similar to antivirus, Host IPS runs on the actual system being protected. If your Host IPS implements behavioral signatures, it has the ability to protect your systems from day zero attacks.

> **DAY ZERO ATTACKS**
>
> Day zero attacks refer to attacks that were previously unpublished when they are used. Therefore, these attacks are not included in the signature database of many antivirus products.

Another advantage of Host IPS is that it can detect malicious software, such as keyloggers and Trojans, that an attacker might attempt to install on your systems.

A Host IPS system such as Cisco Security Agent (CSA) can be installed on the database systems, as well as all user systems. CSA protects the systems from buffer overflow attacks and from the installation of malicious software. It also alerts the user whenever it appears that software is being installed on the system. These alerts provide a visual indication to the user indicating that software is being installed on the system. This enables users to prevent many malicious applications and spyware from being installed on the system while still allowing them to install other software successfully. CSA can also be configured to protect against many malicious applications automatically (without informing the user).

Internal Attack Against a Management Server

Besides external attacks, you also need to worry about internal people who attempt to access unauthorized resources (either intentionally or accidentally). Because your management systems control the configuration on devices throughout your network, protecting these systems is a vital component of your overall network security strategy. Hopefully, an attacker must compromise several security mechanisms to access your management systems.

Protecting against these internal attacks falls into the following areas or layers:

- Layer 1: The switch

- Layer 2: Network IPS

- Layer 3: Encryption

- Layer 4: Strong authentication

- Layer 5: Host IPS

Layer 1: The Switch

The first layer of protection on your network is the switch ports that connect devices to your internal network. By separating different ports into different VLANs, you force traffic between different VLANs to go through your Layer 3 protection mechanisms, such as ACLs on your routers. When you turn off unused ports or use a port-based authentication system like 802.1x, you decrease the chances that someone can plug into an unused port and gain access to important systems.

802.1X

802.1x is a protocol that requires a device to be authenticated before the port that the device is connected to is allowed to access the protected network. Initially, the port provides the device with access only to the switch itself. Then if the device can authenticate successfully, the switch reconfigures the port and provides the device with greater access to the network.

In this example, the only ports configured for the server VLAN are the three server systems. Furthermore, ACLs limit access to only specific user systems. You can also get benefit by enabling port security on the switch's ports. Port security restricts the number of Ethernet addresses that a specific switch port is allowed to use, along with preventing a device from pretending to be another device's Ethernet address using Address Resolution Protocol (ARP) spoofing (common techniques used by tools such as Ettercap and DSNIFF).

Layer 2: Network IPS

Your Network IPS is constantly monitoring the traffic on your network looking for potential attack traffic. In this example, you can also use your Network IPS to identify anomalous connections to or from your management servers. Sensors running in inline mode can actually prevent connections from or to unauthorized systems. If attackers do compromise one of the servers, they can attempt to establish a connection to an external system on the Internet. This connection can be observed by the Network IPS.

Layer 3: Encryption

Many tools are available to sniff (or capture) the traffic on a network. To prevent successful sniffing, encrypt traffic to your management servers so that you stop an attacker from capturing vital information (such as login credentials). Common encrypted protocols for management include Secure Shell (SSH) and Secure Socket Layer (SSL).

In the example, encrypting the network traffic makes it almost impossible for an internal attacker (who has access to the network) to gain login credentials by using a simple network sniffer unless the attacker is able to successfully initiate a man-in-the-middle attack.

> **NOTE**   Enabling port security, however, can minimize or eliminate the ability of the attacker to initiate a successful man-in-the-middle attack.

Layer 4: Strong Authentication

Strong authentication is important to protect critical assets (such as your management systems). One way to implement strong authentication is to implement one-time passwords. Even if an attacker manages to observe the password during a login attempt, the password could not be used by the attacker to gain access to the management system.

ONE-TIME PASSWORDS

By stealing basic username and passwords, an attacker can log in to vital systems. Using one-time passwords, your accounts are protected even if the password is observed because a new password is generated for each login attempt and is usually valid only for a short period of time. These passwords are generated by a smartcard, token, or computer program.

Layer 5: Host IPS

Finally, Host-based IPS, like CSA, protects the management system from attempts at exploiting vulnerabilities in the operating system or applications running on it. In addition, it can enforce policies that define what applications are allowed to run, which systems they are allowed to communicate with, and which users are allowed to run them. This final line of defense provides a final hurdle for an internal attacker.

The Security Policy

Although some people do not recognize it, your corporate security policy has an important role to play in defense-in-depth. It contains policies, procedures, guidelines, standards, implementation specifications, and requirements that should guide every facet of your security strategy. A typical corporate security policy contains four sections:

- Administrative safeguards

- Physical safeguards

- Technical safeguards

- Organizational framework

Each section defines a layer of security. For example, the administrative safeguards determine who should have access to a protected resource, the physical safeguards determine what physical access controls should protect the resource, and the technical safeguards define the technical countermeasures that should be in place. An IPS would likely be a tool used in the technical safeguards section.

The technical safeguards section also defines implementation guidelines for each layer of technical security. It covers how each layer should be configured, what layers should protect each type of resource, and how the layers are to interact. If you do not already use IPS, be sure to add it to your security policy.

You might find that as you add IPS to your security policy that you have to revise other sections to reflect the IPS' impact on other layers. For example, some IPS can reconfigure other types of devices, like firewalls, in response to an attack. The firewall section of the policy must be updated to define which interface should be reconfigured by the IPS, how the configuration request should be handled, and how the communications channel is to be secured.

The Future of IPS

The desire to become proactive instead of reactive has prompted most of the major improvements in IPS technology over the last few years. For example, movement of IPS devices into the data stream improves their ability to stop attacks before any damage can occur. The transition away from purely signature-based detection methods and into detection methods that can stop new and unknown attacks is another example. Refer to Chapter 1, "Intrusion Prevention Overview," for more information about the historical evolution of IPS.

As time goes on, IPS will likely reach a threshold where it is as proactive as it needs to be. At that time, IPS developers will have to find other ways to improve the technology. This section gives three examples of improvements that might be the future of IPS:

- Intrinsic IPS

- Collaboration between layers

- Automatic configuration and response

Intrinsic IPS

Chapter 7, "Network Intrusion Prevention Overview," covers some of Network IPS' limitations. One of the limitations covered there is that a NIPS device cannot inspect traffic it doesn't see. For a NIPS to be effective, it must bridge or capture the traffic between the attacker and the victim. Host IPS has the same problem in that it cannot protect a device that it is not installed on (see

Chapter 5, "Host Intrusion Prevention Overview"). Therefore, it is likely that in the future, IPS will transition away from a network or host add-on and become an intrinsic part of your network or endpoint.

In the case of Network IPS, this means that it will be built into every device that powers your network. Firewalls, routers, switches, and practically any other device through which network traffic passes will have the capability to inspect and act on that traffic. The only traffic that will escape inspection is that which passes directly from host to host with no intermediary.

On the host side, HIPS will run on a wider variety of operating systems and endpoints like IP phones, mobile phones, personal digital assistants (PDAs), and any other device that can connect to the network. It might be that product vendors will ship their products with built-in HIPS. Also, mechanisms that check for the presence of a HIPS before granting network access will become more foolproof and sophisticated.

Eventually, IPS might cease to exist as a standalone technology. If it's built into everything, it might become a standard feature rather than an add-on.

Collaboration Between Layers

Traditionally, each layer of protection operates separately from all of the others. A few exceptions exist, but for the most part, firewalls do not communicate with the NIPS—the NIPS does not talk to the HIPS, the HIPS does not interface with antivirus, and so on. Each layer has weaknesses for which other layers can make up. In the future, the layers will collaborate together, and the whole will be greater than the sum of the parts. This collaboration will result in

- Enhanced accuracy

- Better detection capability

- Automated configuration and response

Enhanced Accuracy

In the near future, accuracy enhancing interfaces between HIPS and NIPS will appear. When NIPS sees a malicious event, HIPS can corroborate it and vice versa. For example, if a HTTP service attack is detected by a NIPS device, it can ask the HIPS running on the target if a web service is running. If a web service is running, the attack is corroborated. If no web service is running, the attack is marked as a false alarm.

Another example would be the case where HIPS sees anomalous network activity on a host. The HIPS will consult with the NIPS to see if the activity is dangerous or benign. The NIPS can report back that the host from which the activity originated was recently identified as an attacker. The HIPS then knows that the anomalous activity is an actual attack and can respond appropriately.

Currently, CS-MARS is a Cisco product that can read syslogs, application logs, and IPS events and correlate them together to help to perform attack research and also mitigate and isolate attacks. You can find out more information on the MARs product at http://www.cisco.com/go/mars. The result of MARs event correlation is less false positive events from security devices and a much better understanding of what the various security event messages mean when looked at as a collective picture of the state of your network.

Better Detection Capability

An attack has a much harder time avoiding detection if all of the layers through which it has to pass share information with each other. Think of a suspicious-looking person passing through a series of manned checkpoints. If the checkpoints do not communicate, the guard at each stop might think the person looks "funny" but not have enough supporting evidence to take action. However, if the guards communicated, they would all agree that the person is suspicious-looking and should be stopped and questioned.

The same concept will be applied to computer security. In the future, each countermeasure will share information with all of the others. For example, a firewall, a NIPS, and a HIPS all detect suspicious, but potentially not dangerous, reconnaissance activity originating from a single host. They all report their findings to a single collection and correlation device. The device sees three similar reports and sends a message to all three devices indicating that a reconnaissance effort is underway and that the attacking host should be shunned.

The same function might take the form of a "tag" applied to network traffic as it passes through defensive layers. If a firewall detects traffic that is anomalous it adds a "potentially dangerous" flag to the traffic. An IPS sees the flag and knows that the firewall thinks the traffic is strange. If the IPS also determines that the traffic is suspicious, it drops the traffic based on its suspicion and the firewall's tag.

Automated Configuration and Response

In the future, security countermeasures will be able to take collaborative, rather than individual, action during an incident. As it stands, when an IPS detects an attack it takes action according to its configuration settings. Moving forward, when the IPS detects an attack originating from an internal host, it can take its usual action and also configure the network to contain the attack. Routers, switches, and firewalls will be reconfigured by the IPS to make sure the attack cannot propagate throughout the network.

HIPS and NIPS can also work together to configure each other. For example, if a HIPS sees an attack against a protected host, it can notify the NIPS. The NIPS can take that notification and reconfigure itself to take more stringent action against traffic from the attacker. Furthermore, if IPS functionality is integrated into many different devices on the network (such as firewalls and routers), all of these devices can participate collaboratively to maintain a strong security posture on your network.

Summary

No single security countermeasure can always stop all attacks. Effective security requires multiple layers of countermeasure, so that if one is bypassed, the attack still has to get through the next layer, the layer after that, and so on. The concept of utilizing multiple layers of defense is called *defense-in-depth*.

A prime target on your network is your corporate database. Hopefully, this database is housed on your internal network and protected by various security measures. However, an external attacker can attack your corporate database in various ways. Some of the attack paths and mechanisms include the following:

- Accessing the database server from Internet

- Accessing the database server from a compromised internal system

- Accessing the database server from compromised DMZ web server

- Accessing the database server from a worm attack

Protecting against these external attacks falls into the following areas or layers:

- Layer 1: The Internet perimeter router

- Layer 2: The Internet perimeter firewall

- Layer 3: The DMZ firewall

- Layer 4: Network IPS

- Layer 5: NetFlow

- Layer 6: Antivirus

- Layer 7: Host IPS

Besides external attacks, you also need to worry about internal people who attempt to access unauthorized resources (either intentionally or accidentally). Protecting against these internal attacks falls into the following areas or layers:

- Layer 1: The switch

- Layer 2: Network IPS

- Layer 3: Encryption

- Layer 4: Strong authentication

- Layer 5: Host IPS

Your corporate security policy has an important role to play in defense-in-depth. It contains policies, procedures, guidelines, standards, implementation specifications, and requirements that should guide every facet of your security strategy. A typical corporate security policy contains four sections:

- Administrative safeguards

- Physical safeguards

- Technical safeguards

- Organizational framework

Part II: Host Intrusion Prevention

Chapter 5 Host Intrusion Prevention Overview

Chapter 6 HIPS Components

Host Intrusion Prevention Overview

Host Intrusion Prevention is a relatively new category of technology in the security marketplace. Since its inception, it has gained broad acceptance, and its use is expected to grow rapidly in the future. Despite this momentum, the category is not as clearly defined as more established technologies like firewall and antivirus. Ambiguous technical literature, vague buzzwords, and rapid product evolution confuse the marketplace to the point that it is extremely difficult to even determine which products are actually Host Intrusion Prevention Systems (HIPS).

A good way to differentiate Host Intrusion Prevention products from other categories in the marketplace is to clearly define the capabilities a product should have to be a part of the category. For example, a motorcycle must have the capability to roll on two wheels whereas a car must be able to roll on four. If a vehicle has only two wheels, then it cannot be in the car category.

Another area of general confusion is what problems HIPSs can solve. A quick look at the way vendors describe their own products reveals that many do not clearly state what benefits their products offer and how they can solve a realistic business or security problem. The capabilities offered by HIPS are exciting, but irrelevant if you don't have a problem to solve and a product capable of solving it.

Even if you have a problem that a HIPS can solve, you sometimes can find better ways to resolve the issue. It would be a waste to purchase and implement a HIPS product when a simple process change or a tool you have already implemented would address the problem more effectively. Before you can use HIPS correctly, you must understand where it provides benefit and where it is limited.

This chapter describes Host Intrusion Prevention so that you understand its

- Capabilities

- Benefits

- Limitations

Host Intrusion Prevention Capabilities

A recent search of the Internet listed over 700,000 pages containing the words *Host Intrusion Prevention*. We found hundreds of different Host Intrusion Prevention products among the results. Knowing which products are actually HIPS and which are not presents a challenge, especially given the overwhelming volume of available information. The challenge is exacerbated by the lack of a formal definition for the category that is accepted by all HIPS vendors.

To help you distinguish HIPS products from the rest, this section lists the capabilities you can look for to determine whether or not a product is a HIPS. This section does not attempt to define standards of quality for HIPS, just a specific set of capabilities. We believe that to qualify as a HIPS, a product should have the following capabilities:

- Blocks malicious code actions

- Doesn't disrupt normal operations

- Distinguishes between attacks and normal events

- Stops new and unknown attacks

- Protects against flaws in permitted applications

Blocking Malicious Code Activities

A HIPS must be able to do more than generate an alert or log when malicious code attacks a host. It must be able to actively block the actions of the malicious code. If the actions are blocked, the attack will not succeed. HIPS products should also keep a log and be able to generate alerts so that users will know what the HIPS did, but the differentiating requirement is that it be able to take action.

For example, one way for malicious code spread from a system it has compromised to other hosts is to copy itself to open network shares. Some security tools might be able to detect the malicious code's copy attempt but not take action against it. A HIPS should be able to detect the attempt and actively block it.

Not Disrupting Normal Operations

One way to secure a host is to unplug it from the network. Disconnecting it from the network would indeed make it more secure, but it would also deprive it of the network services business users rely on. Disconnection is not a very usable security countermeasure because it completely disrupts normal operations.

HIPS is similar in that it must be able to operate without disrupting normal operations. For example, e-mail attachments might pose a security risk because the attachment could contain malicious code. One way to mitigate the risk is to strip all messages of their attachments. However, e-mail attachments are often an essential part of normal operations. A product that deletes all e-mail attachments does not qualify as a HIPS product because it disrupts operations.

Distinguishing Between Attacks and Normal Events

A security product that treated attacks as normal events and normal events as attacks would be virtually useless. HIPS products must be accurate enough to correctly determine which events are attacks and which are normal. You should expect some false positives when you first implement HIPS, but you should find mechanisms within the product to remove the false positives without removing the product's capability to detect attacks.

Stopping New and Unknown Attacks

You can employ numerous methods to stop a published and well-known attack. For example, you can apply a software patch to the host to remove the vulnerability the attack uses. You can also update your antivirus signatures or reconfigure your network appliances to prevent the attack from entering your network. For each new vulnerability or attack, you might need to repeat the update and reconfiguration process.

A technology that requires update or reconfiguration to stop a new and unknown attack (see the note that follows) is not a HIPS. HIPS products must be able to stop new and unknown attacks without reconfiguration or update. The way the HIPS product stops the attack or its success rate is not relevant information in this section. It simply must have the capability.

> **NOTE**   New and unknown attacks are attacks for which the target is unprepared. The target might be unprepared because a patch has not been applied or security countermeasures have not been configured to mitigate the attack. The target might also be unprepared because attack has not been seen "in the wild," so no updates or reconfiguration instructions are available.

Protecting Against Flaws in Permitted Applications

To derive benefit from hosts and networks, organizations must allow applications to run on the hosts and access the network. A product that prevents permitted applications from using the resources it needs does not meet the "doesn't disrupt normal operations" criteria. By the same token, a HIPS must not allow the permitted application to be compromised by an attack. Thus, HIPS products must have the capability to protect against flaws in permitted applications.

Internet-facing web servers, for example, are permitted to accept connections from unknown hosts on the Internet. That makes it easier for attackers to take advantage of any flaws in the web server application. A HIPS should be able to allow the web server to accept connections from the Internet but also prevent the web server from being compromised.

Host Intrusion Prevention Benefits

Host Intrusion Prevention products can address or mitigate a variety of different problems. Proper use and selection of HIPS products should include a process where you match problems your organization is facing with the benefits HIPS products provide. Before you can enter into the process, you need to know how exactly how HIPS products can benefit your organization and what problems they solve.

This section concentrates on some of the benefits provided by HIPS, including the following:

- Attack prevention
- Patch relief
- Internal attack propagation prevention
- Policy enforcement
- Regulatory requirements

Attack Prevention

HIPS products can stop well-known and new attacks. The ability to stop a well-known attack is not particularly notable because a wide variety of countermeasures can do so. Increasingly complex and rapidly propagating viruses, worms, and Trojan horses (see Chapter 1, "Intrusion Prevention Overview") make it incredibly difficult for organizations to adequately update and reconfigure their existing countermeasures in response to new attacks. If an organization is the victim of a widespread virus, worm, or Trojan incident, cleanup and remediation costs in terms of time, lost productivity, and damaged data are usually extensive.

Thus, the most important benefit provided by HIPS is that it can stop both well-known and new attacks. This drastically reduces cleanup and remediation costs. Also, other benefits, like patch relie,f are derived from new and unknown attack prevention.

Patch Relief

Every day, new security vulnerabilities are discovered and patches are created to eliminate the new vulnerabilities. Organizations spend a great deal of time and money deploying these new patches. Patching is, in some cases, a very large information technology budget item.

VULNERABILITIES AND PATCHES

Vulnerabilities are nothing more than openings or exposures that can be exploited. *Exploits* take advantage of vulnerabilities, whereas *attacks* use exploits for nefarious purposes. Patches are used to eliminate vulnerabilities.

A good analogy is the doorway to your home. It is a vulnerability, or opening, that can be used to gain entry to your house. An attacker who walks through the door has exploited the vulnerability, and if the attacker were to steal something from inside, that would be an attack. To patch the vulnerability, you could lock the door or brick it up.

Two factors conspire to make patching so costly. The first factor is that a tremendous number of vulnerabilities to patch exist, and new ones are unearthed constantly. The second is that the time between the discovery of a vulnerability and the creation of an exploit that takes advantage of it is shrinking (see the following note). This means that companies have more vulnerabilities to patch and less time in which to do it. Each individual patch costs money to deploy, and companies cannot wait to deploy multiple patches at once because an exploit might be available any minute.

The second factor is that the shrinking vulnerability to exploit window means that organizations have very little time to test patches before they are deployed. An improperly written patch can "break" the program being patched. This is a risk organizations run every time they roll out a patch they did not have time to fully test.

> **NOTE**   The *vulnerability to exploit window* is the time between the discovery of a vulnerability and the availability of an exploit that takes advantage of the vulnerability. The longer the window is, the more time the vendors and customers have to create and deploy patches to remove the vulnerability.

A HIPS can stop new and unknown attacks, so patching does not have to be as high of a priority. If you are already protected against the vulnerability that the patch addresses, you have time to test patches to discover their impact on their environment. Also, you might be able to save time and money by applying multiple patches together instead of having to deploy them one by one. For example, the application of a Windows Service pack that contains dozens of patches might cost less than applying the patches in the service pack individually.

Internal Attack Propagation Prevention

The Internet is a very common way to launch an attack against a host, and many organizations focus their attentions on the Internet attack vector. However, once a single host has been compromised, it becomes the attacker. The propagation vector changes from Internet to host and becomes internal host to internal host.

Furthermore, hosts like laptops are portable and are protected from the Internet while they are in the office, but are vulnerable when they are connected to the Internet at home or sharing a public network with potentially malicious users. If a host is infected while it is outside of the corporate office and connected to the corporate network, the attack vector is once again internal host to internal host. Thus, hosts must be able to defend themselves against attack without the benefit of network security countermeasures.

The only feasible way to address the issue of internal attack propagation is to use software that resides on the host itself instead of the network. HIPS can prevent a protected host from attacking others, and it can prevent the host from being a victim of an attack.

Policy Enforcement

While the primary benefit of HIPS rests in its ability to secure an endpoint, many HIPS products are also able to enforce corporate computer security policy. Corporate security policies contain procedures and guidelines that, if followed, mitigate the risk of attack. Some organizations do not have security policies, but those that do often have a hard time making sure they are being used.

For example, the security policy might state that hosts equipped with both wired and wireless network adapters should never have both in use at the same time. Using both simultaneously does not damage the host in any way, but does present a security risk (see the "Wired and Wireless Network Adapters" sidebar). Some HIPS are able to enforce the policy by shutting down one adapter when the other becomes active.

WIRED AND WIRELESS NETWORK ADAPTERS

Most of the laptop computers manufactured today have a variety of built-in network adapters. That way, the laptop can use physical connections, wireless connections, and possibly Bluetooth at the same time. Although this is a very convenient hardware arrangement for users, it presents three distinct security risks if more than one adapter is active simultaneously.

The first risk is related to non-corporate wireless access points. The user could be connected to the wired network and, at the same time, the wireless adapter could inadvertently connect to an access point that is not under corporate control. Anyone who is connected to the access point can potentially use the laptop to gain unauthorized access to the corporate LAN.

The second risk has to do with ad hoc wireless networking. Ad hoc networking allows two computers with wireless network adapters to connect to each other directly rather than through an access point. If the user is connected to the wireless network and has ad hoc networking enabled, the wireless adapter might automatically connect to another computer. The other computer, which might be in use by an attacker, now has access to data on the corporate network.

The third risk is that the laptop user could use a wireless connection to intentionally deliver confidential data to a storage place that is outside of corporate control. For example, the user could connect the laptop to the LAN and connect wirelessly to a host on the Internet. This arrangement allows the user to very quickly transmit vast amounts of confidential information to an uncontrolled location.

The policy could also state that removable storage devices should not be used to store data. Storing data on removable storage does no harm, but it does make the data much more portable and easier to steal. To enforce the policy, you could remove the floppy drive, optical recorder, Universal Serial Bus (USB) ports, parallel ports, and serial ports from each system before you allow it to be used. Removing all of those devices is tedious and prevents the user from using the devices for uses that are permitted by policy.

Another option to enforce the removable storage policy is to use HIPS to control the flow of data from the hard drive or the network to removable storage devices. You can prevent anything from being written to removable storage, while allowing anything to be read. The devices can be used for legitimate purposes, but the user cannot violate policy. Figure 5-1 displays a message the user might see if the policy was violated.

Figure 5-1 *Using HIPS to Control USB Storage*

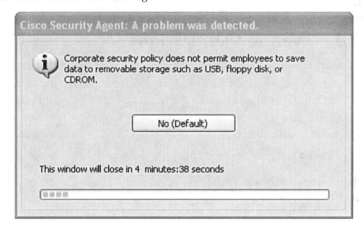

Acceptable Use Policy Enforcement

Another type of corporate policy HIPS can help enforce is the acceptable use policy. Acceptable use policies are different than security policies because they contain instructions related to proper use rather than security. For example, a security policy for company automobiles would enforce the use of seat belts because not using them is dangerous. An acceptable use policy might say that the car should be used for business purposes only. Using the car for personal use is not inherently dangerous as long as the security policy is followed, but it is not the proper way to use the corporate car.

Corporations often have an information technology acceptable use policy stating that employees should not use peer-to-peer (P2P) software to download or share copyrighted materials such as music or movies. Detecting the use of P2P software in an effort to enforce the policy is not always easy. HIPS can, in many cases, solve the problem by detecting and preventing the use of P2P.

A second example of an acceptable use policy relates to the use of the Internet. The policy states that Internet use is reserved for business purposes only. Employees who use the Internet for other purposes, like shopping or downloading pornographic materials, are subject to discipline. HIPS can be used to discern which users have violated the policy. It can also generate evidence to support disciplinary action, such as the name of the user who violated the policy, a list of restricted websites the user visited, and when the user visited them.

Regulatory Requirements

The final problem that HIPS can solve is that it can often fulfill government regulatory requirements. For example, the Administrative Simplification provisions of the United States Health Insurance Portability and Accountability Act of 1996 define standards for the security and privacy of health data. You have many ways to meet the standards, and HIPS products are sometimes a good way.

Host Intrusion Prevention Limitations

HIPS offers many benefits and can be a valuable component in your defense-in-depth security implementation (see Chapter 4, "Security in Depth"), but it is not without its limitations. The key to using HIPS effectively is to be aware of the limitations and account for them. HIPS limitations include the following:

- Subject to end user tampering

- Lack of complete coverage

- Attacks that do not target hosts

Subject to End User Tampering

HIPS products often include safeguards against user tampering, but some tampering methods cannot be mitigated by HIPS. For example, any user that has physical access to a machine also has at least some limited access to all the software installed on it. This presents an opportunity for the user to tamper with HIPS products protecting the host. The user could change the HIPS settings or even disable HIPS entirely.

For example, the Windows operating system includes a troubleshooting tool called safe mode, as shown in Figure 5-2. When safe mode is enabled, much of the software that ordinarily starts when the host is turned on is disabled. In most cases, safe mode also disables HIPS. Once it is disabled, the user can remove it entirely or disable it permanently.

Figure 5-2 *Safe Mode*

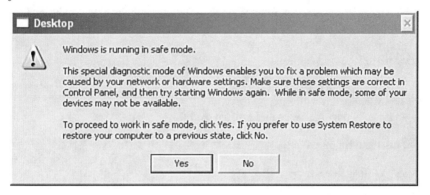

Safe mode is one easy way to meddle with HIPS. You have numerous other ways. A technically savvy user, for example, could physically remove the hard disk from the machine, attach it to another machine, and gain full access to any software that exists on that disk.

Lack of Complete Coverage

HIPS can protect only the hosts on which it is installed. Without help from other tools, it is very difficult to determine which hosts are connected to your network but do not have HIPS running. It is not necessary to have HIPS running on every single host to realize benefit from the tool, but even a few compromised hosts can have a negative impact on the organization as a whole.

Attacks That Do Not Target Hosts

Do not assume that all attacks target hosts. Many of them do, but numerous devices can be attacked that do not qualify as traditional hosts. Devices like IP phones, cellular phones, personal digital assistants, print servers, routers, wireless access points, and switches are all targets. Anything that uses the network is a possible target, and HIPS does not protect everything.

Summary

Host Intrusion Prevention is a relatively new type of technology. As a result, the HIP marketplace is not well-defined. HIPS product literature is abundant, but does not always clearly state what capabilities, benefits, and limitations HIPS products have.

HIPS can be a valuable addition to your arsenal of security countermeasures, but before you can use it effectively, you must have a good understanding of its basic characteristics. To qualify as HIPS, a product must be able to

- Block malicious code actions

- Not disrupt normal operations

- Distinguish between attacks and normal events

- Stop new and unknown attacks

- Protect against flaws in permitted applications

The ability to stop new and unknown attacks is the primary benefit of using HIPS. If an attack can be stopped before it does damage and spreads to other systems, your organization saves money by not having to clean up after the attack, losing productivity, or losing data. HIPS offers other benefits, including the following:

- Patch relief

- Internal attack propagation prevention

- Policy enforcement

- Regulatory requirements

No product is perfect, and HIPS is no exception. It is not suitable for all tasks, should be part of a defense-in-depth implementation, and has weaknesses such as the following:

- Subject to end user tampering

- Lack of complete coverage

- Attacks that do not target hosts

References in This Chapter

Pescatore, J. and Stiennon, R. *Defining Intrusion Prevention*. Gartner Research; 29 May 2003.

CHAPTER 6

HIPS Components

Host Intrusion Prevention System (HIPS) products have two essential elements:

■ A software package installed on the endpoint to protect it, called a client or *agent*.

■ A management infrastructure to manage the agents.

This chapter divides the two major elements into subcomponents, describes them, and illustrates functional approaches for each. Real-world HIPS products are used as practical examples.

Endpoint Agents

Imagine a guard who is assigned to secure the entrance to a building. When someone approaches a protected resource, the guard begins an access control process and stops the person and asks for some form of identification. After the necessary information has been gathered, the guard follows policy and decides whether the person can enter. The policy might say, for example, that employees of ACME Incorporated can enter the building between the hours of 8 A.M. and 5 P.M. (0800 and 1700). After the person has been granted or denied access, the guard simply waits for the next person to approach so that the process can be repeated.

Essentially, HIPS agents apply a similar access control process to computers, as illustrated by Figure 6-1. The process is activated when an operation occurs on a system and can be divided into the following phases:

■ **Identifies the type of resource being accessed**—"Is the resource being accessed the entrance to the building or the elevator?"

■ **Gathers data about the operation**—"Who is this person, who do they work for, and does the picture on the ID look similar to the person?"

■ **Determines the state of the system**—"Is it between the hours of 8 A.M. and 5 P.M. (0800 and 1700)?"

■ **Consults security policy**—"Is this person permitted to access the resource?"

■ **Takes action**—"The person can enter."

Figure 6-1   *Access Control Process*

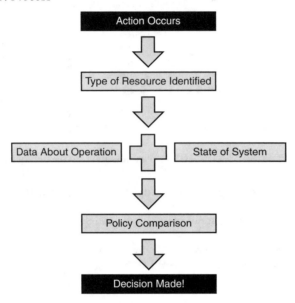

Identifying the Resource Being Accessed

The first phase in the access control process is to identify what type of resource is being accessed. This determination triggers the data gathering phase and changes the type or amount of data to be gathered. If the building entrance is the resource in question, the guard might need to ascertain only the requestor's name. The elevator might require additional information, such as the requestor's company, so that the guard can determine which bank of elevators the requestor should use.

Buildings have thousands of resources. Luckily, not all of them are equally important in the context of security. The resources that are most important are those that attackers could use to gain access to, modify, or damage the building. A catalog of a building's resources could include the flowers near the building, doorways, elevators, windows, fire escapes, and postal address. Attackers are not likely to use the flowers or postal address to attack the building.

In that sense, computer systems are similar to buildings. A HIPS product that identifies and protects every computer system resource would be a secure way to go, although the product would be too cumbersome. To be more efficient, products worry only about the system resources that are the most appealing to attackers. The tough part is to correctly identify the most important resources.

A good way to characterize a resource's level of appeal is to conduct a high-level analysis of attacks that target hosts. Commonalities between them can shed light on subject and help identify important system resources. For example, if different types of attacks tend to use the same sets of resources, those resources are probably more appealing than less commonly used resources.

The first step in the analysis looks at what attacks such as viruses, worms, Trojans, and malicious mobile code actually do. To be successful, attacks must accomplish a set of ordered tasks. This is called the lifecycle of an attack, and it has five phases, as shown in Figure 6-2:

1.   **Probe**—The attack looks for a vulnerability.

2.   **Penetrate**—The attack uses a vulnerability it finds to compromise the host.

3.   **Persist**—The attack installs something on the system.

4.   **Propagate**—The attack uses the compromised host to attack other systems.

5.   **Paralyze**—Damage occurs, either through malicious intent or huge amounts of network traffic because of propagation.

Figure 6-2   *Lifecycle of an Attack*

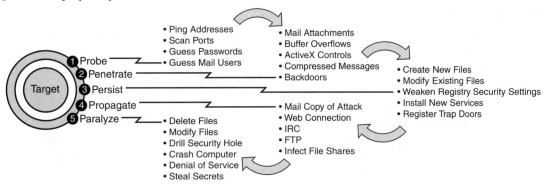

> **NOTE**   Technically, viruses and worms are mobile because they can move from system to system. They could be called malicious mobile code, but in this case, the term refers specifically to dangerous ActiveX and Java programs.

The second part of the analysis matches what the attack does in each phase with the resources it needs to accomplish its activity. For example, the probe phase cannot succeed if the attack cannot access the host via the network. To persist, an attack must be able to modify files, memory, system service configuration, and so on. The propagation phase requires the network once again or some other kind of media like floppy discs, compact discs, and so on.

This mapping of lifecycle phases to required resources yields five critical resource categories. HIPS products should be most concerned with these categories:

- Network

- Memory

- Application execution

- Files

- System configuration

Some HIPS products are able to identify attempts to access all the crucial resource sets, although some cover only portions of the list. Furthermore, each product might identify only particular types of access request. This section delves into these five, touches briefly on some less critical but still important resource sets, and uses real HIPS products as examples.

Network

Before a system can be compromised, an attacker must "find a way" to it by probing for its existence and for vulnerabilities it might have. Barring physical access, in which case you have a problem HIPS can't fix, the only way to probe a system is via the network. Because the network is the *only* way to probe the system, it is the first resource HIPS protects.

> **NOTE** *Vulnerabilities* are weaknesses in a target that can be used to an attacker's advantage. *Exploits* take advantage of vulnerabilities. For example, a front door protected by a flimsy lock is vulnerable. The vulnerability is exploited by breaking the lock and opening the door.

Several important resource subcategories exist within the broader network resource type. The subcategories are generally in step with the relevant layers of the Open Systems Interconnection (OSI) model:

- Application data (Layer 7)

- Establishment of connections from one host to another (Layer 5)

- Network packet headers (Layers 3 and 4)

Not only is the network used to probe and deliver an attack to the host, but it's also the only way to use one compromised system to attack another. The network is so important that some products protect it to the exclusion of other the other critical resource sets. eEye Blink, for example, focuses only on the network and application execution (see the "Application Execution" section later in this chapter).

The McAfee Entercept and Cisco Security Agent (CSA) also cover the network. They both identify inbound connection requests, outbound connection requests, packet headers, and in some cases, packet contents. One difference between the two is that CSA also identifies the number of simultaneously open TCP connections.

Memory

If the attacker or malicious code has probed and found a way to access the system, their next step is to penetrate or deliver an attack payload. The path of least resistance is to use a pre-existing pathway by attaching the payload to an e-mail message, placing it on a network share, sending it with an instant messenger program, or forcing an Internet browser to download it. One problem with this delivery mechanism is that it often requires the user to activate the payload. History has shown that it isn't hard to use social engineering to trick the user to activate the payload. However, the attack has a higher chance of success if it doesn't have to rely on the user to succeed.

SOCIAL ENGINEERING

Social engineering exploits weaknesses in people, rather than weaknesses in computer systems. It's often used to convince computer users to share their passwords or other confidential information with people they should not. For example, an evil-doer pretends to be a help desk technician calling to perform routine maintenance on the target's system. The pretend technician asks the target for the password to access the system, and often the target shares that information without validating that the person's identity.

Another great social engineering example is the "I Love You" worm. The worm payload appeared as an attachment to an e-mail message. Recipients of the message were tricked into invoking the payload by the body of the message which said, "Kindly check the attached love letter coming from me." Naturally, many recipients invoked the attachment hoping to read a sweet love note. Instead, they were infected with a worm.

One commonly used method to deliver a payload without involving the user is the buffer overrun exploit. Buffer overruns, also called buffer overflows, compromise the system memory used by a legitimate running process. The payload replaces the memory used by the legitimate process and is automatically invoked using the privileges of that process.

BUFFER OVERRUNS

Simply put, a buffer overrun happens when an unexpected amount of data is delivered to a vulnerable process running in memory. The memory used by the vulnerable process is replaced by an attack payload. The system automatically invokes the payload, and the payload has the same system privileges as the process it replaced.

Numerous flavors of buffer overrun exist, but the easiest kind to describe is the stack overflow. Stack memory can be thought of as a bucket of memory that programs use to store instructions that will run by the operating system (OS). When a program needs to use stack memory, it takes what it needs by temporarily reserving a slice of the memory, also known as a buffer, and then inserts the instructions. The OS completes the instructions, and then moves on to the next buffer. It refers to a value called a return to know which buffer to run next. Figure 6-3 illustrates this process.

Figure 6-3 *Stack Memory Buffers and Returns*

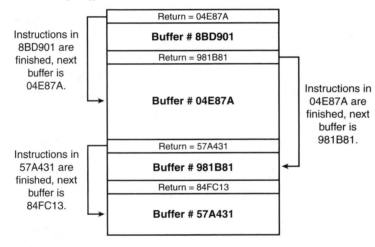

Figure 6-4 shows how a buffer overrun occurs when an attacker delivers, usually via the network, enough data to fill the buffer and overwrite the return. The return now points back into the buffer consisting of the data the attacker delivered. The data contains malicious instructions, which the operating system runs automatically.

Figure 6-4   *Buffer Overruns*

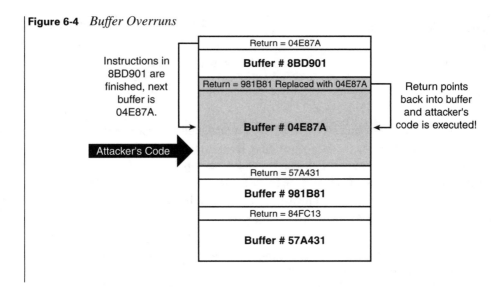

Buffer overrun vulnerabilities and exploits are so commonplace that every major HIPS product protects memory access vigorously. Entercept, for example, closely monitors attempts to access memory and identifies attempts to access other system resources from memory. CSA's approach is similar. eEye identifies memory access attempts by peering inside network data streams to identify patterns indicative of a memory access attempt.

Application Execution

After the attack has delivered and activated its payload, the next step in its lifecycle is to persist, or install itself on the system. Some attacks are not persistent, but worms and Trojans in particular install themselves so that they run whenever the system is running. Installation can be successful only if files and/or configuration settings are modified. The attack often runs itself or other programs to access those resources.

Many products, such as ISS Proventia Desktop, CSA, McAfee Entercept, and eEye Blink, notice when an executable file attempts to become a running process. Entercept and CSA in particular also track the invoking process. CSA adds a level of granularity by being able to identify a process attempting spawn a child process.

> **NOTE**   A *child process* is a new process that is created by an existing process. The original process is called the *parent process*.

> **NOTE** It might seem strange to characterize application execution as a resource. However, programs do not run by themselves. They are invoked by other processes. So in that sense, the application being invoked is a resource for the invoking process.

Files

Things start to get interesting now. The attacker or malicious code has found the system, delivered the payload, and started to persist by installing itself. Malicious code can be installed on a system in only a few ways. A kernel module can be loaded, startup files can be modified, or files might be written to disk. The most effective place to write files is where they can be available for execution every time the system boots. Any directory that is part of the default path will do. Favorites include **X:\windows\system32**, **X:\windows** on Windows OS, and **/usr**, **/usr bin** on UNIX OS.

> **NOTE** Kernel modules are pieces of code that extend kernel functionality but are not actually a part of the kernel itself. They are usually file system or device drivers.

Files are also an important resource during the paralyze phase of the lifecycle. The data they contain might be important. It could be confidential information, critical system files, or log files that identify the intruder. Reading, modifying, or deleting these types of files can severely damage the system and the organization to which the confidential information belongs.

Therefore, HIPS products should monitor file read attempts as well as file write. As an example, CSA identifies directory write attempts, file reads, and file writes. McAfee Entercept takes the same approach, but also offers fine-grained coverage by making a distinction between write and rename, change attribute, create, modify permissions, move, link, and unlink.

System Configuration

Application execution and file modification are two parts of the persistence process. The final part is modification of the system configuration. For example, a Trojan might add itself to the Windows startup folder, the Windows Registry run keys, or **.ini** files so that it runs every time the system is started. UNIX startup **.rc** (run commands) files can also be targeted. The attacker might modify the Windows Registry, UNIX **.conf** files, or security countermeasure settings to weaken operating system security. In some cases, a worm or Trojan can even disable security products, such as antivirus and personal firewalls, or even the HIPS agent itself.

> **NOTE**   The most crucial access attempts are the attempts to access the HIPS agent itself. While they are running, HIPS agents must be able to identify attempts to modify their own files, services, running processes, and configuration settings. What good is intrusion prevention if it can be disabled or modified by an attack?

CSA and Entercept are two examples of products that protect the system configuration by protecting the Windows Registry. CSA identifies any type of write activity. Entercept monitors additional activities such as read, create, delete, modify, change permissions, enumerate, monitor, restore, replace, and load.

Additional Resource Categories

The network, memory, application execution, and system configuration are certainly the most critical system resources to protect. Many other resources are less critical, but still important because they can be useful to attackers. Knowing what resources a product has on its "coverage list" is an important step toward understanding the product's capabilities.

Here is a brief list of some of the additional resources for which HIPS products can identify access attempts:

- **OS kernel**—The kernel is the central portion of the operating system. It can be extended by loading a piece of code, usually a type of driver, separately from the main body of the kernel itself. One category of attack, called a rootkit, is known for loading itself as a kernel module.

- **OS events**—Operating system logs often contain events that can be of interest for forensic or troubleshooting purposes. To make sure that the events in the log cannot be modified, some HIPS products capture events as they are written to the log and store them elsewhere.

- **Windows Clipboard**—The clipboard is not something that malicious code generally uses; however, it is a way to "get around" restrictions placed on certain applications that might access a set of data. An application with permission can copy the sensitive data to the clipboard, and then someone without access to the data removes it from the clipboard.

- **COM component access**—The Microsoft Component Object Model (COM) allows programs to interact with each other easily. COM is used, for example, to copy an Excel spreadsheet into a Word document. Malicious scripts sometimes exploit COM objects such as **Outlook.application** to send e-mail.

- **Devices**—Devices such as keyboards, microphones, and cameras are of particular interest to attackers. An attacker can intercept communications between the keyboard and the OS in an effort to capture passwords and other sensitive information. Some sophisticated attacks also take control of cameras or microphones to spy on the user.

- **Symbolic Links**—Symbolic links are UNIX resources similar to Windows shortcuts. They are special types of file that point to another file or folder. Attackers can use symbolic links to gain access to confidential or important system information.

Gathering Data About the Operation

The next task in the access control process is to gather data about the operation. The operation has been identified as being something worthy of closer examination, but no details have been ascertained as yet. To return to the security guard analogy, consider that the guard knows that someone is trying to use the elevator but doesn't know anything about the person or exactly how the elevator will be used.

To get the details, the guard must know how to get them and what details to get. For example, the guard might ask a set of questions such as, "Who are you?" and "Where are you going?" That's one way to get details. Another approach might be to inspect an identification badge without asking questions. In either case, the guard must also know what data to get from the badge or what questions to ask.

This portion of the book examines how HIPS products gather data and what data they typically gather.

How Data Is Gathered

Data gathering methods differ from product to product. None of the approaches is necessarily better than the others, but each has positives and negatives associated with it. To overcome any negatives and provide more comprehensive protection, most products implement more than one data gathering method. The four most common methods are as follows:

- Kernel modification

- System call interception

- Virtual OSs

- Network traffic analysis

NOTE It might seem like a good idea to install multiple HIPS products so that you can gather data using all of the possible methods. Unfortunately, HIPS products do not usually work well together, and having more than one on a system will likely cause system instability.

Kernel Modification

The kernel modification method is used by trusted OS products such as Sun Microsystems' Trusted Solaris, Security Enhanced Linux (SE Linux) created by the National Security Agency, and PitBull by Argus Systems Group. System objects such as users, processes, files, network interfaces, and host IP addresses are labeled. These labels contain security-related attributes and are called domains.

The OS kernel is replaced or modified so that any time one object requests access to another, the security-related attributes are captured before the operation is allowed. For example, if Process A requests access to File A, the domains associated with each object are captured as the request is processed by the kernel. Figure 6-5 illustrates the kernel modification approach.

Figure 6-5 *Kernel Modification*

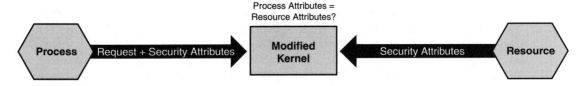

Kernel modification is an older approach that works well with traditional access control models such as mandatory access control (MAC) and role-based access control (RBAC). (See the section, "Access Control Matrix" later in this chapter for more details about MAC and RBAC.) Also, subversion of kernel modifications is difficult because they are tightly integrated with the OS.

One of the downsides of kernel modification is that the new or modified OS kernel might be incompatible with third-party software. If you discover an incompatibility, you have to wait for the HIPS vendor to release a fix before the third-party software can be used. Additionally, the vendor might have to release new product in response to OS updates, which can delay the update process.

System Call Interception

A system call is a request from a process to the operating system kernel when it wants to access an OS resource. A set of interceptors, sometimes called shims, are installed as part of the endpoint agent. The shims sit between processes running on the system and objects they might attempt to access. When a process tries to access a protected resource, the system call is intercepted by the shim before the OS kernel receives it. Information such as the process name, object name, access type, and access time is captured. Figure 6-6 shows a graphical representation of this process.

Figure 6-6 *System Call Interception*

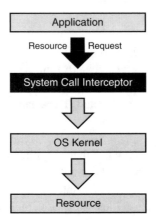

> **NOTE** In the world of carpentry, shims are tapered pieces of material used to fill space between things for support or leveling. In the computer world, shims can be thought of as tapered software components inserted between two other software components.

This is a commonly used method for data collection and is implemented in products such as McAfee Entercept, CSA, and Sana Security Primary Response. Part of the reason for system call interception's popularity is that it is easier to implement than kernel modifications. It is also less subject to third-party software incompatibilities, although they can still occur. One downside of system call interception is that it is not as tightly bound to the OS and opportunities to "get around" it might exist.

A close examination of the CSA explains how system call interception is implemented. During the agent installation, the shims are inserted into the operating system in such a way that they can intercept attempts to access important resources. Important resource categories were listed earlier in the chapter.

In Windows, for example, four shims are installed:

- **CSATdi**—Tdi stands for Transport Driver Interface and is the interface between the network protocols and application programming interface. In the Windows networking model, Tdi corresponds with the transport layer of the OSI model. Essentially, this shim intercepts network connection requests to and from applications running on the system.

- **CSAFile**—This shim captures information about file read/write operations. It uses a Microsoft Installable File System filter.

- **CSAReg**—Registry write actions are intercepted with this shim.

- **CSACenter**—Handles system API calls such as downloading and invoking ActiveX controls, dangerous system calls from stack or heap memory, keyboard IRQ hooking, and media device hooking. It is the most important component of the agent, as it performs several duties beyond system call interception including event management, correlation, and rule enforcement.

Practically speaking, these interceptors install in the system as device drivers and load at the same time as other devices. Figure 6-7 shows the list of loaded drivers on a Windows XP system that is protected by CSA.

Figure 6-7 *CSA Drivers*

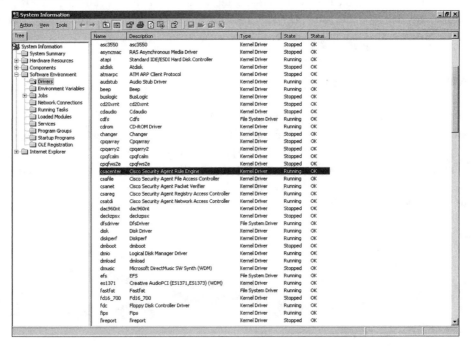

Virtual Operating Systems

The endpoint agent monitors the system for any operation where an application is trying to write an executable file to disk. Before the write operation is allowed, the executable is temporarily placed in a virtual copy of the operating system. This virtual OS is sometimes called a sandbox, because it's a safe place "play."

The executable runs in the sandbox, and any malicious actions it might attempt can be observed before it occurs on the real OS (see Figure 6-8). The virtual OS monitor captures activities such as modifying other files, making network connections, and modifying configuration files. Internet Security Systems Proventia Desktop and Finjan Vital Security for Clients use virtual OSs.

Figure 6-8 *Virtual OSs*

Virtual OSs are potentially a secure way to gather data. Assuming that the executable code is correctly identified and can be placed inside the virtual OS before it runs, the data is gathered without any danger to the actual OS. However, the virtual OS must conform closely with the actual OS in order for the data that is gathered to be accurate.

Network Traffic Analysis

Figure 6-9 shows how in network traffic analysis all network data to and from the protected host is inspected by the endpoint agent. Network packets are re-assembled and analyzed before they are delivered up or down the TCP/IP stack. In most cases, the agent understands commonly used protocols such as HTTP, Simple Mail Transport Protocol (SMTP), FTP, and so on. eEye Digital Security Blink relies primarily on network traffic analysis such as data gathering, although many of the other HIPS products like Entercept and ISS Proventia Desktop make use of some network traffic analysis.

Figure 6-9 *Network Traffic Analysis*

The problem with network traffic analysis is that some traffic cannot be analyzed. Encrypted data, for example, cannot be examined until it has been decrypted. Products that rely solely on this data gathering method must find a way to decrypt the traffic so that it can be examined. However, network traffic analysis is the only way to stop an attack before it arrives on the system. System call interception, virtual OSs, and kernel modification gather data after a potential attack has arrived.

What Data Is Gathered

A wise G.I. Joe character once said, "Knowing *how* to collect data about an operation is only half the battle." The other half is to know *what* data to collect. Exactly which details of the operation are relevant depends on the type of resource that's accessed. For example, the source IP address would not be a relevant piece of information if the type of resource being accessed was a file. The same goes for file name, if the network is being accessed.

For the most part, all HIPS products collect similar data for each type of resource. Table 6-1 shows a few examples.

Table 6-1   *Data Collected per Resource Type*

Type of Resource	Data Collected
All	Time, host identification, access token where applicable, credentials where applicable
Network packet inspection	Source IP, destination IP, packet details, source port, destination port
Network connection request	Process name, source IP, destination IP address, source port, destination port, transport, operation (connect or accept)
File access	Process name, file path, file name, operation (read, write, write directory)
Registry access	Process name, key path, key name, key value, key type
Application execution	Process name, process path, target process name, target process path
Kernel protection	Kernel module name, module hash, code pattern
System event log	Event source, priority, facility (UNIX), event ID (Windows), message pattern (UNIX)
Memory	Process name, function call, buffer return address, buffer contents, target process where applicable

Determining the State

The security guard is almost halfway through the access control process! All the relevant data has been compiled about the operation itself, but the state of the system can alter the outcome of the request. For example, under ordinary circumstances, employees of the ACME Company are allowed to enter the building whenever they want. However, if the building is on fire, they are not.

In practical terms, state conditions determine when a particular security policy is in place. "If the building is not on fire, the normal employee entry policy is enforced. If the building is on fire, the fire employee entry policy is active." State conditions make HIPS policies more restrictive under some circumstances and less under others.

HIPS products commonly use at least one, if not all, the following state types:

- Location

- User

- System

Location State

In this case, location refers to the location from which the system connects to the network. "In the office" and "Out of the office" are obviously useful locations to define. Corporate networks are usually more secure and trustworthy than the Internet or home networks. A more permissive security policy can be active while the host is in the office, and a restrictive policy can be automatically activated as soon as the location state changes to out of the office.

More fine-grained location state conditions could include the following:

- Connected via virtual private network (VPN)

- Austin office

- Europe

- Wireless

The location of the system is usually dependant on a combination of variables such as the following:

- Currently assigned IP address

- Assigned DNS suffix

- The availability of the management server

- Type of network interface being used (wired or wireless)

- MAC address

- Status of VPN client

- IP address of DHCP server

The criteria that can be used to define a location vary from product to product. As an example, Figure 6-10 shows the CSA location state configuration screen.

Figure 6-10   *CSA Location State Configuration*

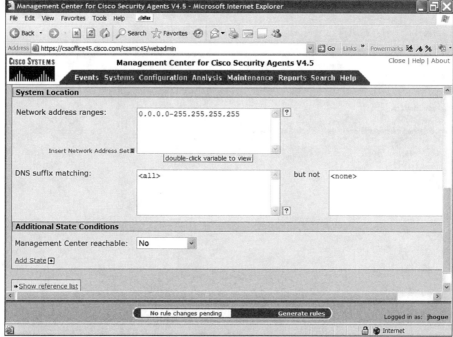

User State

User state is fairly straightforward. User or group names are attached to policies. User states are useful when a particular policy should be overruled for a group of users. Usually, users should not be able to disable the HIPS agent. What if the system is having difficulty and the help desk technician needs to temporarily disable the agent protection to troubleshoot? You could make an exception that is applicable only when a user from the group "Help Desk" is logged on. You could also apply the exception to Administrative users, as shown in Figure 6-11.

Of course, user state conditions rely a great deal on the accuracy of the corporate directory service. Also, strong authentication controls for users who have the ability to stop the agent should be in place wherever possible. Making HIPS policies less secure is a privilege that must be guarded carefully.

Figure 6-11 *CSA User State Configuration*

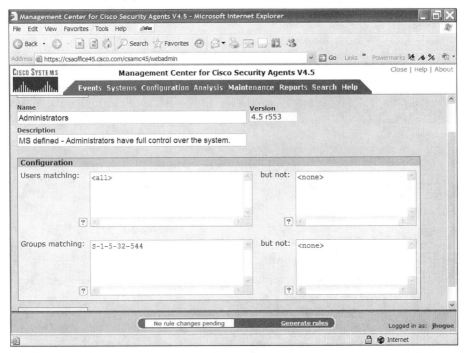

System State

System state is more complicated than the other two states and is something of a catch-all for states that do not fall under the location or user categories. Essentially, it is any previously observed activity or activities that are indicative of an overall condition. That is a vague description, so perhaps the best way to clarify is to give a few examples.

If a host has been repeatedly pinged, port scanned, and connected to by an untrusted host, you can safely assume that it is the target of an attack reconnaissance effort. System state could be set to "Under Attack" and more rigid policies activated until the system is no longer under attack. In a similar vein, a state called "Currently Mapping Network" could be in place if a network scanning process such as Nmap or NBTscan is running and the host is making numerous outbound network connections.

Most HIPS products do not support these types of sophisticated system state conditions. For those that do, what follows is a list of potentially useful ones:

- **Security level**—Some HIPS agent user interfaces (UIs) allow users to set their own security level. The UI might, for example, have a slide bar with off, low, medium, or high choices. When the slide bar is set to medium, policies whose state set contains medium are activated. When the slide bar is set to high, more restrictive policies are enforced.

- **Rootkit detected**—This state is applied when a driver or kernel module (see the sidebar concerning rootkits) attempts to load after the system has booted.

- **Installation process detected**—Less restrictive policies can be activated when a software installation is in process. Conditions indicative of a running installation might be a **setup.exe** or **install.exe** process and the user responding affirmatively when asked if an installation is occurring.

- **System booting**—An endpoint is generally more vulnerable while it is booting because security countermeasures might not be loaded.

ROOTKITS

A rootkit is a type of Trojan horse that intercepts data from terminals, the network, keyboards, and in some cases multimedia devices such as cameras. One of the distinguishing characteristics of rootkits is that they hide their processes, logs, and logins so that they are more difficult to detect. Some rootkits contain backdoor software that allows attackers to remotely access the host on which the kit is installed.

Two different types of rootkit exist, application and kernel. Application rootkits replace existing application executables with fakes. Kernel rootkits load new code into the operating system kernel.

Consulting the Security Policy

Now that the security guard has information about the person attempting to access the building, it's finally time to consult the security policy. The policy should contain a list of criteria required for entry and items that deny entry. The guard matches the captured information with an item on the policy list, assesses the state of the system, and then takes the action associated with the policy object that matched.

You can take many different policy approaches. One possibility is to admit only people who work in the building. A different implementation might say that anyone can enter as long as they do not bring a bomb along. Ideally, an employee who would ordinarily be admitted should not be admitted if the guard sees that person carrying a bomb. Chapter 2, "Signatures and Actions," defines the main categories of signature and explains some of the positive and negative factors associated with each. This section uses the word *rule* to describe the criteria by which HIPS decisions are made, but the word *signature* could also be used. The word *policy,* a collection of rules, is also used. Rules and *policies* replace *signatures* and *signature sets* simply because those words more aptly describe the way most HIPS tools operate. You might notice some overlap, but the intent of this section is to give specific rule examples in the host context. Also, any policy types that do not fall under the categories listed in Chapter 2 are examined. Another important thing to note is that few HIPS products use just one flavor of policy. Several approaches are combined so that the negatives associated with one are overcome another. Also, a combination of policy types makes the product more suitable for use in every situation. You have five essential HIPS policy types:

- Anomaly-based

- Atomic rule-based

- Pattern-based

- Behavioral

- Access control matrix

Anomaly-Based

As defined in Chapter 2, anomaly-based policies are based on deviations from a known and established baseline of typical user traffic and operations. The policy is built when the product monitors the operations performed by users and processes on a protected endpoint for some amount of time. At the end of the learning period, it adds anything it saw to the good and normal activity list. Any subsequent activity the product sees that is not on the good and normal list is denied because different is bad. This is sometimes called a white list, because all activities that are not explicitly permitted are denied.

Sana Security Primary Response is the only HIPS product that relies solely on an anomaly-based policy, although others such as eEye Digital Security Blink use it to some extent. During its learning period, Primary Response monitors the entire host and "learns," for example, that Internet Information Server (IIS), which is the process created when **inetinfo.exe** invokes, is running on the system. Primary Response "sees" all the file write, file read, Registry modify, and network connection operations that the process performs. It detects that IIS has read **index.html** and adds that action to the list of acceptable and normal actions in the security policy. The list might look similar to Table 6-2.

Table 6-2   *Learned Activity List*

Process Name	File Reads	File Writes	Registry Writes	Inbound Connections	Outbound Connections
Inetinfo.exe	\inetpub\index.html \inetpub\wwwroot\site1 \site1.html \inetpub\log\log.txt	\inetpub\log\log.txt \inetpub\tmp\1.tmp	\HKLM\software\ IIS\config\value	TCP\80 TCP\443 TCP\8080	TCP\1433 TCP\1434
Outlook.exe	\application data\user.pst *.wab	\application data\user.pst *.wab	\HKLM\software\ outlook\config	TCP\25	TCP\110

Atomic Rule-Based

Atomic rule-based policies are simply sets of regulations governing the activities of users and processes. Atomic rules contain only one triggering criteria and are composed of five parts:

- **Type**—Type identifies the type of resource the rule intends to protect. A File Access Control rule type, for example, indicates that the rule is invoked when a file access request is identified.

- **Action**—The action that the product takes when the rule is triggered. Log event is one example of an action.

- **Application Class**—Application class refers to the process to which the rule is applied. Usually, they are tied to an executable name. For example, the Web Browsers application class might contain the processes created when **iexplore.exe**, **netscape.exe**, **opera.exe**, or **mozilla.exe** run. The All Applications application class contains all running processes, regardless of the executable that was invoked to create them.

- **Directive**—The kind of access request. The verb varies by rule type, but in a File Access Control rule it could be read, write, rename, modify attribute such as "read-only" or "archive," or a combination of all four. A Network Access Control rule makes a connection or accepts a connection for its verb choices.

- **Object**—The target of the access request. It contains things such as IP address, file, or Registry values.

McAfee Entercept, CSA, ISS Proventia Desktop, and Finjan Vital Security for Clients all use some atomic rules. To make it clear exactly what atomic rules look like, Table 6-3 shows a few examples from CSA.

Table 6-3 *Atomic Rule Examples*

Type	Action	Application Class	Directive	Object
File Access Control	Deny	Web Servers (inetinfo.exe, apache.exe)	Write	HTML files (*.html)
Registry Access Control	Permit	Installation Applications (setup.exe, install.exe)	Write	Windows run keys (HKLM\software\microsoft\windows\currentversion\run, runonce, runonceex)
Network Access Control	Log Event	Web Browsers (iexplore.exe, mozilla.exe, netscape.exe, firefox.exe)	Make a connection	HTTP (TCP/80, TCP/443)
Application Control	Deny	All Applications (*.exe)	Execute	Command shells (cmd.exe, bash, csh, command.exe)

Pattern-Based

Pattern-based policies differ from atomic-rule based policies primarily in the specificity of their triggering criteria. Atomic rules have broadly defined triggering criteria, such as *any* process trying to modify a system executable. Pattern-based rules, also known as signatures, fire when the criteria are far more specific. For example, the signature triggers when it sees a string of data being delivered via the network that is carrying a known attack payload.

McAfee Entercept is a fine example of a product that combines two policy approaches to make up for the deficiencies of each. One of the difficulties with atomic rules is that they can stop an attack but cannot determine exactly what attack they have stopped. Also, atomic rules can suffer from high false positive rates. On the other hand, pattern-based policies cannot identify an attack pattern that has not been seen already.

Entercept combines both atomic rules and patterns. The atomic rules have the ability to stop the new and unknown attacks. After a pattern is available for an attack, Entercept can identify it specifically and avoid false positives. This is called a hybrid approach.

Behavioral

Behavioral policies also make use of rules, but the rules are more involved. Rules contain more than one activity that must occur before a match can be made. Instead of saying that **iexplore.exe** and **netscape.exe** might not invoke executable code, a behavioral rule could say that "Web Browsers" cannot invoke executables. The rule is tripped only if a process is both a web browser and is attempting to invoke executable code.

The process is categorized as a web browser by remembering, or keeping state, on its prior activities. For example, if any process on the system makes an outbound HTTP or HTTPS connection, it is "tagged" as a web browser. It is then subject to the rule that prevents web browsers from invoking executables.

CSA is one product that uses behavioral rules extensively. To help clarify the differences between behavioral rules and other types, Table 6-4 shows a few examples from CSA.

Table 6-4   *Behavioral Rule Examples*

Type	Action	Application Class	Verb	Object
Network Access Control	Add process to application class "Web Browsers" when	Any application	Make a connection	HTTP (TCP/80, TCP/443)
File Access Control	Deny	Web browsers (dynamic app class—defined by previous network access control rule)	Write	System Executables (\windows\system32*.exe)
Network Access Control	Add process to application Class "Network Server Applications" when	Any application	Accept a connection	TCP/*, UDP/*
Application Control	Deny when	Network applications (dynamic app class—defined by previous network access control rule)	Attempt to invoke	Command Shells (cmd.exe, bash, csh, command.exe)

Note that half of these rules do not have an enforcement action. Instead, the process triggering the rule is "tagged" with a description such as Network Server by adding the process to the Network Servers Application class. The actual enforcement is performed by other rules that apply to the Network Servers Application class. This way, you have an implied "If I see X activity *and* I see Y activity, then trigger" statement in the enforcement rule.

Access Control Matrix

The products that collect data using kernel modifications almost exclusively use access control matrixes. An access control matrix lists the labels given to users, processes, and resources on the system. Matrixes are a formal and well-tested way to implement policy.

You find two different types of access control matrix. The first is mandatory access control (MAC), which is used by Argus Systems PitBull and Trusted Solaris. This policy is based on the concept of least privilege. Least privilege means that a user or process should have access only to the resources needed to do its job. A MAC matrix, like the one shown in Table 6-5, has the user and process labels in the columns, and the rows contain the resources. A user or process is able to access only the resources in its row.

Table 6-5   *Example Mandatory Access Control Matrix*

	User	Process
Resource A	Y	Y
Resource B	N	N
Resource C	Y	N
Resource D	N	N

A slightly more permissive type of matrix is the role-based access control (RBAC). SE Linux uses a combination of Type Enforcement, which is a flavor of MAC, and RBAC. RBAC assigns each user a set of roles and each role is authorized to access a set of objects.

Taking Action

The type of resource being accessed is identified, which in turn defines what data should be gathered about the operation. The data is then gathered, the policy is consulted, and it is finally time to take action and enforce the decision listed in the policy. In the security guard example, the action might be to allow access, deny access, or some middle ground such as "detain for questioning."

For HIPS agents, the most obvious actions are permit or deny. However, like the security guard, the agent can take other actions. Not all products support the same actions, but here is a list of some of the possibilities:

- **Permit**—Allow the activity to occur.

- **Deny**—Do not allow the activity to occur.

- **Log Event**—This action is used in conjunction with permit or deny. For example, the activity should be allowed, but also log an event.

- **Drop packet**—Discard the network packet that triggered the rule or matched the pattern. Agents that are capable of network traffic inspection often have this action available.

- **Shun host**—Drop all network traffic, do not accept network connections from, or make connections to, a particular host or set of hosts.

- **Query the user**—Ask the user if the action should be allowed. If performed manually, this action is useful and not malicious. However, if the action is automated, it is probably malicious. Software installation, for example, is fine if the user is actually installing software but dangerous if something or someone malicious is installing software without the user's knowledge. In a situation like that, it's helpful to ask the user, "Are you installing software?"

Management Infrastructure

HIPS agents that have a robust user interface can and sometimes do operate without any kind of central management. Enterprise-class HIPS, however, require a management infrastructure. Typically, the infrastructure is composed of a *management center*, or back end, and a *management interface* used to access the management station.

Security product management stations are high on the typical attacker's target list. If the management station is compromised, the attacker can disable the countermeasure completely or simply reconfigure it in a minor, unnoticeable, and dangerous way. Host Intrusion Prevention agents are immensely powerful, and their management infrastructure should be protected at all costs. To that end, you need to understand the components of a HIPS management infrastructure and the security implications therein.

Management Center

HIPS management centers have three logical elements. The first is a database where event, policy, agent, and other configuration data are stored. The second is an event handling capability, and the final element is policy management.

It's helpful to think of each element separately, because depending on the management model, each component can be installed on a different physical machine. The three most common management models are as follows (see Figure 6-12):

- **Hierarchical**—Also known as "manager-of-managers," this model is best for large companies who have agents distributed across a wide geography.

- **Tiered**—Supports a large number of users but has them report to a single location. Therefore, it is not as well-suited for distributed environments.

- **Single-server**—Single-server implementations are best for small, centralized companies.

Figure 6-12 *Management Models*

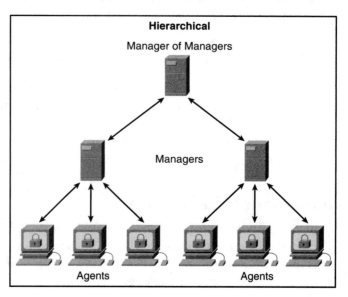

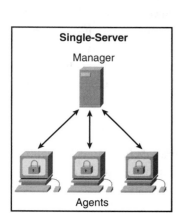

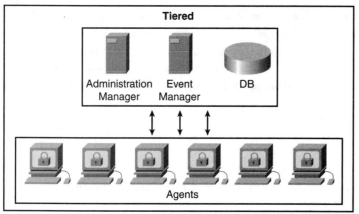

Database

The most critical component of the management center is the database, as it is repository for all policy information. It must be powerful enough to support the number of agents that use it without crashing and secure enough to withstand attack. For these reasons, many, if not all, of the centrally managed HIPS products use some kind of enterprise database such as Microsoft SQL Server or Oracle.

MANAGEMENT MODELS

The most straightforward management model is the *single-server* implementation. In the single-server model, all three management elements are installed on a single server. Many HIPS products, such as Entercept, CSA, and Sana, use this implementation because it is relatively easy to install and configure. On the other hand, scalability can be a problem and most single server management centers cannot support many more than 20,000 agents.

One way to overcome the scalability limitations of a single server is to take the *tiered* approach, where each management element on a separate physical machine. In other words, you have one machine for event handling, one for the database, and a third for policy management. Logically, the three machines act as single entity. In some cases, the database portion can be clustered to further enhance scalability. The downside of a tiered solution is that agents in geographically distributed organizations might have to use limited WANs to deliver events and update policies.

The final management model is *hierarchical*. It is also known as "manager-of-managers" because many submanagement centers report to a central management center. The central manager distributes the policies to the submanagers, synchronizes policies between them, and collects events from them. Ideally, a hierarchical solution should also offer some kind of roaming capability where agents are able to report to the geographically closest submanager. This solution is well-suited for large distributed environments.

Event and Alert Handler

The event handling portion of the management station is also important, but less so than the database because of the fact that HIPS products are supposed to stop attacks before they succeed. HIPS events are almost exclusively informational. They identify what *almost* happened and what action *was taken* rather than give a notification that requires a response. This is in stark contrast with Host Intrusion Detection where the most critical component is the event delivery. HIDS cannot take action, so finding a way to elicit a response from an administrator is crucial.

Event handling covers both event delivery and alert generation. The difference between events and alerts rests in their priority. Events are simply bits of information that might or might not be important. Alerts are any events that are marked, usually by the administrator, as being important and use a higher priority mechanism such as e-mail, pager, or Simple Network Management Protocol (SNMP) messages to deliver them.

Two event-handling models are shown in Figure 6-13. In one, the agents report all their events to the management center, and the management center generates alerts for important events. Alerting is centralized, and events are stored in one location, although a large number of simultaneous events can impact management center performance. Another event delivery approach is to have each agent generate its own alerts. Responsibility for alerting is distributed, so performance is of less concern, although no events are stored centrally.

Figure 6-13 *Event Handling Models*

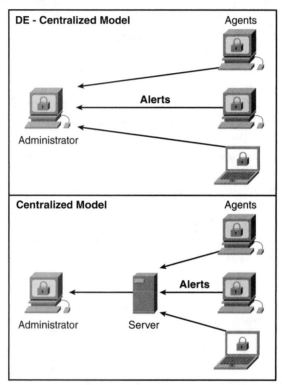

Ideally, events and alerts should be delivered as quickly as possible. If the agents cannot communicate with the alert or event receiver, you might have a delay; however, all HIPS agents should store event information until it can be delivered.

Policy Management

The last piece of the management center is the policy editor. Security policy evolves over time in response to environmental or security-related changes. You use the policy editor to make these changes and distribute them to the agents.

The communications channel used to distribute policy changes must be responsive, reliable, and secure. HIPS products use one or more of the following communications models:

- **Push**—Changes are forced onto the agent by the management center. Agents must listen for pushes constantly so that they are prepared when it happens. The push model propagates changes rapidly, although it represents a security risk because the agents are listening for connections. An attacker could masquerade as a management server and push dangerous policy changes to the agents.

- **Pull**—Agents periodically check with the management center to see if any policy changes are available. In the pull model, policy distribution takes longer because the management center must wait for the agents to check in before the new policy can be delivered. One of the advantages of the pull model is that you stand less risk that agents accept policy changes from unauthorized sources.

- **Push/pull**—Push/pull is the middle ground. The management center can send a message to the agents directing them to "Check Now," which greatly speeds the policy update process. The agents listen for this message, so they are able to receive remote connections However, the risk of a false management center is reduced as long as they are able to connect only to the legitimate management center when prompted to make a policy check. Push/pull is similar to a dial-back modem where the user dials the modem, the modem hangs up, and dials the preprogrammed phone number for the user.

Most HIPS products use some kind of encryption to make sure that the communications between the agents and the management center cannot be overheard (also known as eavesdropping). The encryption also serves the purpose of authenticating the agents and the management console so that the agents cannot deliver events or receive updates from an unauthorized, or spoofed, source. Eavesdropping and spoofing are very common attack vectors, so communications security is very important.

Management Interface

The tool HIPS administrators use to interact with the management center is called a user interface and comes in two forms. It can either be an installed client user interface or a web interface. Although a full user interface sometimes offers more functionality, a web interface is well-suited for remote administration.

In either case, the communications between the management interface and the management center should be as carefully secured as agent to MC communications. You should enforce strong authentication, encryption, and least privilege in addition to layers of defense you usually apply. The endpoint on which the interface is installed should also have a HIPS agent installed to prevent attackers from piggybacking.

Summary

In this chapter, you learned that HIPS products have management infrastructure and agent components. HIPS agents act like security guards and decide whether to allow or deny a person access to a building resource. The guards use an access control process to make the decision and identify the resource the person attempts to access. They continue and gather data about the operation, determine the state of the system, consult the security policy, and finally take action.

HIPS products tackle each phase of the access control process differently. This chapter examined the different approaches in detail. Real HIPS products were used as examples in some cases.

In the first phase of the access control process, the agent identifies the resource being accessed. Commonly identified resources include the following:

- Network

- Memory

- Application execution

- Files

- System configuration

The next phase is the data gathering phase. HIPS products gather data using one or more of the following methods:

- Kernel modification

- System call interception

- Virtual OSs

- Network traffic analysis

HIPS products also determine the state of the system. States in common use include the following:

- Location state

- User state

- System state

The data that was gathered about the resource access attempt and system state is compared to one or more of the following policy types:

- Anomaly-based

- Atomic rule-based

- Pattern-based

- Behavioral

- Access control matrix

The access control process concludes when the HIPS takes action based on the results of the access attempt to policy comparison.

This chapter also addressed the management center and interface components of the management infrastructure. The management center portion was divided into database, event and alert handling, and policy management components. The properties and approaches to each component were discussed. Lastly, the various types of management interface client and management interface security considerations were addressed.

Part III: Network Intrusion Prevention

Chapter 7   Network Intrusion Prevention Overview

Chapter 8   NIPS Components

Network Intrusion Prevention Overview

Network Intrusion Prevention provides a proactive component that effectively integrates into your overall network security framework. Combining Network Intrusion Prevention with other security components, such as a Host Intrusion Prevention System (HIPS), an Intrusion Detection System (IDS), and perimeter firewalls, provides a robust defense-in-depth network security solution.

An Intrusion Prevention System (IPS) provides a powerful addition to your overall network security solution, but it also has its limitations. This chapter focuses on the following topics:

- Network Intrusion Prevention capabilities

- Network Intrusion Prevention benefits

- Network Intrusion Prevention limitations

- Hybrid IPS/IDS systems

- Shared IDS/IPS capabilities

Network Intrusion Prevention Capabilities

Intrusion Prevention technology enables you to stop intrusion traffic before it enters your network by placing the sensor as a Layer 2 (Ethernet layer) forwarding device in the network. This sensor has two interfaces connected to your network (see Figure 7-1). Any traffic that passes through the sensor can then be examined by the sensor's Intrusion Prevention software.

Figure 7-1 *Intrusion Prevention Sensor Deployment*

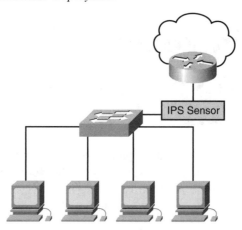

FORWARDING DEVICE
A *switch* is a common forwarding device on a network. It receives traffic on one of its ports and then passes that traffic to another one of its ports. Unlike routing at Layer 3, which rewrites the Ethernet header at each hop, Layer 2 forwarding simply passes the frame to the destination system without modification.

The main differentiator between an IDS and an IPS is the ability of an IPS to drop (or modify) traffic it receives on one of its interfaces, preventing the original traffic from reaching its destination. For efficiency, dropping traffic is usually divided into the following categories:

■   Dropping a single packet

■   Dropping all packets for a connection

■   Dropping all traffic from a source IP

Dropping a Single Packet

The simplest form of Intrusion Prevention involves identifying a suspicious packet and dropping it. The bad packet does not reach the target system, so your network is protected; however, the attacker can repeatedly send the bad packets. For each packet, the IPS needs to analyze the network packets and determine whether to pass or drop the traffic, consuming resources on your IPS device.

Dropping All Packets for a Connection

Instead of dropping a single packet, your IPS can drop all traffic for a specific connection for a configured period of time. In this situation, when a suspicious packet is detected, it is dropped along with all subsequent packets that belong to the same connection. The connection is usually defined as traffic that matches the following parameters:

- Source IP address

- Destination IP address

- Destination port

- Source port (optional)

The advantage to the connection drop is that subsequent packets matching the connection can be dropped automatically without analysis. The drawback, however, is an attacker still has the ability to send traffic that does not match the connection being dropped (for example, attacking another service or system on your network).

Dropping All Traffic from a Source IP

The final dropping mechanism is to drop all the traffic originating from a specific source IP address. In this situation, when the suspicious packet is detected, it is dropped, along with all traffic from the corresponding source IP address for a configured period of time. Because all traffic from the attacking host can be dropped with minimal examination, your IPS device uses very few resources. The main drawbacks are if attackers can spoof the source address and pretend to be an important system, such as a business partner, or if the initial signature is a false positive and valid traffic is denied access to your network.

Network Intrusion Prevention Benefits

Forwarding traffic at Layer 2, the IPS devices on your network can inspect traffic from numerous protocols to identify attacks against your network. By not forwarding malicious traffic, your Network IPS solution can stop this traffic before it reaches the target system. Your IPS also provides the following benefits:

- Traffic normalization

- Security policy enforcement

Traffic Normalization

Besides stopping malicious traffic, your IPS devices can prevent various IDS evasion techniques by normalizing the traffic reaching the systems on your network. Some of the attacks that normalizing TCP traffic can prevent include the following:

- Time to Live (TTL) manipulation

- URG pointer manipulation

- Out of order RST of FIN

- Out of order packets

- TCP window size manipulation

NORMALIZING TRAFFIC

Stateful protocols, such as TCP, operate by a predefined set of rules and states. Some attacks, such as TTL manipulation, utilize the rules to try to evade detection. Normalizing traffic involves manipulating the traffic, such as a TCP stream, to prevent these anomalies. For example, to nullify the TTL manipulation attack, the normalizer engine can force all the outgoing TCP packets to use the smallest TTL observed during the TCP connection.

Normalizing traffic has been initially focused on mitigating various TCP-based attacks. This concept, however, can be applied to numerous protocols. As IPS software evolves, the normalizing capability will grow and incorporate a larger suite of protocols, making it more difficult for an attacker to evade detection and successfully attack systems on your network.

Security Policy Enforcement

Your IPS has the capability to enforce your security policy because your IPS has the capability to modify and drop traffic entering your network. For example, many applications, such as peer-to-peer software, use a destination port of TCP port 80 because this traffic is usually allowed by most firewall policies. The firewall might not be able to distinguish between HTTP traffic going to TCP port 80 and another program, such as Kazaa, using the same port. With an IPS, you can monitor traffic to TCP port 80 and verify its compliance with RFC 2616, "Hypertext Transfer Protocol— HTTP 1.1," thus ensuring that your firewall is allowing only HTTP traffic through for TCP port 80.

Network Intrusion Prevention Limitations

Intrusion Prevention provides a powerful tool to protect your network from attack. The network location where you deploy this technology, however, greatly impacts its effectiveness. For example, assume you are protecting the network shown in Figure 7-2.

Figure 7-2   *Sample Network Configuration*

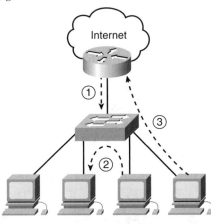

Internal Network

To prevent attacks against your network, your IPS devices must bridge the traffic between the two systems involved in the attack: the attacker and the victim. If you examine the network shown in Figure 7-2, you find three attack vectors:

1. Attacker located on the Internet launching an attack against a system on the internal network

2. Attacker located on the internal network launching an attack against another system on the internal network

3. Attacker located on the internal network launching an attack against a system on the Internet

Protecting against #1 and #3 is easy to accomplish by placing your IPS device between the switch and the router (see Figure 7-3). Any traffic entering the internal network or leaving the internal network now passes through the IPS device and is inspected.

Figure 7-3   *IPS Solution for Attacks Between Internal and External Systems*

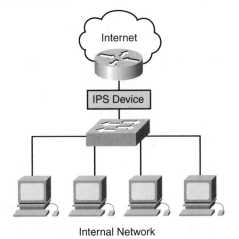

Internal Network

Protecting against #2 using Intrusion Prevention is more difficult. You need an IPS device between the switch and each internal system (see Figure 7-4) to guarantee the attack traffic from any two systems passes through the IPS device.

Figure 7-4 *IPS Solution for Internal to Internal Attack*

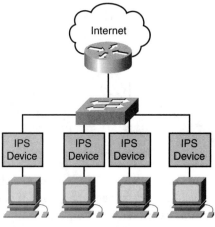

In this situation, it is more effective to use a traditional IDS to passively monitor the traffic going between all the internal systems. A single IDS sensor can perform this monitoring functionality as long as the traffic between the internal systems does not exceed the bandwidth limitations of the monitoring device. You can also utilize a Host-based Intrusion System in conjunction with your Network IPS to effectively monitor all the systems on a single subnet.

Hybrid IPS/IDS Systems

Deploying separate IDS and IPS devices is cumbersome. Protecting your network using hybrid IPS devices, though, enables you to obtain the benefits of both technologies from a single device because IDS and IPS are complimentary technologies.

Using the ongoing network configuration, a hybrid IPS device can provide the IPS protection to prevent an attack coming from or going to the Internet (see Figure 7-5). Using IDS functionality, the same device also can watch for attacks going between two internal systems.

Figure 7-5 *Hybrid IPS Device Providing IPS Protection*

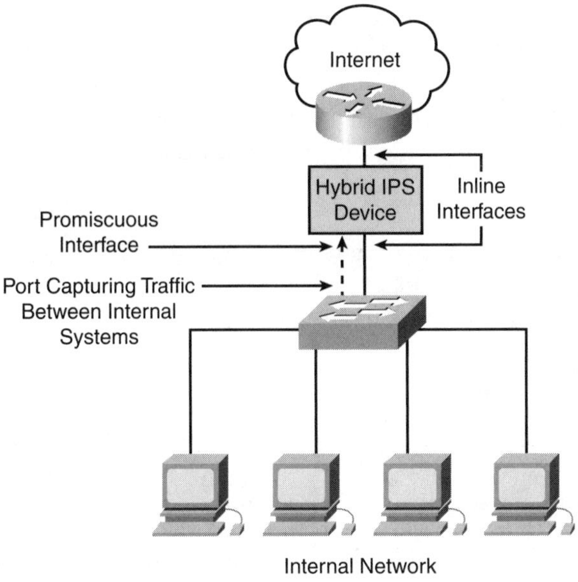

Shared IDS/IPS Capabilities

Although Intrusion Prevention provides some unique capabilities, you should also understand the capabilities shared by IDS and IPS systems, because these two technologies usually are deployed in unison. The combined IDS/IPS capabilities include the following:

■ Generating alerts

■ Initiating IP logging

■ Resetting TCP connections

■ Initiating IP blocking

Each of these items is examined in detail in the following sections.

Generating Alerts

You need to be able to monitor when your network is under attack. Your IDS or IPS should be able to generate alerts to indicate that an attack has been launched against your network even if the intrusion software prevented that attack from succeeding. These alerts enable you to correlate activity on your network between security devices such as IPS and IDS sensors, as well as other infrastructure equipment.

Initiating IP Logging

Sometimes, you want to record the traffic a potential attacker is sending against your network. By analyzing this captured information, you can gain insight into what the attacker is trying to do against your network. Other times, you might want to log traffic that is violating your defined security policy. By seeing which traffic violates the security policy, you can determine what the impact is if you decide to make the security policy mandatory by actively stopping offending traffic.

IP logging refers to the ability to capture the traffic traversing your network. It can be initiated either manually or automatically in conjunction with defined signatures. Most intrusion systems provide IP logging functionality that falls into several categories, such as the following:

- Logging attacker traffic

- Logging victim traffic

- Logging traffic between attacker and victim

The benefits and limitations of these logging options are explained in the following sections.

Logging Attacker Traffic

The most logical logging option is logging traffic from an attacking system. In this situation, you want to monitor all the traffic originating from a specific source IP address. The benefit of logging all of the packets for a specific source IP address is you can examine all of the traffic attackers are launching against your network, not just the traffic to the specific system that initially initiated the logging. The drawback is that logging all the packets from attackers might make analysis more complicated. It also requires more memory or hard drive space to store the information, especially if the attackers are generating a lot of traffic, some of it invalid trying to hide the real attack traffic. Logging traffic from a single host also assumes that the attackers are using a single address from which to launch their attack.

Logging Victim Traffic

Instead of logging the attackers' traffic, you can log the traffic going to a specific target or victim system. In this situation, you focus on all traffic going to the target system, regardless of the source IP address. The advantage of this approach is if the attackers are coming from multiple source IP addresses, you capture all the traffic being sent to the victim machine, not just the traffic from the initial source IP address that initiated the logging. The drawback is, again, the amount of traffic you might capture. If the target system is a large server, you might capture a large amount of information, making it difficult to distinguish attack traffic from normal user traffic.

Logging Traffic Between Attacker and Victim

Another logging option most systems include is the ability to capture all the traffic being sent between two specific systems. This limits the information captured to only the traffic being sent from the attacking system to the victim system and traffic being sent from the victim system to the attacking system. The advantage of this approach is the traffic logged is limited to the IP addresses of the traffic that initially triggered the logging action. The drawback is your captured information provides a limited view of the traffic being sent to the victim as well as a limited view of the traffic being sent from the attackers to your network.

Resetting TCP Connections

One of the original responses incorporated into IDS solutions was the ability to reset a TCP connection, sending a packet with the RST flag set to both systems involved in a TCP connection. By resetting the TCP connection, the attackers lose their TCP session to the victim system. At that point, the attackers need to establish another TCP session to the victim system to continue the attack. This response is particularly effective if the connection is reset before the attackers complete the entire attack, because the attack is never allowed to complete. The drawback is if the attack is already complete by the time the connection is reset, the attackers might have access to the system via a mechanism that is not detected by your security devices, such as a back door opened by the attack. Furthermore, this action is limited to attacks that use TCP-based protocols.

Initiating IP Blocking

IPS devices have the capability to stop traffic before it reaches the target system. IDS devices, on the other hand, passively monitor network traffic by analyzing a copy of the actual traffic. To enable IDS devices to block traffic from attacking systems, they utilize existing infrastructure devices to deploy access control lists (ACLs) on the network. Blocking traffic in this fashion, however, is reactive in that the initial attack traffic has already been sent to the victim system before IP blocking is initiated. If this initial attack traffic succeeds in creating a back door on the victim system, the attackers can easily access this back door undetected from any system. It might not necessarily be the same system used to launch the attack.

An intrusion system usually provides the following IP blocking options:

- Block a specific connection

- Block a specific attacking system

When you are using both of these blocking options, your IPS device needs to know when to remove the blocking action. Automatic blocking actions are performed only for a configured length of time. When the time period expires, your IPS removes the block and traffic from the blocked host is again allowed into the network. IP blocking is not meant to permanently prevent a system from accessing your network. The blocking action simply gives you time to analyze the situation and take the appropriate action to protect your network.

AUTOMATIC BLOCKING

Automatic blocking refers to blocking actions that are initiated in response to the triggering of an IPS signature. Most IPSs also enable you to manually initiate blocking actions. With manual blocking actions, your security operator applies a manual block after analyzing the situation and determining that a specific system (or systems) should be blocked from the network.

One of the downsides of IP blocking is IP spoofing. When using IP blocking, you need to make sure that an attacker cannot use your IP blocking response to deny traffic from valid systems. User Datagram Protocol (UDP) traffic, for example, is connectionless. Many UDP messages are one-way and do not elicit a reply from the destination system. If you configure a UDP-based signature to initiate IP blocking, an attacker using IP spoofing can pretend to be another system. Then, when your IDS blocks the address detected, it is actually blocking traffic from a valid system, maybe one of your business partners.

IP SPOOFING

Sending packets with another system's source IP address is known as *IP spoofing.* Connectionless protocols, such as UDP and the Address Resolution Protocol (ARP), are especially prone to spoofing attacks. By filtering the traffic entering your network (using ACLs and unicast reverse path filtering [uRPF]), you can prevent an external attacker from spoofing traffic that appears to come from systems on your internal network. On some Cisco switches, you can also utilize Layer 2 protections, such as port security and IP source guard, to prevent spoofing at the switch port itself.

ADDRESS RESOLUTION PROTOCOL

On Ethernet networks, data is sent between hosts using Ethernet frames. Hosts tend to send data based on IP addresses. Therefore, a mechanism is needed to translate IP addresses to physical Ethernet addresses. The ARP handles this conversion. ARP provides only the address for the next hop that the packet needs to go through. An IP packet might have to go through several hops before it reaches its final destination. The final destination is determined by the destination IP address of the packet. The designers of ARP did not even consider security during its development, and it is highly susceptible to spoofing attacks; however, attacks are limited to systems with access to the local Layer 2 segment. For more information on ARP, refer to RFC 826, "An Ethernet Address Resolution Protocol."

Numerous programs enable attackers to create packets from any source IP address that they choose. When attackers identify traffic that initiates an IP blocking response, they can then attempt to generate spoofed traffic from a legitimate IP address—your business partners, for example—to see if they can block valid systems from accessing your network.

Summary

IPSs provide a proactive component that integrates very effectively into your overall network security framework. Combining Intrusion Prevention with other security components, such as an IDS and perimeter firewalls, provides a robust defense-in-depth network security solution.

Intrusion Prevention technology enables you to stop intrusion traffic before it enters your network by placing the sensor as a Layer 2 (Ethernet layer) forwarding device in the network. Some of the common dropping actions that IPS provides include the following:

- Dropping a single packet

- Dropping all packets for a connection

- Dropping all traffic from a source IP

One of the main benefits of Network Intrusion Prevention is the ability to stop intrusive traffic from reaching the target system. Other key benefits include the following:

- Traffic normalization

- Security policy enforcement

Network Intrusion Prevention is not without its limitations, such as monitoring traffic between all the hosts on a single subnet. These limitations, however, usually can be mitigated by incorporating Intrusion Detection and host-based analysis in addition to simply using Network Intrusion Prevention. A hybrid IPS provides you with the ability to perform IPS and IDS functionality using the same sensor.

Some of the capabilities shared by both IPS and IDS systems include the following:

- Generating alerts

- Initiating IP logging

- Resetting TCP connections

- Initiating IP blocking

Alerts indicate that events are occurring on your network. IP logging enables you to record the intrusive activity that is occurring on your network. Most intrusion systems provide IP logging functionality that falls into several categories, such as the following:

- Logging attacker traffic

- Logging victim traffic

- Logging traffic between attacker and victim

Resetting TCP connections enables your intrusion system to forcibly terminate TCP connections when intrusive activity is detected. This functionality has limited effectiveness because the attack might have already succeeded in compromising the target system before the connection is reset.

IP blocking is a reactionary response that prevents traffic from an attacking system for a configured period of time. An intrusion system usually provides the following IP blocking options:

- Blocking a specific connection

- Blocking a specific attacking system

CHAPTER 8

NIPS Components

Network-based Intrusion Prevention products use sensors to analyze network traffic at numerous locations throughout your network. These sensors are deployed in various form factors, such as the following:

■ Standalone appliance sensors

■ Blade-based sensors

■ Intrusion Prevention System (IPS) software integrated into the operating system (OS) on infrastructure devices

Regardless of the form factor of your sensors, your sensors must receive the network traffic that needs to be analyzed. Capturing network traffic varies depending on whether you are using in-line mode or promiscuous mode. After your sensors have captured network traffic, their analysis of the traffic falls into the following categories based on the way that the signatures used to analyze the network traffic:

■ Atomic operations

■ Stateful operations

■ Protocol decode operations

■ Anomaly operations

■ Normalizing operations

After it analyzes network traffic, the sensor uses one or more of the following types of actions to respond to the identified traffic:

■ Alerting actions

■ Logging actions

■ Blocking actions

■ Dropping actions

The results of the traffic analysis performed by your IPS sensors are usually monitored via a centralized monitoring console. Similarly, a centralized management application enables you to effectively configure a large number of IPS sensors across your network.

This chapter provides an in-depth explanation of the various Network Intrusion Prevention System (NIPS)/Network Intrusion Detection System (NIDS) components. It divides the major elements into subcomponents and illustrates implementation approaches for each of these subcomponents. Cisco IPS sensors are used as a practical example throughout this chapter to provide real examples of the various NIPS components.

Sensor Capabilities

Your unique network topology identifies which IPS sensors are the most effective devices to analyze the traffic on your network. Some of the factors that impact your IPS sensor selection and deployment include the following:

■ Security budget

■ Amount of network traffic

■ Network topology

■ Security staff to operate the components

Your IPS sensors must monitor traffic, regardless of the unique topology of your network. Besides the amount of traffic that a sensor processes, two other factors significantly impact your choice of IPS sensor: the number of interfaces available on the sensor and the form factor of the sensor. All three of these aspects impact the cost and the efficiency of the sensors that you deploy on your network.

Sensor Processing Capacity

Each IPS sensor can process only a limited amount of network traffic. For example, Table 8-1 shows the bandwidth capacities for several Cisco IPS appliance sensors.

Table 8-1   *Cisco Appliance Sensor Capacities*

Model	Maximum Promiscuous Capacity
IPS 4215	80 Mbps
IPS 4240	250 Mbps
IPS 4255	600 Mbps
IPS 4250XL	1000 Mbps

Different segments of your network support different amounts of network traffic. Your sensors must support the traffic at the specific location in the network at which they are deployed. If you have excess capacity on a sensor, it provides flexibility to handle more traffic as your network grows, although it also makes your NIPS installation more costly because the cost of a sensor is usually directly proportional to the amount of traffic that it can process.

Another way to fully utilize the capacity of your IPS sensors is to use EtherChannel load balance traffic from multiple VLANs across the same trunk line.

The raw bandwidth ratings on an IPS sensor can be misleading because the sensor can process different types of packets and protocols more efficiently than others. Therefore, besides the raw bandwidth that your IPS sensor can handle, you also need to consider the following factors about your network bandwidth when deploying IPS sensors:

■   Average packet size

■   Average number of new TCP connections per second

The ratings indicate the type of traffic that was used to determine the maximum traffic analysis capacity of the sensor. For example, the Cisco IPS 4240 sensor supports a maximum traffic analysis capability of 250 Mbps. The rating is based on the following criteria:

■   2500 new TCP connections per second

■   2500 HTTP transactions per second

■   Average packet size of 445 bytes

■   Running Cisco IDS 4.1 Sensor Software

Sensor Interfaces

Besides capacity, your IPS sensors must also receive network traffic (to be analyzed) via one or more network interfaces. Providing multiple interfaces on a single sensor enables it to monitor multiple network locations. In-line processing (in many situations) requires two interfaces to monitor a single location in your network. Table 8-2 shows the default and maximum interfaces available for several Cisco IPS appliance sensors.

Table 8-2   *Cisco Appliance Monitoring Interfaces*

Model	Default	Maximum
IPS 4215	1 10/100BASE-TX	5 10/100BASE-TX
IPS 4240	4 10/100/1000BASE-TX	4 10/100/1000BASE-TX
IPS 4255	4 10/100/1000BASE-TX	4 10/100BASE-TX

> **NOTE**   As use of in-line monitoring increases, the number of interfaces available on individual sensors keeps increasing. Furthermore, some IPS sensors also enable you to configure in-line processing using a single interface (known as "in-line on a stick").

Although having more network interfaces enables you to monitor more locations throughout your network, you do encounter a break-even point at which the processing capacity of the sensor makes more monitoring interfaces impractical.

For example, suppose that you deploy a Cisco IPS 4240 sensor and use two interfaces for in-line monitoring and the other two interfaces to perform promiscuous monitoring at two other locations in your network. With this configuration, the monitoring interfaces can actually receive 3000 Mbps (1000 Mbps for the in-line pair and 1000 Mbps for each promiscuous interface if the network is totally saturated). Therefore, installing more interfaces on the sensor might not be practical because the potential capacity of the sensor is already being exceeded. Now suppose that you deploy the same Cisco IPS 4240 sensor, although this time, you configure two sets of in-line interface pairs on 100 Mbps interfaces. In this configuration, the monitoring interfaces can receive only a maximum of 200 Mbps (100 Mbps for each in-line pair). In this situation, a couple of more network interfaces can be practical (when using 100 Mbps interfaces). With two more interfaces, you can have a total of three in-line interface pairs. The maximum amount of traffic that these three in-line interface pairs can handle is 300 Mbps, similar to the first example that involved in-line and promiscuous monitoring utilizing on four network interfaces.

> **NOTE**   The interfaces on the Cisco IPS appliances are 10/100/1000BASE-TX interfaces. Therefore, these interfaces can be connected to 10 Mbps, 100 Mbps, or 1000 Mbps interfaces. The sensor automatically detects the configuration speed for each monitoring interface. Understanding the types of interfaces connected to your sensor is important because even a single fully saturated 1000 Mbps promiscuous interface can easily exceed the analysis capacity of the Cisco IPS 4240 sensor.

Sensor Form Factor

The final aspect to consider when you decide on the correct sensor is the network location where you plan to deploy your sensor. The common sensor form factors include the following:

■   Standalone appliance sensors

■   Blade-based sensors

■   IPS software integrated into the OS on infrastructure devices

An appliance sensor can be deployed in almost any network environment, but it does take up rack space. If you use other form factors, such as blade-based sensors, it might fit your network topology more appropriately, especially if rack space is limited.

Standalone Appliance Sensors

The standalone appliance sensors provide the most flexibility when you deploy IPS sensors on your network. These sensors can be deployed at virtually any location in your network. The main drawback to the appliance sensor is that you must make rack space in which to place the sensor. The Cisco 4200 Series sensors are examples of appliance sensors.

Blade-Based Sensors

Blade-based sensors (line cards) enable you to take advantage of existing infrastructure devices to deploy your IPS devices. Blade-based sensors do not take up extra rack space, and they have the advantage of receiving traffic directly from the backplane of the infrastructure device in which it is deployed. One drawback of the blade-based sensors is that they can be costly if you do not already have the existing infrastructure devices deployed on your network; another drawback is limited flexibility in sensor deployment locations. Cisco supports the following different blade-based sensors platforms:

- Cisco Intrusion Detection System Module (IDSM-2)

- Cisco Intrusion Detection System Network Module (NM-CIDS)

- Cisco Adaptive Inspection and Prevention Security Service Module (AIP-SSM)

The IDSM-2 blade operates in the Catalyst 6500 Series family of switches. It provides a maximum of 600 Mbps of traffic analysis capacity. The network module is a line card that provides Cisco IPS functionality into Cisco 2800 or 3800 Series routers. The network module can analyze up to 45 Mbps of network traffic.

The Cisco Adaptive Security Appliance (ASA) integrates a powerful suite of security technologies into a single platform. Some of the functionality built into the ASA includes the following:

- High performance firewall

- Virtual private network (VPN) capabilities

- Worm and virus mitigation

- Adaptive identification and mitigation services architecture

The ASA can also incorporate additional specialized high-performance security services using Security Service Modules (SSMs). These SSMs utilize dedicated coprocessors to perform customized analysis of traffic flows. Advanced intrusion prevention functionality is provided by the AIP-SSM. The ASA AIP-SSM has the following models available:

- Cisco ASA SSM-AIP-10

- Cisco ASA SSM-AIP-20

The intrusion prevention traffic analysis capacity of the modules depends on the ASA appliance in which SSM is installed. Table 8-3 shows the different performance values for the two modules.

Table 8-3   *AIP-SSM Performance Ratings*

ASA Model	SSM	Maximum Performance
ASA 5510	SSM-AIP-10	150 Mbps
ASA 5520	SSM-AIP-10	225 Mbps
ASA 5520	SSM-AIP-20	375 Mbps
ASA 5540	SSM-AIP-20	450 Mbps

IPS Software Integrated into the OS on Infrastructure Devices

When the IPS software is integrated into the software of an existing infrastructure device, the functionality provided is usually limited compared to a standalone appliance sensor because the infrastructure device takes on extra duties and responsibilities. Depending on your network environment, this reduced functionality might not be a problem. Furthermore, because the IPS is part of OS on the infrastructure, deploying the integrated IPS functionality is usually more cost effective (especially for small networks). Newer versions of Cisco IOS (Cisco IOS Release 12.3T and later) incorporate much of the functionality that the appliance sensors provide.

Capturing Network Traffic

Your IPS sensors can process only traffic that they receive on one of their interfaces. in-line processing mode uses pairs of sensor interfaces (or pairs of logical interfaces on a single physical interface), although promiscuous mode requires only a single sensor interface. The following methods of traffic capture are examined in detail in the next sections:

- Capturing traffic for in-line mode

- Capturing traffic for promiscuous mode

Capturing Traffic for In-line Mode

Running a sensor in in-line mode requires that you use a pair of sensor interfaces to bridge the traffic between two separate VLANs (or multiple VLANs when using a trunk). You can also use the sensor to pass traffic between the same VLAN. In this configuration, only traffic passing through the sensor is inspected. A common situation where this configuration is deployed is when you place the IPS sensor between the router and the systems on a specified VLAN. To reach external systems, the internal systems send their traffic through the router. Therefore, external traffic to and from the internal systems must pass through the sensor and be inspected. In this configuration, however, traffic between two internal systems is not inspected by the sensor (because the traffic does not pass through the sensor).

A basic in-line configuration is shown in Figure 8-1. The interface from each router is connected to a different sensor interface. The only way for traffic to pass from one router to the other is if the IPS sensor allows the traffic to pass by taking the traffic it receives on one of its interfaces and bridging it to the other interface.

Figure 8-1 *Basic In-line Configuration*

Router A   Inline   Router B
                         IPS Sensor

BRIDGE

When you bridge traffic, it means that Ethernet traffic (link layer) passes between two interfaces that are each on a specific virtual local-area network (VLAN). Usually, the VLANs are the same, but when establishing an artificial VLAN boundary, the VLANs can be different.

Some typical locations for deploying in-line IPS include the following:

- Between two routers

- Between a firewall and a router

- Between a switch and a router

- Between a switch and a firewall

- Between two switches

You can easily deploy in-line IPS between any two physical interfaces. However, the configuration becomes more difficult with devices such as switches in which the router is integrated into the switch's backplane via virtual interfaces (it does not have physical interfaces). The same situation arises with line cards such as the Cisco IDSM-2, which are also directly connected to the switch's backplane and do not have physical interfaces.

When you deal with devices that are connected to your switch via virtual ports (such as the Multi Switch Feature Card [MSFC] and IDSM-2), you must artificially create a VLAN boundary at which you can deploy your in-line IPS sensor.

Assume that you want to place in-line IPS between the user systems on VLAN 1020 and the Internet (see Figure 8-2).

Figure 8-2 *Simple Network Configuration*

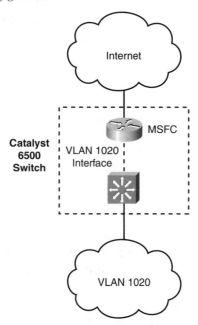

Initially, traffic goes from systems on VLAN 1020 directly to the VLAN 1020 interface on the switch, which allows the MSFC to route the traffic to the Internet. You cannot connect the sensor's interface directly to the MSFC because it has only virtual ports; although if you place the MSFC on another VLAN (for example, VLAN 1030) and use the sensor to bridge traffic from VLAN 1020 to VLAN 1030, you can create an artificial VLAN boundary (see Figure 8-3).

Figure 8-3 *Artificial VLAN Boundary Configuration*

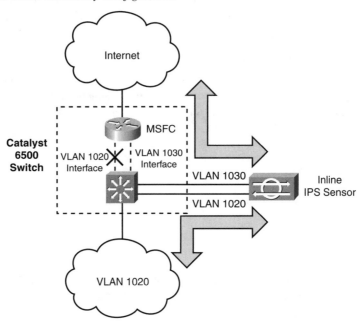

After you create the artificial VLAN boundary, the systems on VLAN 1020 can no longer communicate with the MSFC (because the VLAN 1020 interface on the MSFC is shut down). Now, the systems must rely on the sensor to bridge the traffic (destined to the Internet) to VLAN 1030. After the traffic reaches VLAN 1030, the MSFC can route the traffic to the Internet (refer to Figure 8-3). The same situation also applies to traffic coming from the Internet to systems on VLAN 1020.

Capturing Traffic for Promiscuous Mode

At the network level, your Cisco IPS sensors are the eyes of your IPS. However, to detect intrusive activity, sensors running in promiscuous mode must be able to view the traffic that traverses your network. Via its monitoring interfaces, each of your sensors that operate in promiscuous mode examines only the network traffic that it sees. Unless the monitoring interface is plugged into a hub, your IPS sensor observes only broadcast traffic by default. Therefore, you usually must configure your infrastructure devices to pass specified network traffic to your sensor's monitoring interface. Typical traffic capture devices that you use to pass traffic to your IPS sensors include the following:

■ Hubs

■ Network taps

■ Switches

> **NOTE** Promiscuous interfaces on your IPS sensors do not usually have an IP address associated with them. Therefore, these interfaces are essentially invisible on the network (especially from a Layer 3 or IP perspective).

Besides identifying the infrastructure devices that you can use to pass network traffic to your sensors, this section also examines the following three mechanisms that you can use to configure Cisco switches to mirror traffic to your sensor's promiscuous interface:

■ Switch Port Analyzer (SPAN)

■ Remote Switch Port Analyzer (RSPAN)

■ VLAN Access Control List (VACL)

MIRROR TRAFFIC

To mirror traffic means to take a copy of the network traffic going to a device, switch port, or VLAN and send a copy of that network traffic to another port or VLAN. Copying the traffic does not do anything to the original traffic. The mirrored traffic provides a stream of traffic that can be analyzed by your security systems.

Traffic Capture Devices

To detect intrusive activity, your sensors that run in promiscuous mode must be able to view the traffic that traverses your network. Your sensor's monitoring interface is directly connected to an infrastructure device that mirrors specified network traffic to your sensor for analysis. You can use the following three link-layer network devices to pass traffic to your sensors:

■ Hubs

■ Network taps

■ Switches

A hub is a simple link-layer device. Whenever a device connected to the hub generates network packets, the hub passes that traffic to all the other ports on the hub. Figure 8-4 shows how when Host A sends traffic to Host C, all the other devices connected to the hub also receive a copy of the traffic. The other devices connected to the hub simply ignore the traffic that does not match their Ethernet MAC address.

Figure 8-4 *Hub Traffic Flow*

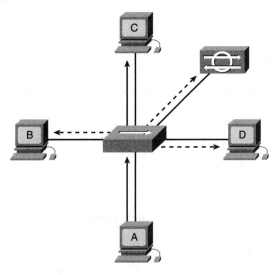

ETHERNET MAC ADDRESS

Just as you can send traffic to a host based on its IP address at the IP layer (network layer), each host also has an address at the link layer known as the Ethernet MAC address. This address is a 12-byte value that indicates the link-layer address that other devices on the same network segment use to send traffic to it. Your network card has a default Ethernet address that the manufacturer assigns, although most systems allow you to change its value.

If the network segment that you want to monitor with your Cisco IPS sensor uses a hub, your sensor can connect one of its monitoring interfaces into a port on the hub to access the network traffic. Unlike other devices that ignore the traffic that does not match their Ethernet MAC address, your sensor puts its interface in promiscuous mode so that it accepts all packets that its network interface card receives.

Sometimes, you need to monitor a network segment between two infrastructure devices that are connected without an intervening switch or hub. In this situation, you can use a network tap to capture the traffic traversing the segment (as well as in-line mode). A network tap is a device that enables you to split a full-duplex connection into two separate traffic flows (each flow representing the traffic originating from one of the two devices). The separate traffic flows can then be redirected to an aggregation switch and eventually to your sensor. Some network taps even eliminate the aggregation switch completely, enabling you to connect the network tap directly to your sensor.

AGGREGATION SWITCH

You use an aggregation switch to combine the multiple traffic flows and pass the traffic to your sensor. When aggregating flows through the switch, however, you must be careful not to exceed the capacity of your sensor. For example, if your sensor is an IPS 4215 appliance sensor, aggregating two 100-Mbps traffic flows can exceed the sensor's capabilities because it is not rated at 200 Mbps (the maximum capacity of the combined two flows).

Figure 8-5 shows a situation in which you want to monitor the network traffic traversing between a Cisco router and a PIX firewall. Initially, these devices are connected to each other directly. To enable you to monitor this traffic, you can install a network tap between these devices (or use in-line mode). The network tap then continues to pass the traffic between the router and the firewall, but also sends a copy of this traffic (via the two specific flows) to your aggregation switch.

Figure 8-5 *Network Tap Traffic Flow*

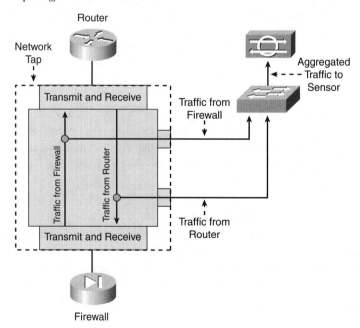

Probably the most common link-layer device on your network is a switch. Unlike a hub, a switch is more selective as to which ports it passes network traffic. The switch maintains a content-addressable memory (CAM) table that maintains a mapping between Ethernet MAC addresses and the port on which that traffic was observed. When the switch receives traffic for an Ethernet MAC address that is not in its CAM table, it floods the packet out all the ports (on the same VLAN) similar to a hub. But after the destination host replies, the CAM table is updated. Now when Host A sends traffic to Host C (see Figure 8-6), the traffic is sent only to Host C (instead of every device connected to the switch). In this scenario, your IPS sensor cannot monitor your network for intrusive activity because the monitoring interface on your sensor does not receive all the traffic traversing your network.

Figure 8-6 *Switch Traffic Flow*

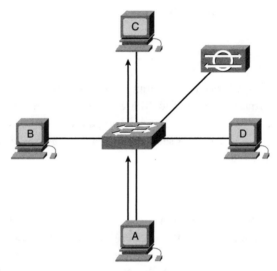

To overcome this problem, you need to configure your switch to mirror specific network traffic to your IPS sensor using a switch capture mechanism. The next section explains the common switch capture mechanisms available on most Cisco switches.

Cisco Switch Capture Mechanisms

With Cisco switches, you can use the following three features to enable your switch to mirror traffic to your IPS sensor's monitoring interface:

- SPAN

- RSPAN

- VACL

> **NOTE** Not all the switch traffic capture features are available on every Cisco switch platform, although all Cisco switches support some form of the SPAN feature. Also, you can use the **mls ip ids** command when you have enabled certain Cisco IOS firewall features to mirror traffic instead of using VACLs.

The SPAN feature enables you to select traffic for analysis by a network analyzer. People refer to SPAN ports by various names, such as port mirroring or port monitoring. Regardless of the name used, the SPAN feature enables you to cause your Cisco switch to pass selected traffic to your IPS sensor's monitoring interface for analysis.

NETWORK ANALYZER

A network analyzer is a device that examines network traffic and provides you with statistics or information about your network traffic. Many network analyzers identify the different types of traffic and their frequency on your network. Using these statistics, you can tune your network to optimize its performance. Your IPS sensor also analyzes the traffic on your network when it watches for intrusive activity.

Sometimes, you want to capture traffic from ports that are located on multiple switches. To accomplish this, you can use the RSPAN feature that is available on certain Cisco switches.

RSPAN allows you to monitor source ports spread all over your switched network. This functionality works similar to normal SPAN functionality, except that instead of traffic being mirrored to a specific destination port, the monitored traffic is flooded to a special RSPAN VLAN (see Figure 8-7). The destination port(s) can then be located on any switch that has access to this RSPAN VLAN.

If you configure RSPAN to monitor traffic sent by Host A (see Figure 8-7), whenever Host A generates a packet to Host B, a copy of the packet is passed by an application-specific integrated circuit (ASIC) of the Catalyst 6000 Policy Feature Card (PFC) into the predefined RSPAN VLAN. From there, the packet is flooded to all the ports belonging to the RSPAN VLAN. All the Inter-Switch Links shown in Figure 8-7 are trunks. RSPAN uses these trunks to support the traversal of the RSPAN VLAN traffic. The only access points to the RSPAN-captured traffic are the defined destination ports (where you would locate your IPS sensors).

Figure 8-7 *Remote SPAN Traffic Flow*

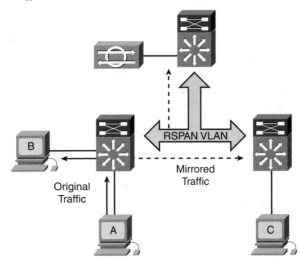

VACL access controls all packets on your Catalyst 6500 switch through the PFC. VACLs are strictly for security packet filtering and redirecting traffic to specific physical switch ports based on the traffic's source or destination VLAN. Unlike IOS ACLs, VACLs are not defined by the direction of the traffic (inbound or outbound).

VACLs are mainly provided to filter traffic on the switch. The **capture** keyword enables you to use a VACL to mirror matched traffic to a designated capture port. This capture option specifies that packets that match the specified *flows* are switched normally and captured and transmitted to the configured capture port. Only permitted traffic is sent to the capture port. When you use VACLs, it enables you to use a fine degree of granularity when specifying which traffic you want to capture (based on VLAN, IP addresses, and ports). You can use VACLs to capture traffic for both IPS modules (blade-based sensors) and appliance sensors.

> **FLOWS**
>
> A flow comprises a traffic stream between a source and destination IP address; a source port and destination port; or a combination of source IP address and source port in conjunction with a destination IP address and destination port. Your VACLs essentially define the flows that represent the traffic on which you want your sensor to perform intrusion detection analysis. Furthermore, your MSFC uses flows to effectively send packets between different VLANs by crossing the switch's backplane only once.

Analyzing Network Traffic

After receiving network traffic, your IPS sensors must analyze that traffic and then perform certain actions based on the results of that analysis. IPS sensor network traffic analysis falls into the following categories:

- Atomic operations
- Stateful operations
- Protocol decode operations
- Anomaly operations
- Normalizing operations

Atomic Operations

Some attack signatures identify situations in which the entire attack signature can be observed by analyzing the contents of a single packet. These signatures are the easiest to process because the IPS sensor has to examine only a single packet to determine if the signature is present. Whenever the attack signature is seen in a packet, the signature triggers, regardless of what traffic came before that packet or the packets that follow that packet.

Stateful Operations

Not all signatures can be processed without maintaining state on the traffic that the IPS sensor has previously observed on the network. For example, most TCP-based signatures require the traffic to be part of a valid TCP connection to actually trigger the signatures. Therefore, the IP sensor must maintain a list of the valid connections that it has seen. This list of valid connections includes information for each connection, such as the following fields:

- Source port
- Destination port
- Current source sequence number

- Current destination sequence number
- Connection state

Usually, this state information is maintained only for a specific amount of time. For example, inactive connections usually time out after a configured length of time. If the space claimed by inactive sessions were not reclaimed after a preset period of time, it would be a small matter for an attacker to consume significant resources on the sensor (by initiating connections and never terminating them). This stale state information would then limit the effectiveness of the sensor to analyze new connections.

Protocol Decode Operations

Instead of searching for known bad text strings, many intrusion systems decode traffic based on a specific protocol definition. This enables the analysis to check for bad values in specific fields of the protocol. When you verify that the traffic matches the protocol specification, it enables signatures to identify traffic that does not conform to the protocol specification, such as peer-to-peer (P2P) traffic with a destination port of 80, which is supposed to be HTTP traffic. Furthermore, decoding traffic for a specific protocol also enables the signatures to more accurately identify attack traffic, thus minimizing false positives.

> **NOTE**   One drawback to utilizing protocol decodes is that not all applications are completely compliant with the RFC. In some situations, this noncompliance can result in the IPS sensor impacting the flow of legitimate traffic.

Anomaly Operations

For anomaly operations, the sensor triggers a signature when it observes traffic that deviates from a configured normal value. For example, assume that the normal amount of Internet Control Message Protocol (ICMP) traffic on your network is 100 K per second, with bursts of 1 M per second for no more than a second. You can create a signature that establishes the normal amount of ICMP traffic based on these parameters. Now, suppose the amount of ICMP traffic is 500 K per second for 5 seconds. This exceeds the normal definition, so the ICMP anomaly signature triggers.

Normalizing Operations

When your IPS sensors operate in in-line mode, you can actually alter the traffic that it receives. This functionality is useful in various situations, such as removing Time to Live (TTL) anomalies in a TCP connection. Normalizing traffic operates as follows:

Step 1   Sensor captures packet on an interface.

Step 2   Sensor analyzes packet.

Step 3   Signature configured for normalization triggers.

Step 4   Sensor generates normalized packet.

Step 5   Sensor transmits normalized packet on outbound interface.

A good example of the way in which normalization modifies packets can be illustrated with the TTL field in a packet. Whenever a source system sends a packet across the network, it initializes the TTL field to a specific value. As each router or other infrastructure device forwards this packet, the TTL is decremented. If the TTL reaches 0 before the packet reaches the target system, the packet is dropped.

An attacker might attempt to send packets that have different initial TTL values in the hope that the packets with smaller TTL values will be processed by the IPS sensor, but not reach the target system. If this happens, the IPS sensor's analysis will be inaccurate because the analysis is not based on the same packets that the target system received and processed (some packets were dropped before reaching the target because of the TTL reaching 0).

Using normalization, the IPS in-line sensor can automatically adjust the TTL values for the packets to match the smallest TTL observed on a specific connection between two systems. Therefore, the analysis performed by the sensor matches the same packets that the host system receives and processes.

Responding to Network Traffic

After they identify potentially malicious activity or security policy violations, your IPS sensors perform specific configured actions. These actions are usually configured on a per signature basis and fall into the following categories:

- Alerting actions

- Logging actions

- Blocking actions

- Dropping actions

Alerting Actions

Alerts or alarms indicate that your IPS sensor has detected traffic that is either suspicious or violates your security policy. These alerts are informative, but they do not solely prevent the observed traffic from traversing your network. A good analogy is a burglar alarm (used by many businesses) that emits a loud noise when the alarm is activated (or sends an alert to a security company). The alarm itself does not prevent the burglar from stealing items from the business. The auditory alarm simply indicates that something suspicious is happening.

Alerts can be transmitted to a monitoring application that is specifically designed to monitor the operation of your IPS sensors. Many systems also enable you to transmit alerts using SNMP traps.

Logging Actions

Logging actions involve your IPS sensors maintaining a record of the traffic that is observed from an attacker after a specific signature triggers. For example, you might configure a specific signature to cause the IPS sensor to capture traffic from an attacking system whenever certain traffic is observed on the network. Logging is similar to using video cameras to visually record what is happening at your business. Similar to alert actions, logging actions do not prevent the attacker from attacking your network, but they do enable you to capture evidence on what the attacker is doing. This information might be helpful if you decide to prosecute the attacker who gained access to your network. It can also be used to determine whether an alert is a false positive, especially if your intrusion device logs the initial traffic that triggered the signature.

Blocking Actions

Blocking actions involve access control lists (ACLs) that block traffic coming into your network. Your IPS sensors do not directly perform the actual blocking of network traffic. Instead, your IPS sensors communicate with infrastructure devices on your network to establish the appropriate ACLs. These ACLs are applied for a configured amount of time, and then your IPS sensors communicate with the infrastructure devices to remove them.

Blocking actions originated with the original Intrusion Detection Systems (IDSs) because they passively examined network traffic searching for intrusive activity. The ability to block network traffic enables the IDS to react to attacks because it prevents traffic from an attacker for a specific period of time.

The drawback to blocking actions is that the initial traffic (before the ACL is applied) still reaches the target system. If the initial traffic that reaches the target system successfully exploits a vulnerability in the target system, the attack can exploit this opening after the ACL is removed or from a second system that has another IP address that is not being blocked.

Dropping Actions

With the addition of intrusion prevention, the ability to drop packets became an available action. This dropping action can successfully stop the initial traffic involved in an attack, which enables your intrusion system to truly prevent the attack traffic from reaching the target system.

Sensor Management and Monitoring

To effectively use NIPS on your network, you need to be able to effectively configure your IPS sensors and monitor the alerts and other signature actions. Managing your NIPS sensors normally falls into the following two categories:

- Small sensor deployments

- Large sensor deployments

Small Sensor Deployments

With small sensor deployments, you need to manage only a few sensors. Configuring only a few sensors can usually be accomplished on an individual sensor basis. Monitoring alerts, however, is done across all your sensors to help correlate the events that are happening across your entire network.

In addition to an extensive command-line interface (CLI), each Cisco IPS network sensor runs an IPS Device Manager (IDM) application that enables you to configure the sensor using a secure graphical web-based interface. Both of these options enable you to easily configure your IPS sensors when you deploy only a few IPS sensors.

> **NOTE** The CLI interface on your Cisco sensors is accessible via the console port on the sensor and across the network. The default network CLI access is provided through Secure Shell (SSH). Telnet is also available but disabled by default because of security risks; the traffic is not encrypted.

For monitoring alerts, Cisco provides a simplified version of the CiscoWorks Monitoring Center for Security (also known as Security Monitor) software. Security Monitor provides numerous features, such as the following:

- Device monitoring

- Web-based monitoring

- Custom reporting

Using a compatible web browser, you can access the Security Monitor to administer and monitor the alerts from your IPS devices. Furthermore, you can easily use an extensive list of common reports to support your reporting requirements.

The functionality being provided by Security Monitor is also being integrated into Cisco Security Monitoring, Analysis and Response System (CS-MARS) software. The CS-MARS software provides a high-performance solution that supplies the following functionality:

- Network-intelligent correlation

- Incident validation

- Attack visualization

- Automated investigation

- Leveraged mitigation

- Compliance management

Eventually, MARS will become the primary software utilized to correlate security events from Cisco intrusion devices.

Large Sensor Deployments

If you deploy a large number of sensors across your network, configuring each sensor individually can become impractical. Just tuning a signature (across all your sensors) is an extremely time-consuming task unless you can automate the process.

Cisco provides the CiscoWorks Management Center for IPS Sensors (IPS MC) software to manage large deployments of IPS sensors. With the graphical web-based application, you can easily and efficiently configure large groups of sensors. For example, you can create a new signature and apply it to all the sensors that are members of a specific group of sensors.

As with small sensor deployments, you use CS-MARS or Security Monitor to monitor large sensor deployments. If you use the full version of the Security Monitor software, you can receive intrusion events from up to 300 Cisco IDS/IPS-capable devices, such as the following:

- Sensor appliances

- IDS modules

- Router modules

- IOS routers

- PIX firewalls

Summary

Your unique network topology identifies which IPS sensors are the most effective devices to analyze the traffic on your network. Some of the factors that impact your IPS sensor selection and deployment include the following:

- Security budget

- Amount of network traffic

- Network topology

- Security staff to operate the components

The main factors to consider when you purchase a sensor to operate on your network include the following:

- Sensor cost

- Sensor processing capability

- Number of monitoring interfaces

Depending on your unique network topology, you need to determine where you want to deploy your IPS sensors (within your network). When you make these decisions, you need to consider the form factor of the sensor to determine which type of sensor meets your needs. Some common sensor form factors include the following:

- Standalone appliance sensor

- Blade-based sensor

- IPS software integrated into the OS on an infrastructure device

Regardless of the type of IPS sensor that you deploy on your network, your IPS sensors can process only traffic that they receive on one of their interfaces. Capturing network traffic for your IPS sensors is usually based on the following two categories:

- Capturing traffic for in-line mode

- Capturing traffic for promiscuous mode

In-line processing mode uses pairs of sensor interfaces. Because the sensor is bridging the network traffic at the link layer, you do not need to do any special capturing of the network traffic. Some typical locations for deploying in-line IPS include the following:

- Between two routers

- Between a firewall and a router

- Between a switch and a router

- Between a switch and a firewall

- Between two switches

Promiscuous mode requires only a single sensor interface, although you must make sure that a copy of the traffic that's examined is passed the monitoring interface. Typical traffic capture devices that you use to pass traffic to your IPS sensors include the following:

- Hubs

- Network taps

- Switches

Cisco switches provide the following three mechanisms to mirror traffic to your sensor's promiscuous interface:

- SPAN

- RSPAN

- VACL

After receiving network traffic, your IPS sensors must analyze that traffic and then perform certain actions based on the results of that analysis. IPS sensor network traffic analysis falls into the following categories:

- Atomic operations

- Stateful operations

- Protocol decode operations

- Anomaly operations

- Normalizing operations

After identifying potentially malicious activity or security policy violations, your IPS sensors perform specific configured actions. These actions are usually configured on a per signature basis and fall into the following categories:

- Alerting actions

- Logging actions

- Blocking actions

- Dropping actions

To effectively use NIPS on your network, you need to effectively configure your IPS sensors and monitor the alerts and other signature actions. Managing your NIPS sensors normally falls into the following two categories:

- Small sensor deployments

- Large sensor deployments

Managing a few sensors can usually be accomplished on an individual sensor basis. If you deploy a large number of sensors across your network, configuring each sensor individually can become impractical and usually requires the deployment of a management tool to manage the various sensors on your network.

For small sensor deployments, Cisco IPS sensors have both a CLI and web-based interface that you can use to configure individual sensors. To configure large sensor deployments, you need to use a tool such as the IPS MC.

In both small and large deployments, you want to monitor the alerts across all your sensors so that you can correlate the events happening at various locations in your network. Cisco provides CS-MARS and Security Monitor to monitor both large sensor and small sensor deployments.

Part IV: Deployment Solutions

Chapter 9   Cisco Security Agent Deployment

Chapter 10   Deploying Cisco Network IPS

Chapter 11   Deployment Scenarios

Cisco Security Agent Deployment

A Host Intrusion Prevention System (HIPS) can be an invaluable tool that has the capability to address many of the computer security challenges you might face today. Before you research, evaluate, and purchase a HIPS product, you should have an idea of what's involved in a HIPS deployment. Be sure your expectations related to the deployment are correct.

This chapter helps you know what to expect during a HIPS deployment. It describes the tasks and decisions you need to make during an implementation of a real-world HIPS product, the Cisco Security Agent (CSA). The decisions made by a fictional company, the ACME Corporation, are used as examples at each stage in the deployment project.

ACME is headquartered in Austin, Texas. It employs approximately 9500 persons. It uses nearly 10,000 desktops and 300 servers. The company has sizable offices in New York, New York; Atlanta, Georgia; Chicago, Illinois; Portland, Oregon; and San Diego, California. The company also has manufacturing plants in DeKalb, Illinois; Midland, Texas; Gary, Indiana; and Huntsville, Alabama. Also, somewhere around 20 small sales offices are scattered around the U.S. ACME makes a wide variety of small home appliances, such as blenders, toaster ovens, irons, electronic clocks, and so on. It sells these items to retail establishments.

CSA deployment has seven major phases:

Step 1   Understand the product

Step 2   Predeployment planning

Step 3   Implement management

Step 4   Pilot

Step 5   Tuning

Step 6   Full deployment

Step 7   Finalize the project

NOTE   This chapter is not a deployment guide and should not be used as a best practices reference. It accurately describes many of the decisions you would have to make during a CSA deployment, but it is not a full-blown deployment guide.

Step1: Understand the Product

Before you implement the product, you should learn as much as possible about it. It's tempting to dive right in without taking the time for research, but during your deployment, you have to make important decisions about how to use the product. If you are well-informed, you are more likely to make good decisions. Product documentation, reviews in trade magazines, and reports from research organizations are a good places to start. If those are not enough, you should consider instructor-led training.

Therefore, the first phase of ACME's CSA deployment is to learn about the product. ACME is already familiar with the fundamental components and capabilities of an Intrusion Prevention System (IPS), which are covered in Part II, "Host Intrusion Prevention." The goal for its research was to identify which of those components and capabilities CSA has.

Components

ACME wants to be sure it identifies all of CSA's functions, so it divides the product into parts and chooses to examine each part individually. As with most HIPS, CSA has endpoint agent and management components.

Cisco Security Agents

ACME starts with the endpoint agents. Chapter 6, "HIPS Components," illustrates the access control process that HIPS agents apply to the hosts on which they are installed. ACME is familiar with the phases in the process, so it chooses to list the phases and determine how CSA operates at each stage. ACME determines that CSA does the following:

1. **Identifies these types of resources that are accessed**—Network, memory, application execution, files, system configuration, operating system kernel, operating system events, the Windows clipboard, COM components, devices, and symbolic links.

2. **Gathers data about the operation**—CSA uses system call interception and network traffic analysis.

3. **Determines these system states**—Location, user, and system.

4. **Consults these types of security policy**—Atomic rule-based and behavioral.

5. **Can take action by**—Permit, deny, log event, drop packet, query the user, and terminate the process.

For example, a web page can contain malicious code that causes the browser to infect the computer with a virus when the browser accesses the page. If a user opens such a web page, CSA intercepts the system calls that are initiated by the browser. In this case, the malicious code forces the browser (c:\windows\explorer.exe) to write to a file called c:\windows\system32\virus.dll. It then determines the state of the computer and compares the activity and state with the defined policy. The policy contains an atomic rule that denies all applications from writing executable files and .dlls to the Windows system folders, so CSA denies the operation.

CSA Management

After ACME feels that it has a sufficient grasp of the endpoint agent components, it moves on to the management. The CSA documentation shows that CSA is a centrally managed product. The management model shown in Figure 9-1 can be single-server or tiered, and the policies are distributed using a pull or push/pull communications mechanism. The management infrastructure is accessed using a web browser interface.

If any of the terms in this section are not familiar to you, please refer to Chapter 6.

Figure 9-1   *CSA Management Architecture*

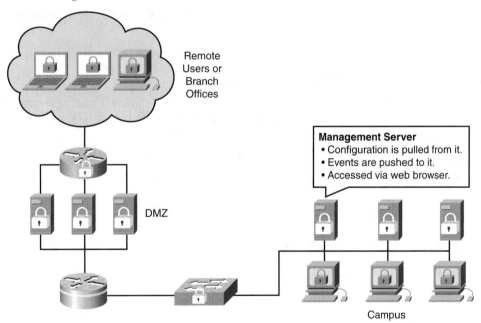

Capabilities

ACME used the CSA documentation it had, what it gathered from its sales team, and what it learned about CSA's components to make a list of CSA's capabilities. It checked to ensure that CSA has all of the capabilities required of a HIPS product:

■   Block malicious code actions

■   Not disrupt normal operations

- Distinguish between attacks and normal events

- Stop new and unknown attacks

- Protect flaws in permitted applications

Next, ACME made a high-level list of the CSA's capabilities:

- Stop new and unknown attacks

- Patch relief

- Internal attack propagation prevention

- Policy enforcement

- Regulatory requirements

For more information about IPS capabilities, please refer to Chapter 5, "Host Intrusion Prevention Overview."

Step 2: Predeployment Planning

Good planning is a critical factor in the success of any deployment. Planning should start well before the implementation begins, and the plan should be continually reviewed and updated during the entire project. ACME invites the relevant stakeholders to a series of HIPS project planning meetings. During the meetings, it intends to address the following:

- Review the security policy

- Define project goals

- Select and classify target hosts

- Plan for ongoing management

- Choose the appropriate management architecture

Review the Security Policy

Chapter 4, "Security in Depth," goes into some depth about corporate security policies. Your security policy guides all of your major decisions during a CSA deployment. If you don't have a security policy, you should strongly consider creating one. Without it, your deployment is likely to take much longer and be far more difficult.

Luckily, ACME has a well-documented and up-to-date security policy. It started its planning session with a review of the security policy in light of CSA's components and capabilities. The intent of this review session was to begin thinking about the following:

- The items in the security policy CSA might be able to address

- How the guidelines relevant to product implementations might impact the CSA deployment

- If the security policy needs to be updated to reflect CSA capabilities

- The policy changes that will govern the operation of CSA at ACME

Define Project Goals

It is important to have a concrete set of measurable goals before the implementation begins. Goals give the stakeholders something to actively work toward and a way to measure the progress of the project. You also use them to restrict the scope of the project. Any decision or product functionality that does not contribute to the achievement of one the goals should not be a part of the implementation.

Most of the goals you define for the project such as deadlines, budgets, and so forth are the same for any project. However, two goals are related specifically to CSA deployments:

- Balance

- Problems to solve

Balance

The first goal you should define is, in a general sense, where you want to fall in the security versus manageability spectrum. This spectrum refers to the idea that for the most part as security increases, the resources needed to manage the security increase as well. Also, increased security can have an undesirable impact on the user experience. Try to characterize your organization's overall philosophical approach to security. To make this characterization, think about the following:

- What people, time, and dollar resources your organization can expend for security efforts

- The expectations users have of their computing experience

- The organization's overall vulnerability level

- The value of the information the security tools protect

- The likelihood of attack

Classify your organization as restrictive, balanced, or permissive. Here are some firewall implementation examples to further illustrate this process:

- A **restrictive organization** implements tight ingress and egress controls. Users are able to establish outbound connections through the firewall only on specific ports using specific protocols. Inbound connections from the Internet are limited by port, protocol, and destination IP address. Restrictive organizations have the resources to make frequent changes to the firewall configuration in response to new needs. Users are accustomed to having their change requests declined and having to wait for approved changes to occur. The information protected by the firewall is so critical and at such high risk that the restrictive approach is necessary.

  Example organizations include banks, government intelligence agencies, and utility companies.

- **Balanced organizations** allow any outbound connection through the firewall except for connections that are known to be dangerous or against acceptable use policy. Inbound connections are also filtered, but only to the extent that inbound connections are permitted into the demilitarized zone (DMZ) on specific ports and using specific protocols. All other inbound connections are denied. A balanced organization has a limited set of resources to expend managing the firewall, so the configuration is designed to require few changes over time. Users are not accustomed to making change requests, and the few they do make are approved and implemented rapidly. The information protected by the firewall is important and at risk, but not enough to require a restrictive approach.

  Example organizations include manufacturing, consulting companies, and retail.

- Finally, **permissive organizations** allow all outbound connections through the firewall. Virtually all inbound connections are also permitted, except for those that are known to be dangerous. Permissive organizations have extremely limited resources to expend managing the firewall, so the configuration is designed to require almost no changes over time. Users never need to make change requests because almost everything is permitted. The information protected by the firewall is not particularly important, and the risk of attack is low.

  Example organizations include portions of educational institutions and volunteer groups.

When ACME started to characterize their organization, it quickly realized that it fits the classic profile of a balanced organization. At ACME, all the following were true:

- It allows almost any outbound connection through the firewall, except for certain types such as common peer-to-peer file sharing connections.

- All inbound connections through the firewall are blocked, except for a small number of DMZ applications.

- Each member of the information security staff is trained to manage multiple technologies and projects because there aren't enough of them to dedicate resources to any one technology.

- A procedure to request changes to the firewall configuration is in place, but it is fairly simple. Most of the time, the requestor just sends an e-mail to the security staff requesting the change.

- Most of the information behind the firewall is not confidential. ACME does have trade secrets, financial information, and employee personal information that should be protected, but that's all the highly confidential material.

Furthermore, ACME's review of the corporate security policy supported this characterization.

Problems to Solve

The second goal you should define clearly is the purpose of the implementation. Start by identifying the problems CSA should solve. Maybe the only problem you want CSA to address is the threat of new and unknown malicious code. Perhaps your corporate security policy includes some restrictions that CSA could enforce. Try to make as thorough and detailed a list as possible. As you make the list, identify which problems are immediate and urgent and which problems can be solved over the long term.

Here are some sample problems:

- Prevent mobile users from attaching infected machines to the corporate network

- Control the flow of confidential data out of the organization

- Control the internal propagation of new and unknown viruses, worms, and Trojans

- Conserve network bandwidth by preventing the use of peer-to-peer (P2P) file-sharing applications

- Protect employee personal data

- Maintain host performance characteristics by controlling spyware and adware

- Enforce relevant corporate acceptable use policies

At ACME, the list of security-related problems to solve never seems to shrink. Every time one problem is solved, another is added to the list. At a stakeholders' meeting, ACME puts its list of 30 or so potential security initiatives on the whiteboard and eliminated the ones that CSA could not help with. They ended up with seven problems that CSA could solve.

After some discussion, the stakeholders decide that as a balanced organization with limited resources, they should not try to tackle all seven problems at once. Instead, they put the seven in order of importance and eliminated the bottom four. That left three goals for the implementation:

1. ACME got hit badly with the last major worm. It had to restore many of its systems from backup, which cost the company a lot of money—not to mention the downtime during the incident! Most of all, ACME wants to protect its hosts against infection by new malicious code.

2. P2P file-sharing applications are becoming a real nuisance because they are using a significant percentage of ACME's available Internet bandwidth. Also, some of the downloaded files are copyrighted, which is a liability for the company. ACME tried to block the connections using its firewall, but it wasn't successful because the P2P programs can use any port. ACME would like to prevent users from downloading music from the Internet using P2P file-sharing applications.

3. Over the last few years, ACME has had to take its e-commerce servers down to be patched much more frequently. The final goal is to reduce the frequency with which it has to update the e-commerce servers with security-related patches.

Select and Classify Target Hosts

Now that you have established your goals for the project, move on to the next predeployment tasks, which are as follows:

- Select target hosts
- Classify selected hosts

Select Target Hosts

Before you can start installing the agent, you must decide which hosts should be protected by it. If you purchased enough agent licenses to cover all of your hosts, the decision is easy. Your decision is more difficult if you bought a smaller number of licenses, but it's likely you had a group of target hosts in mind when you made the purchase. In either case, you should start your deployment with hosts where you think the deployment has a high likelihood of success and that provides benefit to your organization.

Ultimately, ACME plans to install CSA on all 10,000 desktops and 300 servers. However, ACME decided to buy an initial 1500 desktop and 20 server licenses to prove the concept before buying the rest. It was tough to decide which hosts to protect first with CSA.

ACME consulted its goals to select the hosts that, if protected, would contribute the most to the achievement of the goals. It started with the server licenses, and decided to put the agent on 20 of their Microsoft IIS web servers. Its B2B e-commerce site is hosted by those servers. Having CSA on them would reduce the number of times they need to be patched.

Selecting only 1500 desktops out of 10,000 was more of a challenge. ACME earmarked 1000 licenses for the mobile laptops because they are so vulnerable when they are remote and not protected by the corporate security countermeasures. Infected laptops were the source of 8 of the last 10 virus incidents at ACME. If those laptops could be protected while they are remote, it would dramatically increase ACME's protection against malicious code.

The remaining 500 licenses were reserved for the desktops in the manufacturing areas. Each desktop is used by several employees that work in manufacturing. They are supposed to be used only for e-mail and a few other programs, but almost every one has P2P software installed. They generate lots of file-sharing traffic and should be locked down so that they can be used only for legitimate purposes.

Classify Selected Hosts

After you've selected your target hosts, you should loosely classify them by placing them in *restrictive*, *balanced*, or *permissive* groups. These groups are used later to help you decide which CSA security policies should be applied. They also help you know how much effort is required to deploy and subsequently manage the policies you choose.

To classify a host or set of hosts, answer three questions:

- Does the company lose money when this host is unavailable?

- How much control does the user have over the system configuration?

- Are new software packages installed on the system frequently?

NOTE   Don't confuse host classification with the balance goal you set in when you defined project goals. The goal you set there should influence only the way you classify hosts. If you have a situation where you think a group of hosts falls somewhere between restrictive and balanced, apply your organizational classification to help you decide. Think of the organizational classification as a "rounding rule." If the organization as a whole is permissive, round downward. If it's restrictive, round upward.

Here are some samples:

- When **restrictive systems** are unavailable, the company loses a great deal of money. The user has virtually no control over the system configuration. New software packages are rarely installed. When they are, the installation happens only during scheduled maintenance windows and only after thorough testing.

  Examples include call center desktops, kiosks, point of sale, and manufacturing automation systems.

  Protection and Ongoing Management—Restrictive hosts are rigorously protected, but require a fair amount of ongoing management especially when new software is deployed on them.

- When **balanced systems** are unavailable, the loss of productivity indirectly costs the company money. Users have some control over their system configuration, but they are not allowed to install their own applications. Software is installed using a software distribution system such as SMS, Altiris, Radia, or ZENworks. New software is deployed on a fairly regular basis.

  Examples include standard corporate desktops and servers.

  Protection and Ongoing Management—Good protection against new and unknown attacks with some amount of ongoing management as new applications are deployed or updated.

- When **permissive systems** are unavailable, the company might lose some money because of some loss in productivity. Users have complete control over their system configuration, and they are allowed to install whatever applications they want.

  Examples include field laptops and IT desktops.

  Protection and Ongoing Management—Reasonable expectation of protection with very little ongoing management as new applications are deployed or updated.

ACME had an easy time classifying its hosts. When the e-commerce servers are down, it costs the company lots of money. New software is rarely installed on them, and they should be meticulously protected. They are externally accessible. Therefore, ACME classified its e-commerce servers as restrictive systems.

The manufacturing desktops don't cost the company much money when they are down, users are permitted to install software whenever they want, and they are protected by other ACME security countermeasures such as firewalls and Network Intrusion Detecction Systems (NIDS). ACME classified the desktops as permissive, with the caveat that they should not be allowed to download music from the Internet.

Finally, the field laptops were put in the balanced group. The laptops need good protection against attacks because they are often unprotected by corporate security. At the same time, the users need to have some control over their system configuration when they are in the field.

Plan for Ongoing Management

It is a good idea to think about the ongoing management of CSA after it has been implemented. You should try to decide who takes over CSA administration when the project is finished. Also decide where the administrators are to be physically located, and who has responsibility for what types of administration. You should plan for ongoing management at this stage in the project so that you can involve the future administrators in the deployment early on. That way, they are prepared when it is finished.

ACME decided that two members of the corporate security team are to be responsible for CSA policy administration, event handling, and incident response. The servers, the operating system, the server agent software, and the software that make up the CSA Management Center (MC) is to be under the control of the server team. The desktop team is expected to install and troubleshoot the agent software on the desktops and laptops after the project is finished. All of the personnel who manage CSA post-deployment are located at ACME headquarters.

Choose the Appropriate Management Architecture

The final predeployment planning task is to architect the solution that manages the HIPS agents. You should be careful and take your time finishing this task. If you don't plan well and realize later that your management should be different, it is usually difficult to change after agents are deployed and actively managed. At least five factors affect your choice of management architecture:

- **Number of agents**—The number of agents the management solution should support. Make sure to plan for future needs when you select the number. For example, if you want this solution to be in place for at least 3 years, the number of agents it should support is the number of agents you expect to have deployed in 3 years. You might want to deploy only 10,000 agents right now, but in 3 years you might have 40,000.

  Remember that the CSA MC can be implemented in a single-server or tiered manner. A single server supports up to 20,000 agents. You have two ways to support more than that. One is to deploy several single-sever CSA MCs. The other is to tier the management. The choice you make depends on the following factors.

- **Geographical distribution**—Your company might have only one location, it might have several offices within one country, or it could have hundreds of branches across the globe. Also consider how many employees are at each branch, how much network bandwidth each location has, and how many mobile employees you have.

If your company is widely distributed and the branches have limited network connections, single-server management centers at each location might be your only option. It is a costly option from a budgeting and administrative perspective. You have to buy hardware for each location, make sure that security policies are synchronized between sites, and CSA administrators have to treat each location as a separate entity which increases the management burden.

If the company is not distributed or is but has respectable network connections between the branches and headquarters, a single-tiered CSA MC makes more sense. Large organizations can have a number of network operation centers (NOCs) that would be suitable for single or tiered MCs as needed for the number of agents each NOC is expected to support.

- **Administrative model**—In the prior section of this chapter, "Plan for Ongoing Management," you identified the people managing the HIPS after the implementation is finished. The location of the people who manage the solution and what agents they are responsible for can impact your management architectural choices.

  For example, if you choose to have headquarters personnel manage CSA, it is logical to locate the management solution at headquarters. If you have multiple branches and choose to have personnel at each branch administer their own location, a CSA MC at each branch is more appropriate. Time zones and international locations might also influence your decision.

- **Budget**—The amount of money you have earmarked for the management solution.

- **Uptime requirements**—Your organization might have a policy that requires all management solutions to meet certain availability requirements. To achieve the requirements, you might need to consider management architectures that are more suited to high availability and fail more gracefully than others. Tiered management with a database cluster is the best choice for high availability.

Although ACME has licenses for only 1520 hosts, it would eventually like to put CSA on all 10,300. It decided to start with a server big enough to handle that many agents, even though it wouldn't be managing that many at first. The documentation indicates that a single-server CSA MC supports up to 20,000, so the single-server architecture seemed like the best choice.

Before ACME made a final decision, it consulted with the server team. Together, they decided that a single-server will work. The budget is limited, the administrative model fits, and the bandwidth between most ACME sites is respectable.

Step 3: Implement Management

In this phase, you use the plans from phase 2 to begin the actual implementation. In a CSA deployment, the agent installation packages are generated by the management center. You cannot begin installing agents without the CSA MC. Therefore, the first component you must deploy is the CSA management. You face four subtasks in this phase of the project:

Step 1   Install and secure the CSA MC

Step 2   Understand the MC

Step 3   Configure groups

Step 4   Configure policies

Install and Secure the CSA MC

You should have designed your management architecture in the planning phase. Procure the necessary hardware and software, but before you actually build it, make sure it can be installed in a secure manner. It is critical to secure your CSA MC as much as possible. Security management servers are appealing targets for attackers. An attacker can use a compromised security management server for all kinds of nefarious purposes.

To secure the CSA MC, make sure it is protected as many security countermeasures as possible. Chapter 2, "Signatures and Actions," describes many of these. For example, the CSA MC should at least be in a secure physical location, protected by a firewall, and have a CSA running on it.

NOTE   Make sure to consult the CSA MC documentation to ensure that your countermeasures don't prevent it from working. For example, the agents use certain network ports to communicate with the management center. If your firewall blocks those connections, CSA will not work properly.

As soon as the security countermeasures are ready to go, consult your architecture plan and build your CSA management solution.

The ACME project team worked with the security and server teams to securely implement the CSA MC. They attached the single server to the network they usually use for management devices because that network is protected by NIPS and a firewall. Along with the operating system and the CSA MC software, they also installed an agent. When everything was running to their satisfaction, they configured the firewall to allow agents and administrators to communicate with the MC.

Understand the MC

After you have your CSA MC (or MCs) up and running, you can begin to experiment with the interface. You will use it often throughout the project, so take some time to explore and become familiar with it. When you have a task to perform, you won't have to fumble around looking for the correct menu or button to click.

Also, make absolutely sure you are familiar with the way security rules are assigned to hosts. The CSA MC does not assign rules directly to each host because it is not efficient to manage a set of rules for each host. Instead, rules are assigned using a hierarchical structure of related "organizational units" (see Figure 9-2). You should be familiar with five basic organizational units:

- **Hosts**—Systems that are running agents that the CSA MC manages. Each host is a member of at least one group.

- **Groups**—Collections of similar hosts. For example, hosts that are all desktops might be grouped together.

- **Policies**—A set of rule modules that have a common purpose and depend on each other to work properly. Policies are attached to groups. A policy can be attached to more than one group, and a group can have more than one policy attached.

- **Rule modules**—A body of rules that perform a particular function. Rule modules are attached to policies, and a single rule module can be attached to more than one policy.

- **Rules**—An atomic or behavioral security control (see Chapter 6). Attached to rule modules. A rule can be attached only to a single rule module.

Figure 9-2 *CSA Organizational Units*

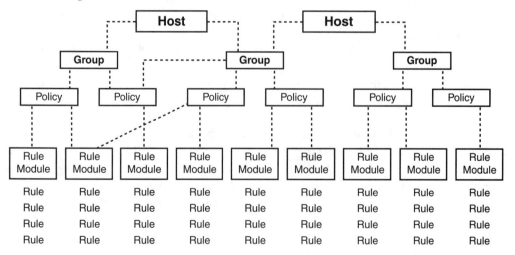

The CSA MC is preconfigured with a useful and robust set of "default" groups, policies, and rule modules. They represent "best practice" configurations, and you should use them wherever possible. Examine the defaults, so that you can determine what they do, how they are arranged, and which ones you might use. Figure 9-3 is an example of one group with its connected policies and rule modules.

Figure 9-3   *CSA Groups, Policies, and Rule Modules*

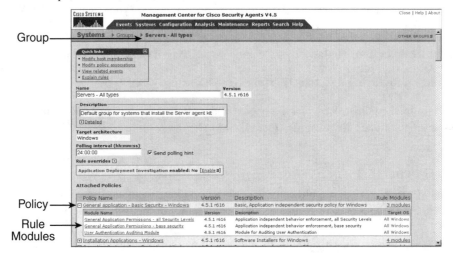

Configure Groups

Your next task is to configure the groups you are going to use for your hosts. There are two types of groups:

- **Policy group**—Used to assign policies to hosts.

- **Secondary group**—Has no policies attached and is used to filter reports, event logs, and alerts.

Policy Groups

Start with the policy groups. Use the relevant default policy groups wherever possible. Using the default groups saves time, and they already have the appropriate security policies attached. For example, if you are deploying agents to desktops you should use the "Desktops—All Types" group or the "Servers—All Types" group for servers.

As a general rule, you should make copies of the default groups you plan to use. Add something to the group name, such as a ticker symbol or a company acronym to mark it as yours. For example, the "Desktops—All Types" could be copied and renamed "ACME Desktops—All

Types." Copying and renaming the built-in groups helps you to differentiate your groups from the defaults and keeps the defaults intact in case you need them later.

ACME decided to use default policy groups and consulted its host classifications to help it decide which ones to choose. The restrictive hosts would be in more restrictive groups, although the balanced would be in fewer and more permissive groups. It made a list:

- **E-commerce web servers (restrictive)**—Servers—All Types, Servers—IIS Web Servers, Servers— Externally Deployed, Systems—Mission Critical

- **Mobile laptops (balanced)**—Desktops—All Types, Desktops—Remote or Mobile

- **Manufacturing desktops (permissive)**—Desktops—All Types

ACME finished the task by making copies of the seven policy groups and adding "ACME" to the name so it could easily recognize them later.

Secondary Groups

After you configure your policy groups, it is a good idea to create some secondary groups. You should base the secondary groups on any combination of the following criteria that seems useful:

- **System function**—Examples include e-commerce applications, back office servers, corporate desktops, remote laptops, or e-mail servers

- **Business groups**—Examples include finance, operations, marketing, technical support, or sales

- **Geographical location**—Base these groups on the physical location of the hosts

> **NOTE** Hosts generally belong to more than one group. A business critical web server in Austin, Texas, for example, might belong to the Windows Server, IIS Web Server, Mission Critical Servers, and Austin Servers groups. The first two groups might be used to apply policies, while the Austin Servers group is used just to filter events and reports.

As you define and create your groups within the CSA MC, consider that each policy group represents a distinct set of hosts and, more importantly, a distinct set of policies. The number of different policy sets you have deployed directly impacts the amount of time you spend managing CSA after the deployment is completed. Using fewer policy sets results in less time spent managing CSA.

One advantage of using a large variety of policy sets allows you to define granular policies that better meet the security needs for each host. Granularity often translates into enhanced security. The cost of enhanced security is additional management burden.

Try to strike a balance between manageability and security. Use the permissive, balanced, and restrictive classifications you gave each group of hosts to help you. If a host is in the permissive category, use fewer policy groups. If it is in the restrictive category, use more.

For example, a permissive server might be a member only of the Servers—All Types group. A restrictive server might be a member of Servers—All Types, Systems—Mission Critical, and Servers—Externally Deployed. Each additional policy group adds additional security policies that increase the protection from attack.

ACME created a chart listing the system function, classification, relevant policy groups, business group, and geographic location for each set of hosts (see Table 9-1).

Table 9-1   *ACME Host Classification Chart*

System Type Group	Classification	Business Groups	Location Groups
E-commerce web servers	Restrictive	Operations	HQ
Mobile laptops	Balanced	Sales Marketing	Remote
Manufacturing desktops	Permissive	Manufacturing	HQ DeKalb Fort Worth

After some discussion, the team decided it didn't want to use location as a filtering or alerting criteria, so it had no need to create those groups. The team created seven secondary groups:

- ACME E-Commerce Web Servers

- ACME Remote Laptops

- ACME Manufacturing Desktops

- ACME Operations

- ACME Sales

- ACME Marketing

- ACME Manufacturing

Configure Policies

The last task before you deploy your first agent is to select and configure the policies that the agent enforces on your hosts. If you used the default policy groups, all of the policies you need are already configured and applied to the hosts based on their group membership. If one of your project goals is to enforce corporate security policy, you need to customize the default policy configuration slightly.

Here are some examples of corporate security policy items that would prompt CSA policy customization:

- **HIPS agent must run at all times**—The CSA default policies allow users to disable the agent. If your policy states that the agent must run at all times, you should change the defaults so that users cannot disable the agent.

- **Users should not use corporate resources to download music**—One of the default rule modules is called Music Prevention Download. Implement this module to enforce the acceptable use policy.

- **Secret company information should not leave the company**—The Data Theft Prevention module can be used to control the movement of secret company information.

Because ACME chose to use the default policy groups, the policies it needs are already configured and are applied to the hosts based on their group membership. The one exception was the manufacturing desktops, which needed the Music Prevention Download rule module. ACME made the change and left the rest of the policies alone.

Step 4: Pilot

The next major phase in the project is to conduct a pilot test. Use the pilot to evaluate the operation of the security agents, the choices you made during the first two phases, and your deployment procedures. You can use the test results to make any necessary adjustments before you move to a wider deployment. This section covers the pilot test:

- Scope
- Objectives

Scope

For the pilot test, deploy the agent on a relatively small number of hosts. The number is up to you, but any number between 10 and 50 will work. Make sure to install the agents in Test Mode.

> **NOTE**   Test Mode is a configuration option in the CSA MC. When Test Mode is turned on for a set of hosts, the agents on the host do not actively enforce policies. Instead, they log only policy violations.

Choose the hosts for the pilot test carefully. If you are not going to install the agent on all of your hosts, make sure to use hosts that are within the scope of the overall project. Also, try to select a few hosts from each of categories on which you intend to deploy the agent. For example, if you plan to install the agent on remote laptops and database servers, try to pilot test on a few of each.

Finally, do your best to test on machines that are operated by "friendly users." Friendly users are people who are more willing to try new technologies. Also, friendly users are ready to provide positive and negative feedback about the technologies they try.

ACME installed the agent in test mode on four remote laptops, four manufacturing desktops, and one e-commerce web server. The web server was a semi-production server because the server team was nervous about installing something new on its production systems. It would, however, become active if one of the others failed. Because it was configured as though it were a regular production server, it served as a good pilot host.

Objectives

You should accomplish the following objectives during the pilot test phase:

- **Test software compatibility**—You always run the risk that CSA, at a basic level, is incompatible with one of your standard software packages. The pilot test is an opportunity to find incompatibilities and resolve them before you expand the deployment.

- **Begin tuning**—The CSA default policies are designed to operate in a wide variety of computing environments. However, no environment is alike. You invariably experience false positives, which are instances where the CSA policy mistakenly treats normal activity on a host as dangerous.

  While your agents are running in Test Mode, use the CSA MC's event log to identify false positives. When you encounter one, you can "tune" it out by configuring CSA to treat it as a normal occurrence. Leave your agents in Test Mode long enough to tune all of the false positives you find.

■ **Gauge user experience**—After you have tuned the CSA policy to the point that you see few or no false positives, you should turn off Test Mode. The agent should be in Full Enforcement Mode, so that you can measure the impact is has on the pilot test users' computing experience. You might want to conduct a survey of the users to get their feedback, both positive and negative.

When all of the objectives are complete, evaluate the results of the pilot test. If a procedure didn't work well, try to improve it. If the users had a bad experience with CSA, determine why and address the issue. Essentially, you should fix any problems you encountered during the pilot test before you move on to the tuning phase.

ACME CSA pilot test went well. The test lasted for two weeks, and during that time, it didn't encounter any compatibility issues. It was able to eliminate most of its false positives, and at the same time, ACME became even more familiar with the CSA management interface.

During the last four days of the pilot, ACME took the agents out of Test Mode so that the users could see how they liked CSA. The results from an informal survey were encouraging. The only complaint was that the agent asked the users too many questions that they didn't know how to answer. The project team made some changes to the policies, so that the users would be asked fewer questions in the future.

Step 5: Tuning

The purpose of the tuning phase is to eliminate false positives. You do this by increasing the number and variety of hosts on which the agent is deployed. The larger number and the wider variety of configurations should lead to more false positives. This is good, because you want to identify as many false positives as possible so that you can tune them out.

Ideally, agents should be installed in Test Mode on several systems from each category. Eventually, your total number of agents should be around 10 percent of the final target number. For example, if you are deploying agents on Apache web servers, standard corporate desktops, and Microsoft SQL servers, you should distribute agents on several hosts from each category. If the total number of combined hosts is 1000, the total number of agents deployed in this stage should be around 100.

After the agents are installed, look at the CSA MC event log at least one time per day. When you find false positives, use the Event Management Wizard (see Figure 9-4) to modify the policy to allow the activities to occur. Continue the tuning process until you no longer see false positives in your event log.

Figure 9-4   *False Positive and Event Management Wizard*

Event Management Wizard

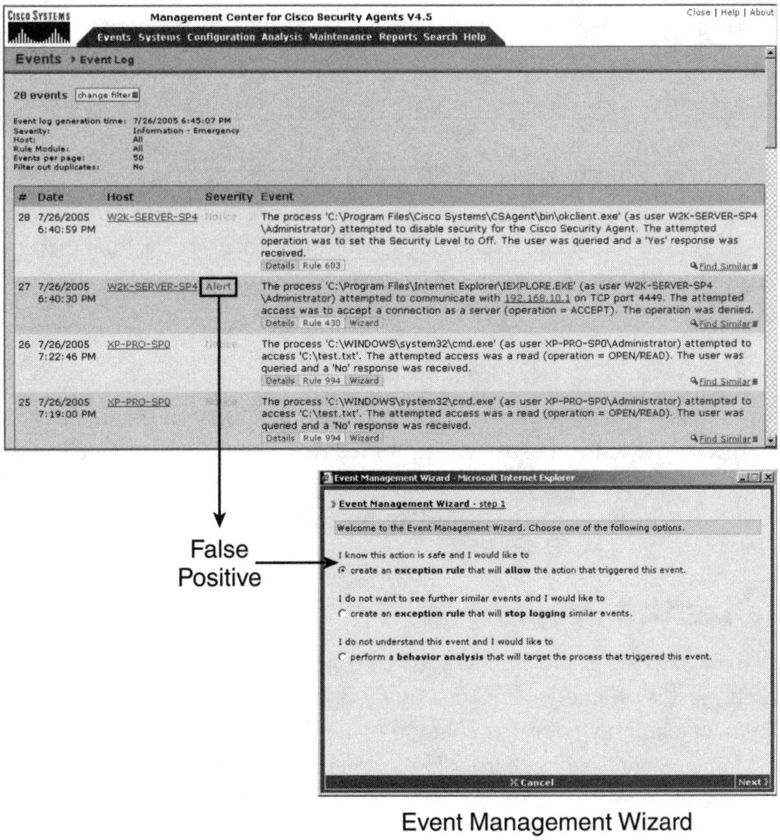

The tuning phase is critically important to the success of the CSA deployment. If you do not adequately tune your policies, a false positive when the agents are not in Test Mode can cause a critical application to fail.

ACME increased its agent count to 150. This time it included 95 remote laptops, 50 manufacturing workstations, and 5 full production e-commerce web servers. Over the course of 4 weeks, it eliminated all of the false positives encountered. ACME was confident that it had an adequately tuned policy and was ready to move to the next phase.

Step 6: Full Deployment

After you are confident that you have correctly tuned the CSA policies, you should begin the full deployment phase. In this phase, you gradually install agents in Test Mode on the rest of the hosts within the scope of the project. As you expand your installation, you might encounter additional false positives. Tune them out as you go along.

> **NOTE** This phase is a good time to make sure your users are aware of what will be installed on their systems, how it works, and what to expect during the deployment. Classroom training, company-wide notes, posters, and announcements are all ways to raise user awareness of the project.

Eventually, you have agents running in Test Mode on every host you want to protect. When you are ready, select a group of hosts to take out of Test Mode. Let them run for a long enough time for you to feel comfortable that everything is working properly. Take another group out of Test Mode and continue taking groups out of Test Mode until all of the agents are fully protecting the hosts.

ACME took all of the hosts involved in the tuning phase out of test mode without incident. It proceeded to install agents in test mode on the remaining hosts at the rate of about 200 per day. Each set of freshly installed hosts was run for a day to check in test mode for any false positives they might have missed. If they didn't find anything to tune, they took the hosts out of test mode the following day. In 10 days, they had all of their agents fully deployed.

Step 7: Finalize the Project

Although the agents are deployed and fully operational, you must tie up a number of loose ends before the project is officially over. First of all, operational control of CSA must transition from the deployment team to whoever is going to manage CSA moving forward (see the "Plan for Ongoing Management" section earlier in this chapter for more information). Also, you need to establish procedures to govern the day-to-day operation of CSA. Here are a few examples:

- **Change control**—This procedure establishes the checks that are in place for CSA configuration changes. It controls how changes are requested, who reviews the changes, and by what criteria they are reviewed.

- **Backup and restore**—A procedure defining the frequency and type of backup performed on the CSA MC. It also outlines the proper way to restore the CSA MC if needed.

- **Log archive**—This procedure describes how long CSA event logs should be kept, when they should be archived, what types of events should be archived, and where the archive is stored.

- **Incident response**—A procedure to manage situations where CSA stops an attack. It should detail who is notified, how they are notified, and any steps that should be taken in response to the attack.

- **Disaster recovery**—The corporate disaster recovery procedure should be modified to include any necessary CSA items.

■ **Policy review**—Guidelines for events that trigger a security policy review. For example, if the CSA policy prohibits software installation, but a user's job requires the ability to install software, this should trigger a policy review.

Summary

Before you embark upon a HIPS deployment, you should have realistic expectations about what is involved. This chapter used a real-world HIPS product as an example to illustrate the decisions that need to be made at each phase in a HIPS deployment. CSA deployment has seven major phases:

Step 1   Understand the product

Step 2   Predeployment planning

Step 3   Implement management

Step 4   Pilot

Step 5   Tuning

Step 6   Full deployment

Step 7   Finalize the project

Understand the Product

The first task in any HIPS deployment is to make sure you fully understand the product you intend to deploy. Review Chapters 5 and 6, so that you are familiar with the potential components, capabilities, and benefits of the HIPS products. Then, determine which components, capabilities, and benefits your product has specifically. Also be sure to investigate the product's management capabilities.

Predeployment Planning

The planning phase of a HIPS deployment should occur before anything has been implemented. During this phase, you should address the following:

■ **Review the security policy**—Determine what, if any, impact your corporate security product has on the HIPS implementation.

■ **Define project goals**—Decide what the goals are for the implementation.

■ **Select and classify target hosts**—Decide which and what types of hosts are to have an agent.

■ **Plan for ongoing management**—Begin to plan for post-implementation of the product.

■ **Choose the appropriate management architecture**—Design the management solution.

Implement Management

The next phase—to implement the management architecture—you designed during your planning. You should make sure to secure the management tool because it is a target for attack. When the tool has been implemented and secured, familiarize yourself with the interface, configure groups of hosts, and configure security policies if needed.

Pilot

During the pilot, you deploy agents on a small group of hosts for a relatively short period of time. The pilot gives you a chance to test software compatibility, begin tuning, and gauge users' impressions of the product. Any issues you encounter during the pilot test can be fixed before continue the deployment.

Tuning

The purpose of the tuning phase is to locate and eliminate false positives. Deploy more agents to increase the likelihood of encountering a false positive, so that you can tune it out. During the tuning phase, you should have agents on approximately 10 percent of your total hosts. When you are confident that you have eliminated all of the false positives, move on to the next phase.

Full Deployment

In this stage, you gradually deploy agents on all of the remaining hosts. If you find any last-minute false positives, tune them out. Eventually, you have agents protecting all of the targeted hosts.

Finalize the Project

In the final phase of your HIPS deployment, create procedures to govern:

- Change control

- Backup and restore

- Log archive

- Incident response

- Disaster recovery

CHAPTER 10

Deploying Cisco Network IPS

Network Intrusion Prevention Systems (NIPSs) can be an invaluable tool that has the capability to address many computer security challenges that you might face today. Before you research, evaluate, and purchase NIPS products, you should have some idea of what's involved in a NIPS deployment to be sure your expectations related to the deployment are correct.

This chapter helps you know what to expect during a NIPS deployment. It describes the tasks and decisions you need to make during the deployment of real-world NIPS devices, the Cisco IPS Sensor Software. A fictional company, the ACME Corporation, is used as an example to show how decisions are made at each stage in the deployment project.

ACME is headquartered in Austin, Texas. Figure 10-1 shows the network configuration for the ACME network. The entire network is not shown, only samples of the various remotes sites.

ACME employs approximately 9500 persons. It uses nearly 10,000 desktops and 300 servers. The company has large sales offices in New York, New York; Atlanta, Georgia; Chicago, Illinois; Portland, Oregon; and San Diego, California. There are also manufacturing plants in DeKalb, Illinois; Midland, Texas; Gary, Indiana; and Huntsville, Alabama. ACME has around 20 small sales offices scattered around the U.S. It makes a wide variety of small home appliances such as blenders, toaster ovens, irons, electronic clocks, and so on. They sell these items to retail establishments.

Figure 10-1 *ACME Network Configuration*

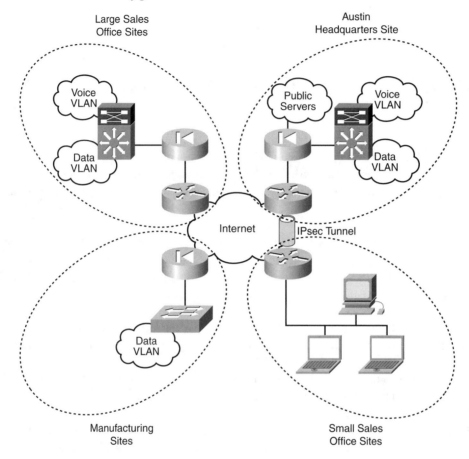

You NIPS deployment involves the following five major phases:

Step 1   Understand the product

Step 2   Predeployment planning

Step 3   Sensor deployment

Step 4   Tuning

Step 5   Finalize the project

> **NOTE**   This chapter is not a deployment guide and should not be used as a best practices reference. It accurately describes many of the decisions you would have to make during a Cisco NIPS deployment, but it is not a full-blown deployment guide.

Step 1: Understand the Product

Learn as much as you possibly can about the product you're about to implement before you start. It's tempting to dive right in without taking the time for research, but during your deployment, you have to make important decisions about how to use the product and where to deploy sensors. Your likelihood to make good decisions goes up if you are well-informed. Product documentation is a good place to start, and if you need more assistance, consider instructor-led training.

> **NOTE** When researching an IPS product, you need to make sure that you understand its true capabilities, which are sometimes inflated by the basic marketing literature. Product comparisons done by various security groups are usually a source of valuable information on actual product capabilities.

Therefore, the first phase of ACME's NIPS deployment is to learn about Cisco IPS Sensor Software. ACME is already familiar with the fundamental components and capabilities of IPS, which are covered in Part II, "Host Intrusion Prevention." The goal for its research is to identify which Cisco IPS sensor components and capabilities ACME can use to protect its network. Therefore, it researches the following topics about the Cisco IPS solution:

- Sensors available

- in-line support

- Management and monitoring options

- NIPS capabilities

- Signature database and update schedule

Sensors Available

ACME wants to be sure it identifies where Cisco NIPS devices can be integrated into its network infrastructure. ACME also wants to identify the functionality provided by the various Cisco IPS devices. Therefore, it examines the various Cisco IPS sensors and platforms. Cisco supports a wide variety of sensors, including the following:

- Cisco IPS 4200 Series appliance sensors

- Cisco Catalyst 6500 Series IDS Module (IDSM-2)

- Cisco IDS Network Module

- Cisco IOS IPS sensors

Cisco IPS 4200 Series Appliance Sensors

The core of Cisco NIPS support is the Cisco IPS 4200 series appliance sensors. The major characteristics of the appliance sensors are shown in Table 10-1.

Table 10-1 *Appliance Sensor Characteristics*

Sensor	Maximum Traffic Analysis	Monitoring Interface	Command and Control Interface	Optional Interface
IPS 4215	80 Mbps	10/100BASE-TX	10/100BASE-TX	4 10/100BASE-TX
IPS 4240*	250 Mbps	4 10/100/1000BASE-TX	10/100BASE-TX	4 10/100/1000BASE-TX (in the future)
IPS 4250XL	1000 Mbps	Dual 1000BASE-SX interface with MTRJ	10/100/1000BASE-TX	1000BASE-SX (fiber)
IPS 4255*	600 Mbps	4 10/100/1000BASE-TX	10/100BASE-TX	1000BASE-SX (fiber) or 4 10/100/1000BASE-TX (in the future)

NOTE The sensors marked by an "*" are the newest appliance sensors added to the Cisco IPS solution. These sensors provide high reliability by incorporating flash for storage instead of a regular hard disk. Also, the sensors can be managed via the console port in addition to the Ethernet command and control interface.

These appliance sensors can be deployed at various locations throughout your network. Each of these sensors runs the same sensor software. The major differences among the appliance sensors involve the following factors:

- Maximum traffic analysis capability

- Number of interfaces

- Type of interfaces

- Cost

Cisco Catalyst 6500 Series IDS Module

For networks that utilize Catalyst 6500 series switches, Cisco provides the Cisco Catalyst Series IDS Module (IDSM-2). This module plugs directly into the Catalyst switch, which enables the sensor to analyze traffic directly from the switch's backplane. The IDSM-2 provides the following capabilities:

- Merged switching and security into a single chassis

- Ability to monitor multiple VLANs (similar to the appliance sensors)

- No impact on switch performance
- Detection and prevention capabilities equal to appliance sensor
- Utilization of the same code base of the appliance sensor
- Potential operation in in-line mode (running Cisco IPS 5.0 Software or greater)

NOTE   Running Cisco IPS 5.0 Software, the IDSM-2 is capable of operating in in-line mode only for a single VLAN, because it does not support trunk traffic passing through the blade. This limitation should be removed in a future software release.

The basic characteristics of the IDSM-2 sensor are as follows:

- **Performance**—600 Mbps
- **Monitoring interfaces**—2-gigabit interfaces
- **Command and control interface**—1-gigabit interfaces
- **TCP Reset interface**—1-gigabit interface
- **Optional interface**—No

NOTE   The TCP Reset interface is an interface that the IPS Software can use to generate TCP Reset packets in conjunction with the TCP Reset signature action. In some IDSM-2 configurations, the monitoring interfaces can receive only incoming traffic. In these configurations, the TCP Reset interface provides an alternate interface through which to support the TCP Reset action.

Unlike the appliance sensor, the IDSM-2 is a switch card. Therefore, to deploy the IDSM-2, you must have a Catalyst 6500 family switch. Furthermore, to successfully utilize your IDSM-2 as another component in your overall Cisco IPS solution, your switch operating system must match one of the following requirements:

- Catalyst OS 7.5(1) or later (on Supervisor Engine)
- Cisco IOS Release 12.1(19)E or later

Cisco IDS Network Module

The Cisco IDS Network Module for access routers provides sensor functionality that is deployed in access routers such as the Cisco 2600XM, 2691, 3660, and 3700 Series routers. The following are the technical specifications for the Cisco IDS Network Module for access routers:

- **Performance**—Up to 45 Mbps
- **Monitoring interface**—Router internal bus

- **Command and control interface**—10/10 10/100BASE-TX

- **Optional interface**—No

> **NOTE**   The Cisco IDS Network Module runs the Cisco IPS 5.0 Software but does not support in-line processing. It can operate only in promiscuous mode.

Cisco IOS IPS Sensors

Certain versions of Cisco IOS Software incorporate intrusion detection functionality into the software. When you use the Cisco IOS IPS functionality, the deployed router is known as a router sensor. Cisco IOS IPS is able to detect a limited subset of attacks compared to the appliance sensor. The software and hardware requirements for Cisco IOS IPS are as follows:

- Cisco IOS Release 12.0(5)T or greater

- Cisco 830, 1700, 1800, 2600, 2800, 3600, 3800, 7100, 7200, and 7500 Series routers

> **NOTE**   Beginning with Cisco IOS Release 12.3(T), Cisco IOS IPS uses the same signature engines that are available with the appliance sensors. Although you cannot check for all the signatures that an appliance sensor does (because of performance reasons), you can configure a limited set of signatures to watch for (choosing from virtually all the signatures available on the appliance sensor). You can also download pretuned signature definition files (.sdf files) that you can use on routers to optimize the IPS functionality based on the amount of RAM installed on the routers. These ".sdf" files identify a core set of IPS signatures to enable on the router.

In-Line Support

Beginning with Cisco IPS 5.0 Software, Cisco sensor software supports attack prevention by operating in in-line mode. In-line mode enables your sensor to drop malicious traffic when it is detected. The following Cisco IPS sensors support in-line mode functionality:

- IPS 4215

- IPS 4240

- IPS 4255

- IDSM-2

- IOS IPS sensors

> **NOTE**   In-line functionality is not supported on the network module. Furthermore, adding this functionality to the network module is not planned.

For more information about network in-line capabilities, refer to Chapter 7, "Network Intrusion Prevention Overview," and Chapter 8, "NIPS Components."

Management and Monitoring Options

After ACME feels that it has a sufficient grasp of the sensor components, it moves on to its network management plan. The Cisco documentation shows that Cisco NIPS can be managed either centrally or on a per device basis. To access the management system for both graphical options, use a web-browser interface.

Command-Line Interface

Each sensor comes with a text-based command-line interface (CLI). This IOS-like interface enables you to configure your sensor and debug its operation. Using the CLI is helpful when you initially set up a sensor and to debug its operation. Although you can configure most sensor parameters using the CLI, most people prefer to use the graphical interfaces to perform most configuration changes. The CLI is accessed using either the console port on the sensor or across the network via the Secure Shell (SSH) protocol.

IPS Device Manager

Each sensor comes with the IPS Device Manager (IDM) software. This software enables you to configure the sensor through a graphical web-based interface. Using IDM, you can also analyze the events that are happening on the sensor and manually initiate IP blocking and logging.

IDM provides a limited monitoring capability. Using this monitoring functionality, you can observe the events that occur on a single sensor. In most situations, however, you want to correlate events from multiple sensors, so you use Cisco Security Monitoring, Analysis and Response (CS-MARS) product to observe IPS events from multiple devices.

> **NOTE**   Previously, Cisco also had another event-correlation software product called Security Monitor. This software is being replaced by the CS-MARS product.

CiscoWorks Management Center for IPS Sensors

The centralized management approach for Cisco NIPS is the CiscoWorks Management Center for IPS Sensors (IPS MC). IPS MC is a component of the virtual private network (VPN)/Security Management Solution (VMS) software. IPS MC enables you to configure and manage hundreds of IPS sensors across your entire network from a single management system.

> **NOTE** VMS is being replaced by Cisco Security Manager (CSM). CSM provides a more scalable graphical interface that enables operators to more efficiently provision their devices and security policies. CSM will play key role in the Cisco Security Management Solution. For more information, refer to Cisco.com.

CS-MARS

When you are deploying a large number of Cisco IPS sensors, you need an efficient way in which to monitor the alerts from these devices. CS-MARS provides this functionality. Using CS-MARS, you can correlate and analyze events from multiple sensors deployed throughout your network through a graphical interface. Additionally, CS-MARS provides correlation with alerts from other network hardware and software devices, including firewalls, routers, switches, host security, NetFlow, antivirus, and more, from various vendors. This type of correlation greatly enhances the accuracy of information provided to the security analyst.

CS-MARS provides numerous features, such as the following:

- Device monitoring
- Web-based monitoring platform
- Custom reporting and correlation capability
- Traffic anomaly detection
- Mitigation recommendations
- Topology awareness

With CS-MARS, you can receive events from a virtually unlimited number of devices, including the following:

- Sensor appliances
- IDS modules
- Router modules
- IOS routers
- PIX firewalls
- NetFlow
- Authentication servers (such as Cisco Secure Access Control Server [ACS])
- Host security software (such as Cisco Security Agent [CSA])

- UNIX hosts

- Windows hosts

Using a standard web browser, you can access the CS-MARS to administer and monitor the alerts from your IPS devices. Furthermore, you can easily use an extensive list of common reports to support your regulatory and other reporting requirements.

NIPS Capabilities

ACME used the Cisco documentation it had, what it had been able to gather from its sales team, and what it learned about Cisco IPS network components to make a list of Cisco NIPS capabilities. ACME checked to be sure that Cisco NIPS solution had all the capabilities commonly available in a robust NIPS product. The major IPS functionality that ACME identified for a robust IPS is as follows:

- Operate in in-line mode and promiscuous

- Support multiple sensor platforms

- Support centralized management

- Support a large signature base

- Support customized signatures

- Provide logging functionality

- Provide IP blocking functionality

- Provide alerting functionality

Next, ACME made the following high-level list of the NIPS functionality that it needs:

- Known network attacks prevention

- Anomalous traffic identification

- Internal attack propagation prevention

- Policy enforcement

- Regulatory requirements enforcement

NOTE   For more information about NIPS capabilities, refer to Chapter 7 and Chapter 8.

Signature Database and Update Schedule

To be effective, an IPS needs to detect a wide variety of different attacks and security policy requirements. Furthermore, updates to the IPS signature database need to be released regularly. Finally, the IPS vendor must quickly provide signatures for serious attacks once they are identified.

ACME samples the Cisco signature database and identifies that it includes more than 1000 signatures and more than a dozen different signature engines that enable ACME to efficiently develop various custom signatures to support a wide range of signatures unique to ACME's network and security policy. Cisco also regularly releases signature updates to enhance the functionality of the Cisco IPS. Finally, ACME discovers that Cisco released Signature Update S183 (to address the Microsoft "plug-and-play" vulnerability) only 45 minutes after Microsoft released its bulletin outlining the problem.

After reviewing the signature database and signature release history, ACME is comfortable that the Cisco IPS signatures are maintained in a timely manner.

Step 2: Predeployment Planning

Good planning is a critical factor in the success of any IPS deployment. Planning must start well before the implementation begins, and the plan needs to be continually reviewed and updated during the entire project. ACME invites the relevant stakeholders to a series of NIPS project planning meetings. During the meetings, they take care of the following:

- Review the security policy

- Define deployment goals

- Select and classify sensor deployment locations

- Plan for ongoing management

- Choose the appropriate management architecture

Review the Security Policy

Chapter 4, "Security in Depth," describes corporate security policies. Your security policy guides all of your major decisions during a NIPS deployment. If you don't have a security policy, strongly consider creating one. Without it, your deployment is likely to take much longer and be far more difficult. Additionally, if you need to take corrective actions with an employee, a written policy describing what is considered acceptable use might also be required.

Luckily, ACME has a well-documented and up-to-date security policy. It started its planning session with a review of the security policy in light of Cisco NIPS components and capabilities. The intent of this review session was to begin thinking about the following:

- The items in the security policy Cisco NIPS might be able to address.

- If the security policy needs to be updated to reflect NIPS capabilities.

- The policy changes that govern the operation of Cisco NIPS at ACME.

Define Deployment Goals

It is important to have a well-defined set of measurable goals before the implementation begins. Goals give the stakeholders something to actively work toward and a way to measure the progress of the project. You also use them to restrict the scope of the project. Any decision or product functionality that does not contribute to the achievement of one the goals should not be a part of the implementation (unless you decide to add a goal that it does address).

Most of the goals you define for the project, such as deadlines, budgets, and so forth, are the same for any project. However, two goals are related specifically to NIPS deployments:

- Security posture

- Problems to solve

Security Posture

The first goal you should define is, in a general sense, where you want to fall in the security versus operability spectrum. This spectrum refers to the idea that, for the most part, as security increases, the ease of operability decreases, which can result in an undesirable impact on the users of your network. Try to characterize your organization's overall philosophical approach to security (commonly known as your security posture). To characterize your security posture, think about the following:

- What people, time, and dollar resources your organization can expend for security efforts

- The functionality that users need to perform their jobs

- The organization's overall vulnerability level

- The value of the information the security tools protect

- The likelihood of attack

A NIPS typically operates so that all traffic is permitted by default, and only malicious traffic is denied, while a firewall typically has opposite operation. A firewall typically permits only traffic that has been specifically allowed and denies everything else. NIPS can certainly be configured to operate more like a deep-inspection firewall, just as a firewall can be configured to be more permissive. Using the following implementation examples to illustrate the process, try to classify your organization as *default deny* or *default allow*:

■   A **default deny organization** starts by denying everything. Then, necessary applications and their traffic are permitted only after they have been approved. The approval process determines that specific applications are both vital to business operation and do not adversely impact the overall security of the network. Users are only able to establish outbound connections through the IPS on specific ports using specific protocols. Inbound connections from the Internet are limited by port, protocol, and destination IP address (if allowed at all). Default deny organizations have the resources to make frequent changes to the IPS configuration in response to changing needs. Users are accustomed to having their change requests declined and having to wait for approved changes to occur. The information protected by the IPS is so critical and at such high risk that the default deny approach is necessary.

Example organizations include banks, government intelligence agencies, and utility companies.

■   **Default allow organizations** start by allowing everything. Then, when traffic is determined to be a significant security risk, it is denied on the network. Virtually all inbound connections are also permitted, except for those that are known to be dangerous. Default allow organizations have extremely limited resources to expend managing the IPS, so the configuration is designed to require almost no changes over time. Users never need to make change requests because almost everything is permitted. The information protected by the IPS is not particularly important, and the risk of attack is low.

Example organizations include portions of educational institutions and some volunteer groups.

> **NOTE**   Many attacks, such as worms, indiscriminately attack IP addresses on the Internet. These IP addresses might belong to a wide range of organizations, making any organization the potential target of an attack.

When ACME started to characterize its organization, it quickly realized that it more closely matches the profile of a default allow organization. At ACME, the following statements are true:

- It currently allows almost any outbound connection through the firewall, except for certain types such as common peer-to-peer (P2P) file-sharing connections, and anticipate using the IPS in the same mode.

- All inbound connections through the firewall are blocked except for a small number of demilitarized zone (DMZ) applications.

- Each member of the information security staff is trained to manage multiple technologies and projects because there aren't enough of them to dedicate resources to any one technology.

- A procedure is in place to request changes to the firewall configuration, but it is fairly simple. Most of the time, the requestor just sends an e-mail to the security staff requesting the change. This same procedure is expected to work with IPS.

- Most of the information behind the firewall is not confidential. ACME does have trade secrets, financial information, and employee personal information that should be protected, but that's about it.

- ACME is not subject to any specific regulatory requirements.

Problems to Solve

The second goal you need to define clearly is the purpose of the implementation. Start by identifying the problems NIPS should solve. Maybe the only problem you want NIPS to address is to identify if internal ACME users are launching attacks against fellow employees or other systems on the Internet. Perhaps your corporate security policy includes some restrictions that NIPS could enforce (such as preventing peer-to-peer applications from sending traffic through your firewall using port 80). Try to make as thorough and detailed a list as possible.

The following list indicates some sample problems that can be solved using either host or NIPS:

- Prevent mobile users from infecting other machines when they attach their system to the corporate network

- Control the flow of confidential data out of the organization

- Control the internal and external propagation of viruses, worms, and Trojans

- Conserve network bandwidth by preventing the use of P2P file-sharing applications

- Enforce corporate acceptable use policies

At ACME, the list of security-related problems that need to be solved never seems to shrink. Every time one problem is solved, another is added to the list. At a stakeholders' meeting, they put their list of 20 or so potential security initiatives on the whiteboard and eliminated the ones that NIPS could not help with. They ended up with eight problems that NIPS could solve.

After some discussion, they decided that as a *default allow* organization with limited resources, they should not try to tackle all eight problems at once. Instead, they put the eight problems in order of importance and eliminated the bottom four. The following goals were left for the implementation:

1. ACME went through a lengthy legal battle in which one of its employees attacked various Internet servers from the ACME network. ACME barely managed to avoid serious monetary damages. It would like to detect and stop attacks launched from its internal network toward other systems on the Internet. P2P file-sharing applications are becoming a nuisance because they are using a significant percentage of ACME available Internet bandwidth. It tried to block the connections using its firewall, but it wasn't successful because the P2P programs can use any port. It wants to prevent users from downloading music and movies from the Internet using P2P file-sharing applications.

2. ACME just deployed Voice over IP (VoIP) to the headquarters facility and the large sales offices. ACME is afraid that the VoIP network might be attacked from internal or external users. It wants to detect and stop common attacks launched from the data VLAN (which houses the users' computers) to either the voice VLAN or the server VLAN.

3. ACME wants to prevent the spread of network worms and viruses both on the internal networks and from the Internet. This protection supplements the Host Intrusion Prevention Systems (HIPS) and antivirus software already installed on many of the hosts throughout ACME's network.

Select and Classify Sensor Deployment Locations

After having established your goals for the project, move on to the next predeployment task, which is to determine where and which type of IPS sensors to deploy on the network. ACME decides to break down the sensor deployment into the following four types of sites:

■   Austin headquarters site

■   Large sales office sites (New York, Atlanta, Chicago, Portland, and San Diego)

■   Manufacturing sites (DeKalb, Midland, Gary, Huntsville)

■   Small sales office sites

Austin Headquarters Site

The headquarters site is a major component of the ACME network. All the other sites communicate with each other via the headquarters network. The core of the headquarters network is a

Catalyst 6500 switch. ACME decides to deploy two IDSM-2s in this switch to monitor the internal VLANs at the headquarter's facility. It also decides to deploy a Cisco IPS 4255 sensor to monitor the public servers and attacks outside the perimeter firewall, because many of these attacks are not seen on the internal network (they are blocked by the perimeter firewall). Because the number of attacks directed toward the outside of the firewall is likely to be high, ACME decides to initially focus only on virus and worm detection. Gradually, ACME plans to add other important signatures as well.

> **NOTE**   ACME's security policy clearly outlines which traffic is allowed to its publicly accessible servers, such as its web server and mail server. ACME plans to utilize IPS to provide analysis on this allowed traffic to gain an extra measure of protection against attacks that use these easily accessible traffic channels. The Cisco IPS 4255 sensor running in in-line mode prevents many attacks directed to the corporate web server.

The IDSM-2 sensors can detect attacks launched from the data VLAN to either the server VLAN or the voice VLAN. Cisco IPS also supports signatures that detect P2P traffic. These signatures can identify and stop traffic for common P2P applications. The Cisco IPS 4255 sensor can monitor all the attacks being launched against the ACME network.

Large Sales Office Sites

ACME has five large sales office sites in the following locations:

- New York, New York

- Chicago, Illinois

- Portland, Oregon

- San Diego, California

- Atlanta, Georgia

ACME decides to use a single Cisco IPS 4255 at each large sales office. Each of these sensors is deployed with four monitoring interfaces. This enables each sensor to operate in in-line mode at the following locations:

- Access to data VLAN

- Access to voice VLAN

When the Cisco IPS 4255 supports eight monitoring interfaces, ACME plans to add the four more interfaces and use one of the new interfaces to promiscuously monitor attacks detected outside the perimeter firewall and two more to provide in-line monitoring for the server VLAN.

Manufacturing Sites

ACME has four manufacturing facilities located in the following cities:

- DeKalb, Illinois

- Midland, Texas

- Gary, Indiana

- Huntsville, Alabama

At each manufacturing site, ACME decides to deploy a Cisco IPS 4240. Each sensor uses two interfaces to operate in in-line mode at the inside of the perimeter firewall. Another interface operates in promiscuous mode to monitor attacks outside the perimeter firewall.

Small Sales Office Sites

ACME has approximately 20 small sales offices spread across the United States. Each of these sites is connected to the headquarters facility over an IPsec tunnel. ACME decides to implement IOS-IPS in the perimeter router at each small sales office.

Plan for Ongoing Management

It crucial to think about the ongoing management of your NIPS after it has been implemented. Try to decide who is going to take over sensor administration when the project is finished. Also, decide where the administrators are to be physically located and who has responsibility for what types of administration. If you can plan for ongoing management at this stage in the project, you can involve the future administrators in the deployment early on, so that they are ready to go when it is finished.

ACME decided that four members of the corporate security team are to be responsible for sensor administration, event monitoring, and incident response. All NIPS devices are to be managed and monitored from the ACME headquarters. All the personnel who are to manage sensor post-deployment are located at ACME headquarters. Using CS-MARS, the security personnel are able to correlate all of their security-related events, such as NetFlow data and syslog messages as well as IPS alerts.

Choose the Appropriate Management Architecture

The final predeployment planning task is to architect the solution that is going to manage the NIPS sensors. Be careful and take your time finishing this task. If you don't plan well and realize later that your management should be different, it can be difficult to change after sensors are deployed and actively managed. At least five factors affect your choice of management architecture:

- **Number of sensors**—The number of sensors the management solution should support. Make sure to plan for future needs when you select the number. For example, if you want this solution to be in place for at least three years, the number of sensors it should support is the number of sensors you expect to have deployed in three years.

  Remember that the IPS MC can be implemented in a single-server manner. A single server supports up to 300 sensors. To support more sensors than that, you must deploy several IPS MCs.

- **Geographical distribution**—Your company might have only one location, it might have several offices within one country, or it could have hundreds of branches across the globe. Consider how many sensors are at each branch and how much network bandwidth each location has.

  If your company is widely distributed and the branches have limited network connections, you might decide to manage the branch sensors individually (instead of centrally from your headquarters location). Managing and monitoring each branch individually increases the burden of correlating events across your entire network.

  If the company is not distributed or is but has reliable network connections between the branches and headquarters, a single IPS MC probably makes more sense. Large organizations might have a number of network operation centers (NOC), which would be suitable for single IPS MCs as needed for the number of sensors each NOC is expected to support.

- **Administrative model**—In the prior section of this chapter, called "Plan for Ongoing Management," you identified which people manage the NIPS after the implementation is finished. The location of the people who manage the solution and what sensors they are responsible for can impact your management architectural choices.

  For example, if you choose to have headquarters personnel manage branch sensors, it is logical to locate the management solution at headquarters. If you have multiple branches and choose to have personnel at each branch administer their own location, branch sensor management can be handled on an individual sensor basis unless the number of sensors requires the deployment of an IPS MC at the larger branch locations.

- **Budget**—The amount of money you have earmarked for the management solution. The budget also includes the number of people that you plan to use to configure and monitor your IPS solution.

- **Uptime requirements**—Your organization might have a policy requiring all management solutions to meet certain availability requirements. To achieve the requirements, you might need to consider management architectures that are more suited to high availability and fail more gracefully than others.

The entire ACME NIPS solution involves the following sensors (see Figure 10-2):

- Two IDSM-2 (headquarters)

- One IPS 4255 (headquarters)

- Five IPS 4255 (large sales offices)

- Fout IPS 4240 (manufacturing sites)

- Twenty IOS-IPS Sensors (small sales offices)

Figure 10-2 *ACME IPS Network Configuration*

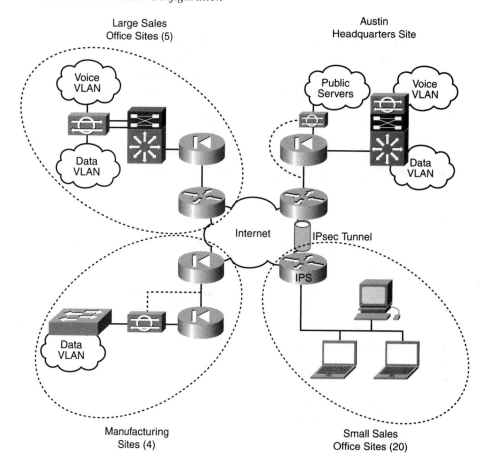

These sensors can easily be managed by a single IPS MC system.

Step 3: Sensor Deployment

In this phase, you use the plans from phase 2 to begin the actual implementation. You face four subtasks in this phase of the project:

Step 1   Understand sensor CLI and IDM

Step 2   Install sensors

Step 3   Install and secure the IPS MC

Step 4   Understand the management center

Understand Sensor CLI and IDM

The initial sensor installation involves configuring the sensor through the CLI. Using the CLI, you configure the basic network parameters and allow access to the sensors from your management system. You can also perform numerous sensor configuration tasks using the IDM, which is a graphical web-based interface that is part of the sensor software. Understanding both of these interfaces is vital to successfully deploying Cisco IPS sensors on your network.

Install Sensors

The physical deployment of the in-line sensors involves the following two steps:

- Configuring the sensor

- Cabling the sensor

Configuring the Sensor

Before you can connect an in-line sensor into your network, you need to enable the interfaces that are to be used for your in-line pairs. You also need to configure the network parameters for the command and control interface so that you can access the sensor from your management platform.

> **NOTE**   From the sensor CLI, you need to configure a few basic parameters, such as the management interface characteristics. These parameters are configured by running the **setup** command. The remaining sensor configuration can be performed using the GUI management tools.

Cabling the Sensor

After the initial software configuration, you need to physically connect the in-line sensor at your deployment locations in the network. Typical in-line deployment locations include the following:

- Between two routers

- Between a firewall and a router

- Between a switch and a router

- Between a switch and a firewall

Install and Secure the IPS MC and Understand the Management Center

You should have designed your management architecture in the planning phase. Procure the necessary hardware and software, but before you actually build it, make sure it is going to be installed in a secure manner. It is critical to secure your IPS MC as much as possible. Security management servers are appealing targets for attackers. An attacker can use a compromised security management server for all kinds of nefarious purposes.

To secure the IPS MC, make sure it is protected with as many security countermeasures as possible. Chapter 2, "Signatures and Actions," describes many of these. For example, the IPS MC should at least be in a secure physical location with restricted access, protected by a firewall, and have a CSA running on it.

> **NOTE**   Consult the IPS MC documentation to make sure that your countermeasures don't prevent it from working. For example, the sensors might use certain network ports to communicate with the management center. If your firewall blocks those connections, IPS MC cannot properly manage and monitor your sensors.

As soon as the security countermeasures are ready, consult your architecture plan and build your NIPS management solution.

The ACME project team worked with the security and server teams to securely implement the IPS MC. It attached the single server to the network it usually uses for management devices because that network is protected from the regular network. It also verified connectivity to the command and control interfaces on its deployed sensors.

Step 4: Tuning

One purpose of the tuning phase is to reduce false positives. The default sensor installation generates alerts for its signatures, but it does not perform any actions, such as dropping the traffic or initiating IP blocking. During the tuning phase, you need to monitor the alerts that your NIPS generates and verify that normal user traffic is not causing the alerts.

Tuning your NIPS is an ongoing process. The purpose of the initial tuning involves the following tasks:

- Identify false positives

- Configure signature filters

- Configure signature actions

Besides configuring actions for specific signatures, you can also tune your Cisco IPS appliances using the Risk Rating. Using the Risk Rating and event action override, you can override configured actions for signatures in which the Risk Rating is below a specific value. This helps reduce false positives because the Risk Rating provides a more reliable indicator of event severity. Similarly, you can produce actions in which the Risk Rating is high (even if the signature is not configured for the specific action).

> **RISK RATING**
>
> One of the limiting factors associated with intrusion systems is false positive alarms. False positives generate more work for your security analysts and can reduce their confidence in the alarms that the intrusion system identifies. To reduce the probability of false positives, Cisco IPS version 5.0 calculates a Risk Rating for alerts from 0–100. Instead of relying solely on the severity of the attack detected, the Risk Rating is calculated based on the following factors:
>
> - Event severity
>
> - Signature fidelity
>
> - Asset value of target

NOTE   With CS-MARS, you can also use the CS-MARS appliance to tune all of your correlation rules at on time, regardless of whether the events are from the Cisco IPS appliances, firewalls, open source tools, or other products. This more automated approach is usually more effective and results in a simpler and easier-to-maintain methodology.

Identify False Positives

Many original Intrusion Detection Systems (IDSs) had a significant problem with false positives. As the technology has evolved, the rate of false positives has diminished greatly. Increased accuracy was a vital component to developing an effective Intrusion Prevention solution. The

Cisco Risk Rating represents another mechanism to increase the accuracy of the IPS alerts and reduce false positives.

Nevertheless, you still need to test the default signature configuration to verify that none of the signatures trigger regularly on normal user traffic. After your initial test, you need to continually assess alerts and identify false positives (as well as false negatives) as they arise. This tuning continues as new signatures are applied to the sensors via signature updates.

Configure Signature Filters

Signature filters enable you to exclude alerts for signatures when the traffic involves specific systems. For example, you might want to configure a shared message block (SMB) signature to generate an alert only if the traffic involves a system that is external to your network. SMB traffic between systems on your network is common traffic that you want to allow. This same traffic, however, from an external Internet system is usually indicative of malicious activity. So, in this situation, if you set up a filter, the alerts are limited to only SMB traffic that involves an internal and external system.

Configure Signature Actions

One of the most powerful aspects of your NIPS sensors is their ability to generate an action whenever a signature fires. Besides generating an alert, your sensor can perform one or more of the following actions:

- Drop traffic (in-line mode only)

- Block traffic

- Log traffic

- Reset a TCP connection

> **NOTE** Firing too many actions for too many signatures can also be one of the significant weaknesses of an IPS. Each of these actions consumes resources on the IPS devices, thus potentially impacting its performance. Cisco IPS enables you to limit the configured actions by using the event action override to override the default actions. Utilizing this functionality enables you to make sure that actions are not invoked lightly.

Using these actions to stop attacks and block traffic from attacking systems enables your IPS to take an active role in the defense of your network. Setting the actions, however, requires you to examine your security posture and security policy. For example, depending on the accuracy and severity of a signature, you might decide to limit the actions to alerting and logging. For other signatures, you might decide that the signature severity warrants the drop action.

Step 5: Finalize the Project

Although the sensors are deployed and fully operational, you have a number of loose ends to tie up before the project is officially over. First of all, operational control of your sensors must transition from the deployment team to whoever is going to manage sensors moving forward (see the section, "Plan for Ongoing Management" earlier in this chapter). Also, you need to establish procedures to govern the day-to-day operation of your NIPS sensors. Here are a few examples:

- **Change control**—Establishes the checks that are in place for sensor configuration changes. It controls how changes are requested, who reviews the changes, and by what criteria they are reviewed.

- **Backup and restore**—Defines the frequency and type of backup performed on the IPS MC. It also outlines the proper way to restore the IPS MC if needed.

- **Log archive**—Describes how long sensor event logs should be kept, when they should be archived, what types of events should be archived, and where the archive is stored.

- **Incident response**—Investigates sensor alert needs to be developed. Whenever an alert is generated, someone needs to examine the alert and verify that the attack was successfully stopped. If your sensor alerts only on malicious traffic, you also need to examine attacked systems to verify that they have not been compromised. Using CS-MARS can simplify this process because many of the steps that an operator performs to analyze an attack are automatically handled by CS-MARS.

Summary

Before you embark upon a NIPS deployment, have realistic expectations about what is involved. This chapter used a real-world NIPS product as an example to illustrate the decisions that need to be made at each phase in a NIPS deployment. You have to perform five major Cisco NIPS deployment phases:

Step 1	Understand the product
Step 2	Predeployment planning
Step 3	Sensor deployment
Step 4	Tuning
Step 5	Finalize the project

Understand the Product

The first task in any NIPS deployment is to make sure you fully understand the product you are going to be deploying. Review Chapters 7 and 8 so that you are familiar with the potential components, capabilities, and benefits associated with NIPS products. Then, determine which components, capabilities, and benefits your product includes. Also, be sure to investigate the product's management capabilities.

Predeployment Planning

The planning phase of a NIPS deployment must occur before anything has been implemented. During this phase, you need to

- **Review the security policy** — Determine what, if any, impact your corporate security product has on the NIPS implementation.

- **Define goals** — Decide what the goals are for the implementation.

- **Select and classify sensor deployment locations** — Decide where and what types of sensors are to be deployed on your network.

- **Plan for ongoing management** — Begin to plan for post-implementation of the product.

- **Choose a management architecture** — Design the management solution.

Sensor Deployment

The next phase is to deploy the sensors you chose during your planning session. Along with deploying your sensors, you also need to install your management software and make sure that access to the management tool has been secured, because it is a prime target for attack.

Tuning

One purpose of the tuning phase is to locate and eliminate false positives. Another aspect of tuning is to create necessary filters to overcome known false positive situations. Finally, tuning involves configuring signature actions. Generating one or more of the following actions when signatures fire helps to fully utilize the functionality that your IPS sensors provide:

- Drop traffic (in-line mode only)

- Block traffic

- Log traffic

- Reset a TCP connection

Finalize the Project

In the final phase of your NIPS deployment, you need to create procedures to govern the following:

- Change control
- Backup and restore
- Log archive
- Incident response

CHAPTER 11

Deployment Scenarios

Every Intrusion Prevention System (IPS) deployment is different. The company type, which is characterized by things such as its size, vertical, and emphasis on security, accounts for many of the differences. This chapter examines an assortment of IPS deployment scenarios; each scenario uses a different type of company as an example. The following six company types are examined:

- Large enterprise

- Branch office

- Medium financial enterprise

- Medium educational institution

- Small office

- Home office

In each scenario, you read about the following:

- The company background and recent computer security incidents

- The factors that limit the IPS project

- The goals for the project that are derived from the problems to solve and the corporate security policy

- High-level Host Intrusion Prevention System (HIPS) implementation planning

- High-level Network Intrusion Prevention System (NIPS) implementation planning

Large Enterprise

In 1974, Premium Airways transported its first passengers in two propeller-driven airplanes. Since then, Premium has grown to become a national carrier with hundreds of jets in service. Most of the company's 40,000 computers are located on the headquarters campus in Tulsa, Oklahoma.

The other 10,000 hosts are scattered at airports all over the United States. Some of the systems are kiosk-type machines that passengers use to check in. Others are used by the airline operations staff at each airport. Also, each gate has a computer that is used to scan boarding passes before the passenger gets on the plane.

All of Premium's airport computers, whatever their function, connect back to the data center in Tulsa. They use a site-to-site virtual private network (VPN) to communicate with a large Microsoft SQL database cluster. Each airport has its own VLAN. Aside from that, the administrative and airport computers are not separated.

This lack of separation proved to be a problem six months ago during a very severe virus incident. Somehow, a system at headquarters was infected by the Slammer worm. The worm propagated rapidly to almost all of the SQL database servers, including the cluster that supports the airport systems.

SLAMMER WORM

The SQL Slammer worm attacked Microsoft database servers with unprecedented speed. It infected most of its estimated 75,000 victims within the first 10 minutes. For more information on the SQL Slammer worm, refer to Chapter 1, "Intrusion Prevention Overview."

As a result, Premium had to delay and even cancel some flights because the database that supports boarding pass scanners, check-in kiosks, and gate personnel was down. Not only that, but the worm generated so much traffic that the overall network performance was significantly reduced. Remediation was difficult because many of the network links were saturated.

Premium lost a great deal of money that day. Refunds had to be paid to passengers, the whole schedule had to be changed because planes weren't where they were supposed to be, and airplanes cost money to operate even if they aren't flying. Premium's reputation also suffered a blow when the reason for the delayed and cancelled flights made front-page news.

To make sure this wouldn't happen again, Premium re-evaluated its entire security strategy. One of the projects that came out of the re-evaluation was to implement IPS. Premium started off its IPS deployment with a meeting where the stakeholders:

- Identified limiting factors that would impact the IPS project

- Used the corporate security policy to identify goals for the project

- Started high-level HIPS implementation planning

- Started high-level NIPS implementation planning

Limiting Factors

The stakeholders at the meeting recognized two company practices that would limit the way IPS could be deployed:

- Premium Airlines classifies technology products as either "emerging" or "standard." Emerging technology is any product that has not been running in production at headquarters for at least a year. Even if the technology has been publicly available for over a year, Premium classifies it as emerging until it has run at Premium for a year and become a standard. Emerging technology cannot be deployed at the airports for fear of implementing an unproven product on mission critical systems.

  In this case, HIPS is categorized as emerging technology, so it cannot be used at the airports. NIPS is a standard because it has been in production at headquarters for a little over a year.

- The corporate security policy doesn't allow users to disable host security countermeasures such as antivirus software.

Security Policy Goals

During the security re-evaluation in the wake of the Slammer worm, Premium's security policy was revised. The revision included three provisions that were in direct response to what it learned during the Slammer incident:

- Greater effort must be made to prevent viruses from infecting headquarters hosts. Antivirus software is not a sufficient countermeasure for this task.

- The airport systems must, wherever possible, be isolated from headquarters systems. If isolation is not possible, rigorous controls must be in place to prevent headquarters security incidents from affecting airport systems.

- The IT security team had a difficult time identifying the origin of the Slammer worm. It took several days to determine that the attack came from an internal host rather than the Internet. The security policy was modified to require a tool be in place to help IT security quickly determine if an attack came through their Internet connections or from an internal source.

HIPS Implementation

Premium used the limiting factors and goals it had established to start HIPS implementation planning. It was too early to get into the details, but it wanted to define:

- Target hosts

- Management architecture

- Agent configuration

Target Hosts

The team immediately excluded airport hosts from the HIPS implementation for three reasons:

- Airport hosts are not particularly vulnerable to attack because they run only an operating system and one or two applications and are kept in locked cases.

- As part of the overall project, they will be isolated from headquarters. If the headquarters systems are infected by something, isolation should reduce the risk that the infection spill over into the airports or vice versa.

- HIPS is an emerging technology that can't be installed at the airports for a year anyway.

All of the 30,000 hosts at headquarters are perfect candidates for a HIPS product. The first hosts to get protection will be any system that connects to the airports so that they are less likely to be infected by malware. After that, the agent will be deployed to desktops because that is where the Slammer infection originated. Finally, the rest of the hosts are covered.

MALWARE

Basically malware refers to any form of malicious software. Common examples include viruses, Trojans, worms, spyware, and adware.

Management Architecture

Premium Airlines has a good-sized team of computer security experts. A portion of the security team has only one duty—to "clean up" after virus incidents. When the IPS project is finished, Premium Airlines should have fewer virus incidents, so some of the cleanup team can take over HIPS management.

The team also decided that the management architecture should have the following characteristics:

- The management server is to be located in the Tulsa data center. Most of the agents are to be in that office, and the data center is staffed 24 hours per day.

- They need a tiered management server to support 30,000 agents.

- Premium has an out-of-band management network. The HIPS management server should reside on that network. Some network configuration changes will probably be required to secure the server and so that the management server can connect to the agents.

Agent Configuration

The IPS project has three goals: prevent headquarters virus infections, isolate airport systems, and provide a way to identify a virus' origin. The team talked about each goal and identified agent configuration settings for each.

To stop headquarters viruses, the agent configuration has to be fairly restrictive. Also, one of the problems the team had during the Slammer incident was that the network was so saturated that they couldn't push antivirus updates out to their hosts. They had an update that would stop Slammer, but couldn't deploy it. Thus, the agent should be configured so that it can stop viruses without needing updates.

One concern with the restrictive configuration approach is that false positives could be an issue. The group decided that if they had to err, they would prefer false positives over another major virus incident. One team member suggested that one way to handle false positives would be to allow users to turn the agent off. It was a good idea, but the corporate security policy prohibited that.

To isolate airport systems, the agent is to be configured to prohibit network access to the airport systems for any hosts that do not absolutely require it. The hosts that do require access are to have their access restricted to required services. For example, databases that the airport hosts use accept connections only on database ports.

Finally, the HIPS is to be configured to log permitted but unusual network connections between hosts. Ordinarily, network connections that are permitted are not logged. The team decided that if unusual connections were logged, they could use the logs to help them identify the origin of a virus.

NIPS Implementation

Premium deployed NIPS at the headquarter location approximately more than a year ago. This deployment consisted mainly of several sensors to monitor traffic between various operational VLANs on the Premium network (see Figure 11-1). It also deployed sensors to monitor its inbound Internet connections.

Figure 11-1 *Initial Premium Airways Network Configuration*

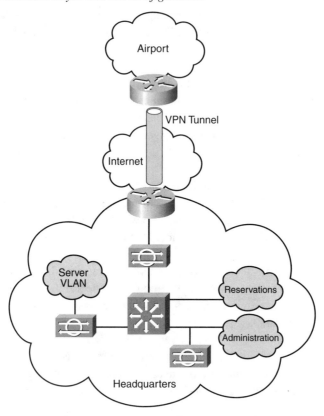

That initial deployment worked well, but Premium did not fully utilize the NIPS functionality because it used its sensors mainly to monitor attacks to the internal server VLAN. Only the sensors protecting the Internet connections were configured for in-line functionality. During this upgrade to the IPS solution, it plans to enhance the NIPS deployment through the following measures:

■ Deploy more sensors at the network core in Tulsa to provide in-line monitoring to all airport VLANs

■ Utilize in-line functionality to more closely regulate inter VLAN traffic at the headquarters facility and traffic destined for airport VLANs

Sensor Deployment

Premium decides to take advantage of its existing NIPS deployment at the headquarters facility. Initially, it monitored only Internet connections and traffic destined to the server VLAN. With this upgrade, it plans to deploy in-line sensors monitoring all airport VLANs. This new NIPS functionality adds 40 sensors to the Premium NIPS deployment.

To increase the separation between the airport systems and other hosts on the Premium network, the in-line sensors are to have custom signatures developed that restrict the connections allowed to access the airport computers. Furthermore, all connections between the headquarters site and any airport site are logged by the NIPS using informational custom signatures (see Figure 11-2).

Figure 11-2   *Final Premium Airways Network Configuration*

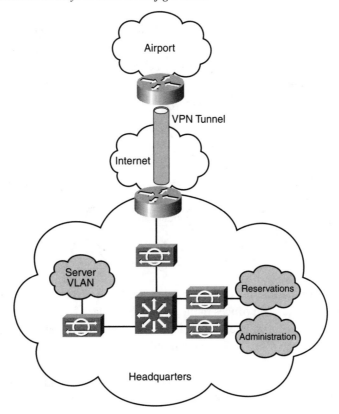

NIPS Management

Premium already has NIPS deployed at its headquarters location. Presently, it is managing these five sensors using a centralized management application via an out-of-band management network. The upgrade adds 40 sensors that need to be managed. The current management infrastructure, however, can support approximately 150 sensors, so it can easily handle the extra sensors.

To improve configuration and monitoring of the NIPS deployment, Premium also decides to add three more people to the current NIPS security staff of one person.

Branch Office

The SafetyNet Insurance agency is a large company with over 20,000 employees. A majority of the employees are independent agents who pay SafetyNet a franchise fee to be allowed to open a brick-and-mortar storefront. One of the branch offices is located in a strip mall in Charlotte, North Carolina.

The office employs 10 agents, 20 support staff, and each has their own computer for a total of 30 desktops. They also have one Windows server that they use for database services and file sharing. A point-to-point VPN over a high-speed Internet connection allows them to transmit paperwork to SafetyNet headquarters. They use the same Internet connection without the VPN for e-mail, web browsing, and so on (see Figure 11-3).

Figure 11-3 *Initial SafetyNet Network Configuration*

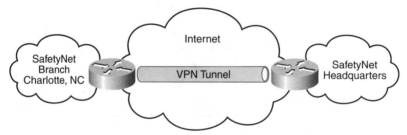

If the computers or the Internet connection need repair, they can call the "computer guy" who services all of the SafetyNet offices in the county. His salary is subsidized by SafetyNet, but the office still has to pay him an hourly wage. Plus, the guy is really busy, so it sometimes takes him a few days to get to the office to solve the problem.

A few weeks ago, the managers in the office decided to make a major investment in computer security. They had three reasons for the decision:

■ Office computers are frequently infected by viruses that come in via e-mail or web browsing. The viruses sometimes propagate through the VPN to SafetyNet headquarters. When the headquarters technicians detect that a virus is coming from a branch office, the response required by headquarters security policy is to drop the VPN tunnel until the branch office computers are cleaned. Headquarters would rather lose the connection to a branch office than risk a major security incident at headquarters.

Headquarters dropped the VPN several times last year, and every time it does, the office has to wait several days until the computer guy can get there and clean the infected systems. During that time, the office can still sell policies, but it has to transmit paperwork and get quotes via fax, which really delays the process and costs business.

- Many of the employees don't have high-speed Internet connections at home, so they use the office computers to surf the web during off-hours. Lately, the company has had to pay the computer guy a tremendous amount of money to remove spyware and adware that was inadvertently installed by employees who were surfing the web.

- A fair amount of employee turnover occurs at this branch. Six months ago, an agent left to work for another agency and took the office's entire client list with her. She used the list to contact many of the SafetyNet policyholders and convince them to move to her agency.

They hired a computer security consultant to help them. He immediately suggested that IPS could alleviate many of their problems.

Limiting Factors

Before the consultant could get started, the office management made him aware of the limitations under which he had to work. They explained that although the office doesn't have a computer security policy, headquarters has one with specific caveats that apply to all branch offices. A few of the guidelines in the policy appeared to be applicable:

- All branch office computers must run virus protection of some kind at all times.

- Branch offices must make a best effort to keep virus protection up-to-date.

- The Internet router, where the VPN is terminated, is supplied and maintained by headquarters. The branch office is prohibited from modifying the operation of the router or VPN in any way.

Security Policy Goals

When the consultant asked them what their goals for the project were, they listed four:

- Make it harder for employees to steal valuable information.

- Reduce support costs related to the cleanup of spyware and adware.

- Cut down on the number of times headquarters has to drop the VPN connection because an office computer is infected with a virus.

- Accomplish all of the goals without significantly increasing ongoing costs.

HIPS Implementation

SafetyNet's consultant used the limiting factors and goals to create an initial HIPS project plan. The plan defined the following:

- Target hosts

- Management architecture

- Agent configuration

Target Hosts

The headquarters security policy requires that all of the branch office systems run virus protection. IPS falls into the virus protection category, so all hosts are targets for HIPS.

Management Architecture

One of the limiting factors SafetyNet shared with the consultant is that they don't want to spend much money keeping the HIPS up-to-date. Also, they don't have the expertise to make HIPS configuration changes after the consultant leaves. To address both of these issues, the HIPS is to be managed by a reasonably priced managed security service provider (MSSP).

The consultant is to do the initial agent deployment and configuration. Once he is finished, the agents are to be configured to report events and receive security settings from the MSSP's management server. Also, the MSSP delivers weekly status reports to the office manager.

Agent Configuration

HIPS can help address all of SafetyNet's goals. To do so, it will be configured to

- Prevent the customer database from being copied to the desktops from the server, printed, or compressed. That way, it's harder to steal.

- Make sure that the only program that can access the customer database is the customer management program. This is so that employees can't use a database management tool of their own to read the database and export it into another program.

- As a theft deterrent, track all accesses of the customer database.

- Reduce virus, worm, and Trojan infections so that headquarters does not drop the VPN connection.

- Stop adware and spyware.

NIPS Implementation

Many of the problems being faced by SafetyNet can be addressed using HIPS. The consultant also decided to utilize NIPS to help minimize the VPN connections from being taken down by headquarters by installing an in-line sensor that drops all virus traffic (using IPS virus signatures) before they leave or enter the Charlotte branch.

Sensor Deployment

The Charlotte branch decides to deploy an in-line NIPS sensor between their network and the VPN router connected to the headquarters. By dropping all known virus-related traffic, they hope to keep the branch VPN operational (even if they have an infected system) while allowing them time to clean the infected system (see Figure 11-4).

Figure 11-4   *Final SafetyNet Network Configuration*

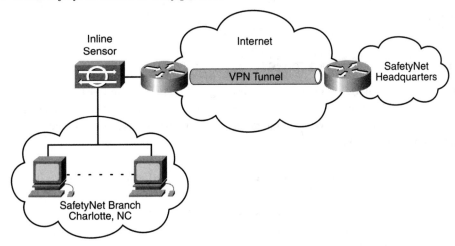

Using an in-line NIPS sensor, the Charlotte branch decides to drop the initial virus traffic (using virus-based signatures) and then block all traffic from the infected host for 24 hours (allowing time for the machine to be cleaned). If the virus is detected over a weekend, the traffic from the infected host is blocked for a longer period of time.

NIPS Management

The Charlotte office decides that the configuration on their sensor is not going to change very often. Furthermore, their research indicates that the virus-based NIPS signatures are accurate (the false alarm rate is very low). Therefore, the Charlotte branch decides to pay a consultant to initially configure the sensor and update the configuration quarterly. They plan to use the same MSSP that is monitoring their HIPS to manage the NIPS deployment.

To test the effectiveness of their in-line sensor, the managers decide to have the consultant configure the NIPS to generate an e-mail to all of the branch managers whenever an infected system is detected.

> **NOTE**   The Charlotte deployment goes very well, and infections not detected by HIPS are blocked by the NIPS sensor. Headquarters notices that during the last year, it has never had to drop the Charlotte branch VPN connection because of an infected system. After investigating the Charlotte solution, SafetyNet decides to protect all of its branches in a similar fashion. Instead of deploying in-line sensors at each branch, it decides to deploy the NIPS sensors at the headquarters site. By deploying sensors at the headquarters location, it can decrease costs and management because traffic from all of the branches can be monitored with fewer sensors (a single sensor can handle multiple branches). Furthermore, the in-line sensors enable SafetyNet to modify its security policy to state that all traffic from an infected system will be blocked for 24 hours instead of all traffic from a specific branch, thereby reducing lost business opportunities.

Medium Financial Enterprise

BLI Bank, headquartered in Green Bay, is a regional bank serving most of northern Wisconsin. The bank has 25 branches, with an average of 20 dumb terminals at each branch. The terminals connect back to a mainframe at headquarters. Branch operations are supported by 500 employees at headquarters who have desktops.

A few years ago, BLI created an investment group in an effort to boost profits. The investment section has 1500 employees, all of whom are located at headquarters. The branch operations and investment groups share a T3 connection to the Internet (see Figure 11-5).

Figure 11-5   *Initial BLI Bank Network Configuration*

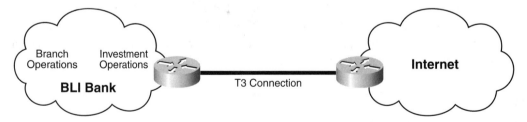

Naturally, computer security is important to BLI, as it should be for any financial institution. BLI doesn't have a particularly large IT staff, but they are qualified. They conduct regular risk analyses, maintain a rigorous security policy, and implement a very good computer security program.

Recently, information security at financial institutions has come under increased government scrutiny. BLI has to comply with several new sets of regulations. It has to find a way to fulfill the requirements in the regulations with very limited IT resources. The staff believes that an IPS can help them accomplish the task with the resources they have.

Limiting Factors

BLI must keep in mind a number of limiting factors as it decides how to use and deploy IPS:

- BLI is a regional bank so it has limited IT resources, but it's subject to the same regulations that apply to large financial institutions with lots of IT resources. It has to maximize the value of IPS by using it to fulfill as many regulatory requirements as it possibly can. At the same time, it has to make sure that it can support the IPS implementation with the small staff they have.

- Right now, the investment and branch operations groups are subject to very different regulatory requirements. The branch operations group is regulated far more stringently. BLI can separate the groups to some extent, but it can't afford two Internet connections. It will have to fulfill the requirements even though both groups share a single Internet connection.

Security Policy Goals

The BLI information security team analyzed the new regulations and modified its corporate security policy accordingly. Then, it reviewed the policy and listed the requirements that an IPS could fulfill:

- BLI must employ a neutral company to conduct remote penetration tests to make sure that BLI's countermeasures are working. BLI must be able to internally verify that the penetration tests are occurring regularly.
- All login failures and successes must be logged.
- All accesses of the mainframe and SQL databases must be tracked.
- Transactional network traffic must be separated from employee traffic such as e-mail and web browsing.

HIPS Implementation

BLI used the goals and limiting factors to come up with a high-level HIPS deployment plan. The plan defined the following:

- Target hosts
- Management architecture
- Agent configuration

Target Hosts

All hosts have to have an agent if BLI is going to enforce the regulatory requirements. The deployment starts with the branch operations machines because they are more important to the regulators. The investment hosts follow.

Management Architecture

The total number of hosts is less than 10,000, so a single management server architecture is appropriate. To prove to regulators that it is enforcing the regulations, BLI wants to be able to capture all HIPS events without losing any. A redundant management server with automatic failover can virtually assure that events are not lost.

Agent Configuration

BLI kept two factors in mind as it planned for the HIPS configuration. The first was that it had to fulfill the regulatory requirements. The second was that it had do so without having to devote many resources to ongoing agent management. It wants to keep the management tasks down to only a few hours per week.

To reduce ongoing management costs, BLI decided to disable all of the IPS features in its HIPS product. It felt that its existing security tools, such as antivirus and firewalls, were stopping malware well enough. The agent would be configured to enforce the following policies only:

- All login failures and successes written to the operating system event log are to be forwarded to the HIPS management console.

- The agent on the SQL database is to keep track of all IP addresses that connect to it.

NIPS Implementation

BLI Bank realizes that HIPS can provide it only a certain degree of protection. Therefore, it decided to supplement its HIPS deployment with a NIPS deployment as well. The NIPS deployment helps enforce network separation along with some regulatory requirements.

Sensor Deployment

BLI Bank has to worry about regulatory requirements as well as the separation between the investment operations and the normal banking transactions. From a network perspective, it decided to deploy in-line IPS sensors at the Internet perimeter and between the investment group and the rest of the bank's network.

The sensor monitoring the investment group not only monitors attacks originating from the investment group systems, but is also configured to drop any connections from the investment group to the bank's network. Only connections from the investment group to the Internet are allowed (see Figure 11-6).

Figure 11-6   *Final BLI Bank Network Configuration*

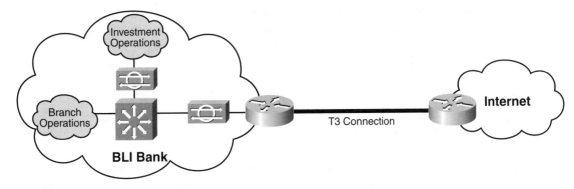

NIPS Management

BLI has a limited IT staff, so it decided to have a consultant initially install and configure its NIPS sensors. After the initial configuration, it feels that its current IT staff can maintain and monitor the IPS sensors.

Medium Educational Institution

Davis State University is a liberal arts school in Pittsburgh, Pennsylvania. Each of the 2300 undergraduate and 400 graduate students is required to have a personal computer. The school employs 500 faculty and staff, has 3 computer labs, and maintains approximately 50 different servers. The students use a T3 Internet connection, and there is a T1 reserved for the faculty and administrators (see Figure 11-7).

Figure 11-7   *Initial Davis State Network Configuration*

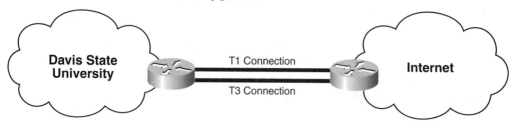

The school is faced with two problems that are proving difficult to solve. The first is that a number of other colleges and universities have recently had very public breaches in their computer security. Specifically, several incidents in the news have reported confidential student data and test scores stolen. The major donors and alumni are pressuring the senior administration to make sure this doesn't happen at Davis State.

The second problem is that a T3 Internet connection should be more than sufficient for 2700 students, but it's not proving to be so. The school IT staff found that the T3 is saturated with traffic that has nothing to do with education. So much traffic is generated by peer-to-peer file-sharing applications, Internet game servers, and software file servers that the T3 is almost unusable for legitimate purposes. Furthermore, the IT staff is concerned that the school might be held liable for any copyrighted material the students download using school networks.

Davis State's tiny information security team determines that an IPS can mitigate both problems.

Limiting Factors

An IPS might be able to mitigate the two problems, but it has to operate under certain restrictions:

■   The school takes a very permissive approach to computer security. The students pay a quarterly fee to use the school computing resources. Davis State administrators feel that if students are paying for a service, they should be able to use it for pretty much whatever legal purpose they want.

■   Educational institutions generally believe in a free exchange of information, and Davis State is no exception. For the most part, computer security should not curtail information exchange.

■   The students and faculty have complete control over their own systems. They can install and use whatever software they want. At the same time, the school has no way to mandate that a particular software package be installed.

Security Policy Goals

Davis State doesn't have much of a security policy, but it does maintain a list of high-level security guidelines. At the request of the administration, two guidelines were added:

- A best effort must be made to prevent theft of confidential student data.

- Davis State IT can restrict (not prevent) the use of certain types of applications such as peer-to-peer file sharing, game servers, and software file servers.

HIPS Implementation

Davis State used the goals and limiting factors to come up with a high-level HIPS deployment plan. The plan defined the following:

- Target hosts

- Management architecture

- Agent configuration

Target Hosts

The students and faculty have complete control over their own machines. They can install whatever software they want, change their system configuration at will, and attach new systems to the network. The school IT department has no way to forcibly deploy HIPS to any student or faculty host. Thus, a HIPS at Davis State cannot solve the bandwidth problem.

The IT department can, however, deploy agents on the machines they administer. Those machines include the servers that store confidential student information. There are only a few of them, but they all will have agents to help achieve the confidentiality goal.

Management Architecture

The single-server management architecture is more than sufficient for the limited number of agents to manage at Davis State. The team elects to install the management server software on a powerful workstation computer.

Davis State has a central IT department, but most of the server administration is decentralized. Departments have their own IT personnel to administer the department's computing resources. Student confidential data is kept on servers administered by a number of different departments. The deployment team decides to create a HIPS administrative account for each department. The accounts are limited so each administrator can configure only agents belonging to his or her department.

Agent Configuration

The agents on the servers are to have a very restrictive configuration. Usually, a restrictive policy requires a great deal of ongoing management. In this case, the servers that store student data run only a few applications, and those applications change very infrequently.

The central IT department creates the initial agent configuration. Each application on the servers has its own custom policy. The policy allows the application to perform only the functions it must in order to work correctly. When the agent is deployed and tuned, the central IT department turns administration over to the departmental administrators. To make sure that the departments don't change the policy too much, the central IT security team periodically checks the status of the policy on each server.

NIPS Implementation

With the open nature of the university network (and lack of control over student's systems), Davis State University decides to focus on a strong NIPS deployment. By regulating traffic at the network level, it can regulate the use of applications (such as peer-to-peer software) without having to directly modify the student's computers.

Sensor Deployment

Davis State University decides to deploy an in-line NIPS sensor at their Internet perimeter (the T3 line). This in-line sensor is configured to drop peer-to-peer traffic using pre-installed signatures. By limiting peer-to-peer traffic, the university hopes to enable everyone to have adequate bandwidth to access the Internet (see Figure 11-8).

It also decided to deploy an in-line IPS sensor to monitor access to the server VLAN and the administrative network. These sensors limit access to the servers and administrative network, as well as log connections to the administrative network.

It also decided to promiscuously monitor other network segments so that it can quickly identify malicious activity on the network. It decided not to use in-line monitoring at these locations because of the open nature of the university.

PROMISCUOUS MONITORING

Sensors running in promiscuous mode detect intrusive activity by examining traffic received on one of their monitoring interfaces. Usually, this requires directing a copy of the network traffic being analyzed to the sensor's monitoring interface. Unlike using in-line mode, sensors operating in promiscuous mode can only react to the traffic that they analyze; at least the initial attack packet will always reach the target system.

Figure 11-8 *Final Davis State Network Configuration*

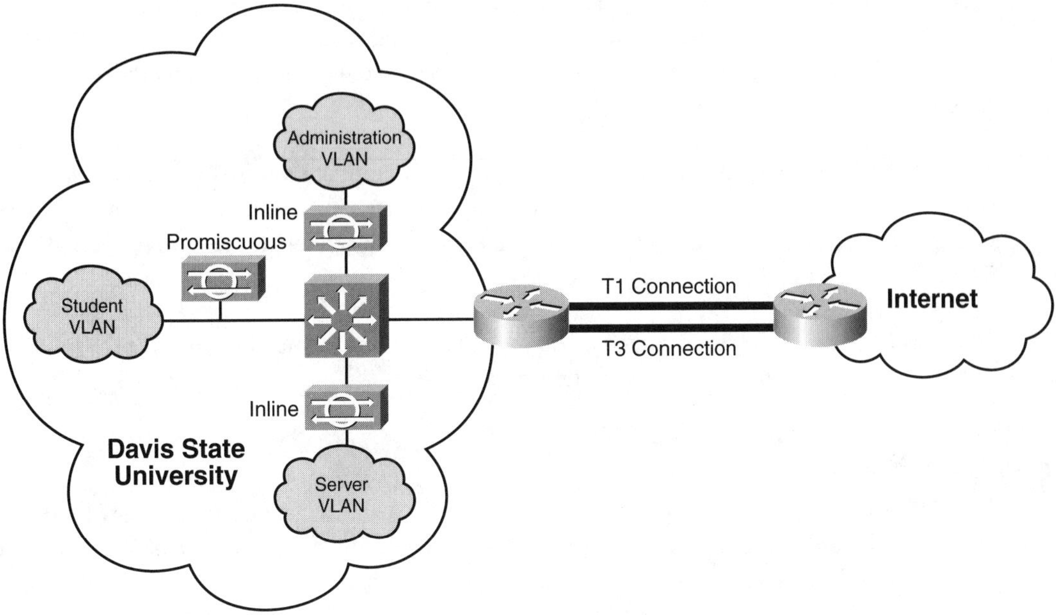

NIPS Management

Davis State University decides to configure its NIPS sensors individually because it manages only a few sensors. The current IT staff is responsible for managing and configuring these new security devices on the network.

Small Office

Jones Hardware of San Antonio, Texas, is a family-owned chain of hardware stores. There are ten stores in all, and one of the stores has some extra offices where a headquarters of sorts resides. Each store has two or three desktops, while the headquarters offices have ten desktops and one Windows server.

The computers at each store are used for point-of-sale transactions, to track inventory, to maintain employee schedules and payroll, and to place inventory orders with headquarters. The stores also have a shared digital subscriber line (DSL) Internet connection so that they can correspond with vendors via e-mail, connect to headquarters, and conduct Internet research. Jones Hardware relies pretty heavily on computers, but has no IT staff at all.

On a recent store visit, the CEO Stewart Jones found that two of the three computers were out of order. The sales clerks were issuing paper receipts, some items were out of stock because the inventory program wasn't available to prompt the store manager to order more, payroll was coming up, and the payroll program was on one of the broken computers. Nobody knew how to fix them.

Jones asked around and discovered that the out-of-order computers were crashing constantly because of virus and spyware infections. They had antivirus on them, but it wasn't being updated consistently. The store manager called a computer consultant to repair the systems periodically. The consultant was paid from the register.

This was a real problem. Jones asked a computer-savvy friend of his how to solve the problem, and the friend suggested that a HIPS might work.

Limiting Factors

If a HIPS were going to solve the problem, it had to do so without supervision of any kind. Jones Hardware couldn't afford to hire even a part-time IT person. Also, the solution had to work on the existing systems without any upgrades or additional hardware.

Security Policy Goals

The chain doesn't have a computer security policy of any kind. Jones did, however, want to establish some goals so that he could measure the success of the HIPS:

- Reduce the virus and spyware infections by 99 percent

- Reduce the computer consultant visits

SPYWARE

Spyware refers to software on your system that surreptitiously monitors your actions and activities (such as the web sites that you visit). It can also steal your identity or allow for the download of other malicious software. Most spyware software is installed on your system without your knowledge.

HIPS Implementation

Jones brought the idea of using IPS to its regular computer consultant. The consultant thought it was an excellent idea and volunteered to select and implement a HIPS product. Jones wanted a high-level project plan and quote before he agreed. The plan was to include the following:

- The target hosts

- The management architecture

- Any configuration suggestions

Target Hosts

All of the computers at Jones Hardware are to be protected by HIPS agents. The store computers are the most important systems, so they are implemented first. When the stores are finished, agents are put on the headquarters systems.

Management Architecture

One of the limiting factors is that the agents have to work without supervision. Therefore, the agents are unmanaged. They have no management server and no local user interface (UI). The consultant prepackages the agents with the configuration in his lab and installs them on Jones' computers.

This unmanaged approach presents some risk. Jones Hardware might require changes to the agent configuration at a future date and have no way to make them. Stewart Jones recognizes the risk, but prefers a theoretical risk over the demonstrated risk of viruses and spyware.

Agent Configuration

The store agents have a restrictive configuration while the headquarters agents take a balanced approach. The stores have a restrictive configuration because they are the most important computing resources Jones Hardware has. Sales might be lost when a store computer goes down. Also, they are running only a few legitimate business applications. If a false positive occurs, it is okay as long as the business applications work properly.

The headquarters agents have a balanced configuration. The users at headquarters are accustomed to having some level of control over their systems. Also, the users at headquarters are more computer literate, so they have some chance of repairing a machine that is infected. The store employees cannot be expected to repair their systems.

In either case, the primary goal of the configuration is to stop viruses, worms, Trojans, spyware, and adware. The agents use the Internet to automatically update any signatures they have. Once the agents are deployed, the consultant will come by periodically to make any needed configuration changes and to verify that the goal of reducing malware by 99 percent has been achieved.

NIPS Implementation

Because of the limiting factor that the IPS operates without supervision, Jones Hardware did not consider deploying a NIPS solution. A NIPS solution would require at least minimal resources to configure and manage the system on an ongoing basis.

Home Office

Alice Smith has been in marketing for 15 years. Two years ago, she decided she wanted to spend more time with her two children. She left her high-level corporate marketing job to start a freelance business at home. Now, she has hundreds of clients that pay her to give them marketing advice and create deliverables like marketing plans, product collateral, and launch campaigns.

Some of her clients were referred to her, but the vast majority found her through the Internet. Alice is fairly computer literate, so when she started her business, she hired a web designer to make her a really slick web site. The site has attracted lots of clients, and she pays the web designer to update it periodically.

The Internet is more than just an advertising tool for Alice. It is the primary way she communicates with her customers. The Internet is an inexpensive and reliable way to exchange ideas, deliver product, and conduct research for her clients.

Lately, she's had some trouble with her computer and Internet connection. It's the kids. She lets them use the computer at night because they have educational games they like and they enjoy web surfing. The problem is that the kids accidentally infect her computer with spyware and viruses.

The infections are bad enough by themselves, but they are made worse because of the following:

- She has had calls from clients complaining that the documents and e-mails she sends them contain viruses.

- Her Internet service provider (ISP) disconnects her from the Internet when they detect virus traffic from her computer. She really likes her ISP because they are very reliable. One of the ways they stay reliable is to disconnect infected users so that they don't infect other users. Unfortunately, she's been disconnected once or twice when she really had to get a deliverable to a client.

- To get the ISP to restore her connection, she has to open a trouble ticket with them. They let her connect to a remediation server that has tools she can use to clean her system. Also, the remediation server has patches that the ISP requires her to apply before they restore her connection.

One of the ISP technicians suggested that HIPS might help her avoid viruses and spyware.

Limiting Factors

The only limiting factor for Alice is that she wants to make sure her children can continue to use the computer at night. They really enjoy it. Plus, it's good for them to have lots of experience with computers.

Security Policy Goals

Alice doesn't have a security policy because she's a one-person company. She does have a few goals for the IPS:

■   Prevent the kids from accidentally deleting client data.

■   Not allow the children to harm any of the programs she uses for work.

■   Stop malware from infecting her machine so that the ISP doesn't cut her off.

HIPS Implementation

The ISP technician that introduced the idea of the HIPS sent Alice a short list of Internet sites related to HIPS. As she read about the capabilities of different products, she kept a running list of her requirements for:

■   Management architecture

■   Agent configuration

Management Architecture

Alice has only one computer, so she cannot use a HIPS product that requires a dedicated management server. Also, she doesn't really want to install a big management package on her existing computer. The best option for her is a product that is designed for the home or small business user. It should be easy to use, have a local user interface for configuration changes, and have useful documentation.

Agent Configuration

Only a handful of HIPS products met Alice's management requirements. Of that handful, only two could do the other things she wanted:

■   The product has to support user-based state conditions. When the kids are logged on to her computer, the user interface should be hidden so that the kids can't turn off the tool. When Alice is logged on, she has to be able to access the HIPS user interface.

- She needs a tool that can prevent read and write operations to the directories where the client data is stored. This policy should be enforced only when the children are using the computer.

- Alice is not a computer expert, so she wants a product that doesn't require much configuration. It should automatically update its configuration as needed via the Internet.

Eventually, Alice found a product that met her needs, bought it, and installed it. After a brief struggle with the user-based configuration, she was able to get it to work the way she wanted. The kids could still use the computer, but it was protected.

NIPS Implementation

Alice did not even consider a NIPS because the website that the technician pointed her to focused solely on HIPS. Because of the limited size of the network, however, an NIPS would not be practical anyway.

Summary

Every IPS deployment is different, and the characteristics of the company doing the deployment account for many of the differences. This chapter examined IPS deployments six different types of company:

- Large enterprise

- Branch office

- Medium financial enterprise

- Medium educational institution

- Small office

- Home office

Each section covered five deployment-related topics:

- The company background and recent computer security incidents

- The factors that limit the IPS project

- The goals for the project that are derived from the problems to solve and the corporate security policy

- High-level HIPS implementation planning

- High-level NIPS implementation planning

Large Enterprise

- **Company background**—Premium airlines had a hard time with the Slammer worm. It initially infected a computer at headquarters, and then spread to the airports. The damage was extensive. Premium decided to implement IPS in an effort to prevent another incident like the Slammer worm.

- **Limiting factors**—Premium classifies a HIPS as an emerging technology because it has not been running at the airline for more than a year. Premium's policy does not allow emerging technologies to be deployed at airports. Also, the security policy does not allow users to disable host security countermeasures.

- **Security policy goals**—Premium wanted to increase malware protection on headquarters hosts, isolate airport systems from headquarters hosts, and implement an easier way to identify the source of a host-based attack.

- **HIPS implementation**—Premium airlines decided to put the HIPS on all of the headquarters hosts, starting with any that connect to airports. The tiered management server is to be located in the Tulsa office. The HIPS agent is to be configured to meet the goals for the project.

- **NIPS implementation**— Premium decided to take full advantage of its NIP capabilities to perform in-line monitoring for traffic entering the major network segments at the headquarters facility. It also added in-line monitoring (at the headquarters facility) for all of the airport locations. The IPS management is performed at the headquarters facility using the existing out-of-band management network, but required the addition of three new security analysts.

Branch Office

- **Company background**—The SafetyNet Insurance branch office in Charlotte, North Carolina, decided to invest in IPS for several reasons. First, when it gets infected by a virus, SafetyNet headquarters drops the VPN connection it uses to process paperwork. Also, employees accidentally install spyware and adware on the office computers. Finally, an agent left to work for another company and took the office client list with her. It'd like to make it harder for employees to steal the client list.

- **Limiting factors**—All of the office computers must run virus protection at all times. The virus protection must be kept up to date. The branch office is not allowed to modify the Internet router or VPN configuration.

- **Security policy goals**—Make it harder for employees to steal valuable information. Reduce the costs associated with removing spyware and adware. Cut down on the number of times headquarters drops the VPN because of a virus-infected host.

- **HIPS implementation**—HIPS is installed on all hosts and managed by a managed security service provider. The agents are configured to protect the hosts from malware and protect the customer database.

- **NIPS implementation**—An in-line sensor is installed between the router that provides the VPN connection to the SafetyNet headquarters. The branch anticipates minimal management of its single sensor so it hires a consultant to initially configure its NIPS and update the configuration quarterly. It plans to use a MSSP to monitor its IPS deployment (instead of performing that function themselves).

Medium Financial Enterprise

- **Company background**—BLI Bank is a regional bank with 25 branches and an investment group. BLI must comply with several new sets of government computer security regulations. The staff believes that IPS can help fulfill the requirements in the regulations.

- **Limiting factors**—The bank has limited IT resources. Also, the investment and branch operations are regulated differently.

- **Security policy goals**—Employ a neutral company to conduct tests to make sure that BLI's security countermeasures are working. All login failures and successes must be logged. All access of the mainframe and SQL databases must be tracked. Transactional network traffic must be kept separated from employee traffic.

- **HIPS implementation**—All hosts have HIPS installed, and they are managed by a single management server. The agents are configured to log login failures and success. They also keep track of which IP addresses connect to the SQL database.

- **NIPS implementation**—BLI Bank's main concern is the mixing of traffic between the bank's branch operations and its investment operations. It installs an in-line sensor between the investment group's network and configures it to prevent cross traffic between the branch operation transactions and the investment group. It also installs an in-line sensor to monitor traffic at its Internet perimeter. Initially, a consultant configures its IPS with the normal IT staff maintaining the IPS after that.

Medium Educational Institution

- **Company background**—Davis State is a liberal arts school in Pittsburgh, Pennsylvania. The school has two problems. The first is that the major donors and alumni are concerned that Davis State is not adequately protecting the students' confidential information. The second is that prolific unauthorized applications are using too much of the school's Internet bandwidth.

- **Limiting factors**—The school takes a permissive approach to computer security. It believes that computer security should, for the most part, not curtail information exchange. The students and faculty have complete control over their systems.

- **Security policy goals**—The school doesn't have a policy per se, but does have a list of guidelines. The guidelines were modified to encourage security for student data and the ability to restrict the use of certain types of applications.

- **HIPS implementation**—The Davis State IT department cannot force students or faculty to install the HIPS, so it is installed only on the hosts IT controls. The agents are managed by a single management server and configured to secure student data.

- **NIPS implementation**— Davis State University deploys in-line IPS to protect the administration VLAN (which includes the faculty) and the server VLAN. The student network is monitored promiscuously only to watch for attack traffic. Davis State's IT department configures its few IPS sensors individually and monitors them for attacks.

Small Office

- **Company background**—Jones Hardware of San Antonio, Texas, is a family-owned chain of hardware stores. The company has a few desktops at each store and a headquarters with ten desktops and one Windows server. The store computers are very important because they are used for point of sale, inventory schedules, and payroll. Unfortunately, the store computers are frequently down because of malware.

- **Limiting factors**—The IPS has to operate without any supervision of any kind, because Jones Hardware cannot afford to hire IT personnel.

- **Security policy goals**—Jones Hardware does not have a security policy. It did set a goal to reduce the malware infections by 99 percent.

- **HIPS implementation**—HIPS agents go on all of company machines. The agents are to be unmanaged and configured to implement a balanced security policy.

- **NIPS implementation**—Because the IPS must operate without supervision, Jones Hardware did not consider deploying a NIPS solution.

Home Office

- **Company background**—Alice Smith is a freelance marketing consultant who works from home. The Internet is one of the primary ways she communicates with her clients. Lately, she's had some trouble with her connection because her kids accidentally infect the computer with malware. When the system is infected, it sometimes tries to infect her clients and causes her ISP to disconnect her Internet connection.

- **Limiting factors**—Alice wants to make sure her children can use the computer at night.

- **Security policy goals**—Alice's goals for the project were to prevent the kids from accidentally deleting client data, harming any of the programs she uses for work, and installing malware.

- **HIPS implementation**—Alice installed an unmanaged HIPS agent on her computer. The agent is configured to hide the HIPS interface and protect client data when the kids are logged onto the computer.

- **NIPS implementation**— Alice did not even consider NIPS because the website that the technician pointed her to focused solely on HIPS. Because of the limited size of the network, however, NIPS would not be practical anyway.

Part V: Appendix

Appendix A   Sample Request for Information (RFI) Questions

Sample Request for Information (RFI) Questions

Requests for Information (RFI) is a document that some companies use to learn more about a product or solution. The information in the RFI helps them select a product that best fits their needs. This appendix contains a list of sample questions you can use if you are preparing an RFI for Intrusion Prevention products. It contains the following sections:

- **Solution**—Covers, at a high level, the solution the vendor proposes, the components of the solution, how they work together, and so on.

- **Support**—Inquires about the support offerings available for the solution.

- **Training**—Discusses any training that might be available for the solution.

- **Licensing**—Examines how the solution is sold.

- **Network Intrusion Prevention**—Goes into depth about the proposed Network Intrusion Prevention product. It covers the way it works, its management, operational considerations, and compatibility with other products.

- **Host Intrusion Prevention**— Goes into depth about the proposed Host Intrusion Prevention product. It covers the way it works, its management, operational considerations, and compatibility with other products.

Solution

1. Describe the proposed solution at a high level, using diagrams if necessary.

2. List the key benefits if your solution.

3. Explain the attributes of your solution that differentiate it from others.

4. List the components that make up the proposed solution.

5. Is there a common management platform for the entire solution or does each component have its own management?

6. Give the version number for each component that is part of the solution.

7. For each component of the solution, list the release date for the proposed version.

Support

1. What documentation is provided with the solution?

2. What support levels does your company offer (such as 24x7)?

3. How can we contact your support organization (phone, e-mail, and so on)?

4. Does your organization have international support capabilities?

5. How quickly should we expect a response to a new support case?

6. What other support services are offered?

7. If your solution requires signature/policy updates, how frequently are updates issued?

8. What is the price for your support offerings?

9. Do you offer software/hardware maintenance? If so, what is included?

10. How will we be notified if a product is at the end of support or end of life?

11. Does your solution have any certifications (Microsoft, ICSA, and so on)?

Training

1. Do you provide training for the solution?

2. If so, what delivery methods are available (instructor-led, online, and so on)?

3. Who delivers the training?

4. What is the price for your training?

Licensing

1. Do you sell the solution directly or do your partners sell it?

2. What is the licensing model (subscription, perpetual, and so on)?

3. What does your solution cost?

4. What, if any, purchase/lease options do you offer?

5. How is licensing enforced?

Network Intrusion Prevention

1. Describe the Network Intrusion Prevention System (NIPS) product at a high level.

2. Is the Network Intrusion Prevention portion of the solution implemented as hardware, software, or both?

   3. What software platforms are supported?

   4. What hardware platforms do you offer?

Functionality

   1. Describe the attack detection techniques your product uses.

   2. Does the product use stateful analysis? If so, describe its use.

   3. What network protocols can be analyzed?

   4. What application protocols can be analyzed?

   5. Can your product operate in both inline and passive mode?

   6. If malicious traffic is detected, what response capabilities does your product have (log, drop packet, and so on)?

   7. How is fragmented traffic handled?

   8. Does the NIPS have any remediation capabilities? If so, describe them.

   9. False positives are an issue for most NIPS products. If we encounter false positives with your products, how do we tune them?

   10. Is there a tuning, learning, or testing mode?

   11. What is the inline throughput and latency for your products?

   12. What is the detection-only throughput and latency for your products?

   13. What information do logged events contain?

   14. Can event severity be modified?

   15. What types of signatures/policies are used (atomic, stateful, and so on)?

   16. What triggering mechanisms does your product use (pattern detection, anomaly-based, behavior-based, and so on)?

   17. Can signatures/policies be applied to specific categories of traffic (VLAN, subnet, IP address)?

   18. Can policies/signatures be customized or created?

   19. Does the product have any application-specific signatures/policies? If so, what applications are included?

   20. What self-defense capabilities does the product have?

   21. Does your product have the capability to detect or stop known attacks? How?

22. Does your product have the capability to detect or stop unknown attacks? How?

23. Does your product have the capability to detect or stop network worms? How?

24. Does your product have the capability to detect or stop Trojans? How?

25. Does your product have the capability to detect or stop spyware? How?

26. Does your product have the capability to detect or stop adware? How?

27. Does your product have the capability to detect or stop viruses? How?

28. Does your product have the capability to detect or stop traditional hacking attempts? How?

29. Does your product have the capability to detect or stop encrypted attacks? How?

30. Does your product have the ability to control bandwidth utilization? How?

31. Does your product have the ability to enforce acceptable use policies (peer-to-peer file sharing, pornography, and so on)?

32. Does your product have the ability to enforce security policies (confidentiality of data and so on)?

33. Can your product isolate malicious traffic/hosts?

34. Can your product overcome evasion techniques? How?

35. Are languages other than English supported? If so, describe the level of support and list the languages.

36. If the product fails, does it fail open or closed?

37. Please describe the current roadmap for future product releases.

Management

1. Is the product centrally managed?

2. Describe the management infrastructure.

3. Does the management solution have a database component? If so, what type of database?

4. What architectural options are supported (single-server, tiered, hierarchical)?

5. How many devices can each architecture (single-server, tiered, hierarchical) support?

6. Describe the high availability and failover capabilities of the management solution.

7. How do administrators access the management interface?

8. How are administrators authenticated?

9. How is administrator-to-management communication secured?

10. Is there an audit trail? If so, describe it.

11. Is role-based administration supported?

12. How many events can one management server store?

13. How many events per second can one management server handle?

14. What are the bandwidth requirements? Describe the communication protocols between the managed devices and the management server.

15. How does management avoid denial-of-service because of event flooding?

16. Can a policy/signature be backed out?

17. What capabilities does the management offer for signature/policy testing before they are deployed?

18. Describe any centralized notification/alerting capabilities.

19. Are events collected in real time?

20. Are alerts delivered in real time?

21. How can alerts be delivered (e-mail, SNMP, and so on)?

22. How is device-to-management communication secured?

23. How is the management infrastructure itself secured?

24. If your product requires updates, how are the updates distributed? Is it automatic?

25. How are configuration changes distributed?

26. Are languages other than English supported? If so, list them.

27. Can logs be exported?

28. Describe any capability to group managed devices.

29. Does the management solution provide detailed status of the devices it manages?

30. What happens if the management solution fails?

Operations

1. Describe any reporting capabilities the product might have.

2. Can custom reports be created?

3. Describe any backup capabilities the product might have.

4. Describe any restore capabilities the product might have.

5. Describe any automatic log archival capabilities the product might have.

Compatibility

1. What operating systems are supported for the management infrastructure?

2. Is the product compatible with asset management solutions? If so, list them.

3. Is the product compatible with any event collection/correlation solutions? If so, list them.

4. Is the product compatible with any third-party management solutions? If so, list them.

Host Intrusion Prevention

1. Describe the Host Intrusion Prevention System (HIPS) product at a high level.

2. Is the Host Intrusion Prevention portion of the solution implemented as hardware, software, or both?

Functionality

1. Describe the attack detection techniques your product uses.

2. Does the product use stateful analysis? If so, describe its use.

3. If malicious activity is detected, what response capabilities does your product have (allow, deny, and so on)?

4. What host resources are analyzed (network, memory, file, registry, and so on)?

5. How is data gathered (system call interception, kernel modification, network traffic interception, and so on)?

6. Does the product conduct packet inspection? If so, describe how.

7. Does the HIPS have any remediation capabilities? If so, describe them.

8. False positives are an issue for most HIPS products. If we encounter false positives with your products, how do we tune them?

9. Is there a tuning, learning, or testing mode?

10. Describe the impact your product has on host performance (processor usage, memory usage, latency, and so on).

11. What information do logged events contain?

12. Can event severity be modified?

13. What types of signatures/policies are used (atomic, stateful, and so on)?

14. What triggering mechanisms does your product use (pattern detection, anomaly-based, behavior-based, and so on)?

15. Can signatures/policies be customized or created?

16. Does the product have any application-specific signatures/policies? If so, what applications are included?

17. What self-defense capabilities does the product have?

18. Does your product have the capability to detect or stop known attacks? How?

19. Does your product have the capability to detect or stop unknown attacks? How?

20. Does your product have the capability to detect or stop network worms? How?

21. Does your product have the capability to detect or stop Trojans? How?

22. Does your product have the capability to detect or stop spyware? How?

23. Does your product have the capability to detect or stop adware? How?

24. Does your product have the capability to detect or stop viruses? How?

25. Does your product have the capability to detect or stop traditional hacking attempts? How?

26. Does your product have the capability to detect or stop encrypted attacks? How?

27. Does your product have the ability to control bandwidth utilization? How?

28. Does your product have the ability to enforce acceptable use policies (peer-to-peer file sharing, pornography, and so on)?

29. Does your product have the ability to enforce security policies (confidentiality of data and so on)?

30. Can your product isolate malicious traffic/hosts?

31. Can your product overcome evasion techniques? How?

32. How are configuration changes distributed?

33. Are languages other than English supported? If so, describe the level of support and list the languages.

34. If the product fails, does it fail open or closed?

35. What happens to the HIPS if the management solution fails?

36. If the host is offline, what happens to the HIPS? Are events cached?

37. Can host software be hidden from the end user?

38. Does the HIPS display any messages to the end user? If so, describe them.

39. Does the installation require a reboot?

40. Do signature/policy/engine updates require a reboot?

41. What format does the HIPS installation package use (InstallShield, MSI, and so on)?

42. What software distribution mechanisms can be used to distribute the HIPS (Microsoft Systems Management Server, Radia, Altiris, CD, e-mail, and so on)?

43. Are administrative rights required for install?

44. Does the product have an unattended silent install capability?

45. Does the product support user-based profiles? If so, describe how they work.

46. Does the product support location-based profiles? If so, describe how they work.

47. Please describe the current roadmap for future product releases.

Management

1. Is the product centrally managed?

2. Describe the management interface.

3. Does the management solution have a database component? If so, what type of database?

4. What architectural options are supported (single-server, tiered, hierarchical)?

5. How many hosts can each architecture (single-server, tiered, hierarchical) support?

6. Describe the high availability and failover capabilities of the management solution.

7. How do administrators access the management interface?

8. How are administrators authenticated?

9. How is administrator-to-management communication secured?

10. Is there an audit trail? If so, describe it.

11. Is role-based administration supported?

12. How many events can one management server store?

13. How many events per second can one management server handle?

14. What are the bandwidth requirements? Describe the communication protocols between the managed hosts and the management server.

15. How does management avoid denial-of-service because of event flooding?

16. Can a policy/signature be backed out?

17. What capabilities does the management offer for signature/policy testing before they are deployed?

18. Does the management solution provide a detailed status of the hosts it manages? If so, describe the details that are provided.

19. Describe any centralized notification/alerting capabilities.

20. Are events collected in real time?

21. Are alerts delivered in real time?

22. How can alerts be delivered (e-mail, SNMP, and so on)?

23. How is device-to-management communication secured?

24. How is the management infrastructure itself secured?

25. If your product requires updates, how are the updates distributed? Is it automatic?

26. How are configuration changes distributed?

27. Are languages other than English supported? If so, list them.

28. Can logs be exported?

29. Describe any capability to group managed hosts.

30. Does the management solution provide detailed status of the devices it manages?

31. What happens if the management solution fails?

32. Can logs be exported?

Operations

1. Describe any reporting capabilities the product might have.

2. Can custom reports be created?

3. Describe any backup capabilities the product might have.

4. Describe any restore capabilities the product might have.

5. Describe any automatic log archival capabilities the product might have.

Compatibility

1. What operating systems are supported for the management infrastructure?

2. What operating systems are supported for the HIPS software?

3. Is the product compatible with asset management solutions? If so, list them.

4. Is the product compatible with any event collection/correlation solutions? If so, list them.

5. Is the product compatible with any third-party management solutions? If so, list them.

6. Does the product support any directory services (Active Directory, Lightweight Directory Access Protocol, Novell eDirectory, and so on)? If so, describe the support.

access control list (ACL)   A method that limits the use of a resource to authorized entities.

Address Resolution Protocol (ARP)   A protocol that translates IP addresses to physical Ethernet addresses.

aggregation switch   A switch that you use to combine multiple traffic flows into a single flow. This single traffic flow can then be analyzed by your intrusion devices running in promiscuous mode. An aggregation switch is commonly used in conjunction with a network tap.

anomaly signature   A signature that triggers when a defined normal level is exceeded (for example, exceeding a defined amount of Internet Control Message Protocol [ICMP] traffic on the network).

atomic signature   A signature that triggers on the contents of a single packet or event. The entire attack signature for an atomic signature occurs in a single packet or event and does not require an Intrusion Detection System (IDS)/Intrusion Prevention System (IPS) to maintain state.

authentication   The verification of a person's or process' identity.

behavior-based signature   A signature that triggers on traffic that deviates from what is considered normal (for example, an e-mail application invoking the command.com executable).

block signature action   Involves an IDS/IPS device that initiates an ACL on another device to block offending traffic.

buffer   A portion of computer memory that temporarily stores data.

Cisco Security Agent (CSA)   A software agent that runs on a host and prevents attacks against the host from malicious applications.

client-server architecture   An architecture in which multiple client system access applications run on a single server system.

content-addressable memory (CAM) table   Maintains a mapping between Ethernet MAC addresses and the switch port on which that traffic was observed.

day zero attack   Attacks that appear in the wild before the vulnerability being exploited is published.

demilitarized zone (DMZ)   A network that is partially protected by a firewall but still provides access to the protected systems from external systems.

denial-of-service (DoS)   A situation in which the goal of the attack is to prevent regular users from accessing a specific resource or application.

distributed denial-of-service (DDoS)   Results when thousands of zombie systems are targeted at a single system or network.

drop signature action   Occurs when an inline sensor drops network traffic (after analyzing it) because it does not forward the traffic that it receives on one of its interfaces.

encryption   Process whereby data is coded so that unauthorized people or processes cannot understand it.

EtherChannel   A functionality that some Cisco switches provide that enables you to configure multiple trunk lines to be members of the same VLAN so that traffic can be load balanced across the multiple trunk lines.

event correlation   Means you develop a complete picture of all the events or attacks that occur on the network (based on time, location, and so on).

event horizon   The maximum amount of time over which you can successfully detect an attack signature.

exploit   A piece of software that takes advantage of a system vulnerability. The result of an exploit can include a DoS, a system compromise, or the theft of data.

false negative   A situation in which an intrusion system fails to generate an alert or alarm after processing attack traffic that it is configured to detect.

false positive   A situation in which an intrusion system generates an alert or alarm after processing normal user traffic.

firewall   A security device that is designed to limit or restrict access to a protected network.

forwarding device   Receives packets on one of its ports and then passes that traffic to another one of its ports based on the destination Ethernet address of the packet (without modifying the packet).

Host Intrusion Prevention (HIP)   Software that runs on computer systems to protect the system. It analyzes activity on the system and prevents attacks from succeeding.

hub   A simple link-layer device. Whenever a device connected to the hub generates network packets, the hub passes that traffic to all the other ports on the hub.

Hypertext Transfer Protocol (HTTP)   A communication protocol that enables a computer to retrieve information across the web from web servers.

incident response   The procedure that you follow when you detect an attack against your network or the compromise of a machine on your network.

inline monitoring   Occurs when you place an IPS sensor as a forwarding device on your network. Because the inline sensor forwards network traffic, it has the ability to drop unwanted traffic that enters or leaves the network.

Internet   The global network that connects millions of computers.

Internet Protocol address (IP address)   An identifier for a computer or device on a TCP/IP network.

Intrusion Detection System   An intrusion monitoring system that passively monitors network traffic looking for malicious activity.

Intrusion Prevention System (IPS)   An intrusion monitoring system that examines network traffic while it acts as a forwarding device for that traffic.

IPS Device Manager (IDM)   A graphical interface that enables you to configure and monitor the operating characteristics of a single Cisco IPS sensor.

kernel   The fundamental part of an operating system that performs basic functions.

keylogger   A hardware device (or software application) that captures the keystrokes that are typed on a system.

log signature action   When a signature fires, the log signature action causes the IPS sensor to record the packets that the attacker generates on the network. The amount of information collected is usually based on either a specified length of time or a specified number of bytes.

malicious code   A piece of code designed to damage a system's availability, integrity, or confidentiality.

managed device   The device that receives and applies the ACL that is generated by a Cisco IPS sensor. The ACL is typically generated in response to signatures configured with the block action.

master blocking sensor   A sensor that controls and initiates the blocking requests for a specific network device.

Microsoft Component Object Model (COM)   A model that defines how objects interact within an application or between applications.

Network Intrusion Prevention (NIP)   Software and hardware that runs on your network. It analyzes network traffic and prevents attacks from damaging the network.

network tap   A device that enables you to split a full duplex connection into two separate traffic flows (each flow representing the traffic originating from one of the two devices).

Network Time Protocol (NTP)   (Refer to RFC 1305); defines a network protocol that enables client systems to synchronize their system clocks by contacting a server system.

normalizing traffic   Involves manipulating the traffic (such as a TCP stream) to prevent or remove anomalies such as out of order packets and malformed Time to Lives (TTLs).

one-time password   A password that is generated for the user that uses a smartcard. It is valid only for a single login and a limited time.

Open Systems Interconnection (OSI) model   A framework of protocols used to facilitate the communication between computers.

out-of-band management   Occurs when you use a network that is dedicated solely to management access (as opposed to using the regular network).

passive monitoring   Occurs when you capture a copy of all the traffic going across a network and analyze the traffic for intrusive activity.

pattern-based signature   A signature that triggers based on a specific pattern (such as a text string or sequence of binary bytes).

peer-to-peer architecture   An architecture in which applications reside on every system, which enables any two systems to interact with each other.

perimeter firewall   The firewall that you use to protect your entire network from the Internet.

personal digital assistant (PDA)   A handheld device that combines computing and possibly networking functionality.

personal firewall   Refers to restrictions that you place on your computer to prevent specific network traffic from accessing your system.

port   An interface through which data passes.

promiscuous monitoring   *See* passive monitoring.

pull model   An architecture in which the management system retrieves events from an IPS device when it is ready to process them.

push model   An architecture in which events are transmitted from an IPS device to the management system when it the IPS device generates them.

regular expression (regex)   A pattern matching language that enables you to define a flexible search pattern.

remote procedure call (RPC) protocol   Enables one system to run applications on another system across the network.

Remote Switch Port Analyzer (RSPAN)   A mechanism provided on some Cisco switches that enables you to capture network traffic from different devices connected to multiple switches.

rootkit   A collection of tools that an attacker installs on a system to enable him to covertly gain access to the system and monitor its operation.

Secure Shell (SSH)   A secure encrypted protocol that you can use to gain command-line access to systems on your network.

Security Monitor   A graphical interface that enables you to monitor and correlate events from many Cisco IPS devices on your network.

security policy   A set of rules that define the security requirements for a network.

signature   Any distinctive characteristic that identifies something (such as a type of attack).

signature action   Refers to the actions that your IPS/IDS devices and software perform after a signature triggers.

signature trigger   The mechanism that IPS software uses to identify malicious or unwanted traffic.

software bypass   A software mechanism by which an inline sensor handles traffic when its IPS analysis engine is not operating.

spam   Unsolicited electronic messages. Usually, these messages are sent in bulk to many people at the same time (known as spamming). Although various electronic media are subject to spam, the most popular media used to transport spam is e-mail.

stateful signature   A signature that requires analyzing multiple packets or events to identify intrusive behavior. To track the multiple events, the IPS must maintain information about the events/actions that it has already observed.

Structured Query Language (SQL)   A popular relational database query language.

switch   A link-layer device that selectively passes traffic to its ports based on the contents of its CAM table.

Switched Port Analyzer (SPAN)   A mechanism supported on Cisco switches that enables you to configure the switch to capture a copy of selected traffic and pass it to a configured destination port for analysis.

TCP Reset Signature Action   Tries to reset a specific TCP connection when malicious traffic is identified in the TCP connection.

Transmission Control Protocol (TCP)   A connection-oriented protocol that begins with a three-way handshake and ensures reliable delivery of data.

triggering mechanism   Refers to the conditions that cause an intrusion system to generate a signature action.

Trojan   A program that performs an external function and then secretly performs another function in the background. The secret function is often malicious.

unicode   A character encoding standard that is designed to provide a universal way to encode characters of any language.

User Datagram Protocol (UDP)   A connectionless protocol that requires little overhead but does ensure reliable delivery of data.

virtual local-area network (VLAN)   A group of devices on one or more LANs that are configured to appear as if they are on a single network.

virus   A malicious software program that usually requires user intervention to spread to other systems.

VLAN access control list (VACL)   A security feature (available on some Cisco switches) that enables you to use ACLs to redirect a copy of network traffic from multiple VLANs to a destination port for analysis.

vulnerability   A flaw or weakness in a computer system that an attacker can use to attack the system.

worm   A self-replicating computer program that impacts the operation of a system similar to a virus.

zombie system   A system that an attacker compromises (usually without the user's knowledge) and is used for various purposes (such as DDoS attacks and sending spam e-mail).

Index

Numerics

802.1x, 78

A

access control matrices, 124
access control process of HIPS endpoint agents
    consulting the security policy, 119–124
    determining system state, 115–116, 119
    gathering data operation, 110
    gathering operation data, 111–115
    identifying access resource, 102
    taking action, 124
ACLs (access control lists), 73
    block signature action, 47
ad hoc networking, 94
aggregation switches, 160
AIC (application inspection and control) signatures, 43
alarm summarization, 46
alarms
    event responses, 61
    false negatives, 59
    false positives, 59
    incident response plans, 66
    true negatives, 60
    true positives, 60
alerts, 45, 61
    false negatives, 59
    false positives, 59
    generating, 141
    risk ratings, 223
    true negatives, 60
    true positives, 60
allow signature action, 47

analyzing network traffic
    via anomaly operations, 165
    via atomic operations, 164
    via normalizing operations, 165–166
    via protocol decode operations, 165
    via stateful operations, 164–165
anomaly operation method of network traffic analysis, 165
anomaly-based detection, 42–43
anomaly-based security policies, 120
anonymous delivery mechanisms, 14
antivirus software, 23–24
    role in layered defense, 76
ARP (Address Resolution Protocol), 144
ARPANET, 9
atomic operation method of network traffic analysis, 164
atomic alerts, 45
atomic rule-based security policies, 121–122
atomic signatures, 34–35
    host-based, 35
    network-based, 35
attacks
    automated response, 26
    characteristics of, 12–13
    CIH virus, characteristics of, 19
    complexity of, 14–15
    event correlation, 65–66
    impact of, 16
    lifecycle of, 103
        application execution, 107
        file resources, 108
        memory resources, 105–107
        network resources, 104–105
        persistence process, 107–109
    Loveletter virus, characteristics of, 19–20

mitigating
   at host level, 23–25
   at network level, 25–26
Morris worm, characteristics of, 18
Nimda worm, characteristics of, 20–22
replacement login, example of, 17
signatures. *See* signatures
SQL Slammer worm, characteristics of, 21
authentication
802.1x, 78
role in layered defense, 79
Auto mode (software bypass), 63
automated response to attacks, 26
automatic blocking, 143–144
automatic summarization, 46

B

balanced systems, 186
behavioral security policies, 122–123
behavior-based detection, 44
benefits of IPSs, 137
HIPS
   acceptable use policy enforcement,
      95–96
   attack prevention, 92
   internal attack propagation
      prevention, 93
   patch relief, 92–93
   policy enforcement, 94–95
security policy enforcement, 138
traffic normalization, 138
"benevolent" worms, 16
blade-based sensors, 153–154
block response, 61
block signature action, 47

branch office IPS deployment, 236–237
HIPS implementation, 238
limiting factors, 237
NIPS implementation, 239–240
security policy goals, 237
buffer overflow vulnerabilities, 22
buffer overrun exploit, 105–107

C

cabling, sensors, 221
capabilities
of Cisco IPS network components, 211
of IPSs
   attack prevention, 27
   regulatory compliance, 27
capturing network traffic
devices for, 158–161
with IPSs, 154
   for Inline mode, 155–157
   for promiscuous mode, 157–158
with RSPAN, 162
with SPAN, 162
with VACLs, 164
characteristics
of attacks
   CIH virus, 19
   Loveletter virus, 19–20
   Morris worm, 18
   Nimda worm, 20–22
   replacement login attack, 17
   SQL Slammer worm, 21
of signatures, 34
Chernobyl, 19
child processes, 107
CIH virus, 19
Cisco Catalyst 6500 series IDSM-2, 206–207
Cisco IDS Network Module, 207

Cisco IOS IPS sensors, 208
Cisco IPS 4200 series appliance sensors, 206
classifying IPS hosts, 185–187
client-server architecture, 8
client-server computing, 7–9
clipboard, 109
collaboration between layers, 81–82
COM (Component Object Model), 109
communications, securing management
    communication, 66–68
comparing IPS and IDS functionality, 136
complexity of attacks, 14–15
conducting pilot tests, 194–196
configuration updates, 62
configuring
    policy groups, 191–193
    secondary policy groups, 192–193
    sensors, 221
corporate security policies, 79–80
    default policy configuration,
        customizing, 194
    reviewing, 212
correlation tools, 65–66
criteria for sensor selection
    form factor, 152–154
    interfaces, 151–152
    processing capacity, 150–151
CSA (Cisco Security Agent), 77
    phases of deployment, 177
        conducting pilot tests, 194–196
        finalizing the project, 198
        full deployment, 197–198
        implementing management, 189–194
        predeployment planning, 180–184
        selection and classification of target
            hosts, 184–188
        tuning, 196
        understanding the product, 178–179
CSA MC (CSA Management Center),
    organizational units, 190–191
CS-MARs (Cisco Security Monitoring,
    Analysis and Response System), 82
customizing default corporate security policy
    configuration, 194

D

day zero attacks, 77
default allow organizations, 214
default deny organizations, 214
defense-in-depth, 71
    corporate security policy, 79–80
    examples of, 72–79
defining goals of IPS deployment, 213–216
delivery mechanism of attacks, 13
deny response, 61
deploying IPSs
    at medium financial enterprises, 240
        HIPS implementation, 241–242
        limiting factors, 241
        NIPS implementation, 242–243
        security goals, 241
    at branch offices, 236–237
        HIPS implementation, 238
        limiting factors, 237
        NIPS implementation, 239–240
        security policy goals, 237
    at home office, 250
        HIPS implementation, 251–252
        limiting factors, 251
        NIPS implementation, 252
        security policy goals, 251
    at medium educational institutions, 243
        HIPS implementation, 245–246
        limiting factors, 244
        NIPS implementation, 246–247
        security policy goals, 245
    at small offices, 247
        HIPS implementation, 248–249
        limiting factors, 248
        NIPS implementation, 250
        security policy goals, 248
    host IPS, 53
        determining factors, 54–55
    network IPS, 55
        determining factors, 56–58
    on large enterprise, 229–230
        HIPS implementation, 231–233
        limiting factors, 231
        NIPS implementation, 233, 236
        security policy goals, 231
    sensors
        large deployments, 169
        small deployments, 168

deployment phases
    of CSA, 177
        conducting pilot tests, 194–196
        finalizing the project, 198
        full deployment, 197–198
        implementing management, 189–194
        predeployment planning, 180–184
        selection and classification of target
            hosts, 184–188
        tuning, 196
        understanding the product, 178–179
    of IPS, 204
        finalizing the project, 225
        predeployment planning, 212–220
        sensor deployment, 221–222
        tuning, 222–224
        understanding the product, 205–211
devices
    failure
        inline sensor failure, 62
        management console failure, 63–64
    intrinsic IPS, 80–81
device-to-device communication, securing, 68
directory traversal attacks, 40
DMZ firewall, role in layered defense, 75
drive-by spamming, 14
drop signature action, 46
dropping
    all packets from source IP address, 137
    all packets on connection, 137

E

encoding mechanisms, 40
encryption, role in layered defense, 78–79
endpoint agents, access control process, 101
    access resource, identifying, 102
    consulting the security policy, 119–124
    determining system state, 115–116, 119
    gathering operation data, 110–115
    taking action, 124
enforcing security policies, 138
EtherChannel, 63
event correlation, 65–66
event horizon, 36
events, 109

evolution of security threats, 6
    client-server computing, 7–9
    Internet, 9
    mobile computing, 10–11
    wireless connnectivity, 10
examples
    of attacks
        CIH virus, 19
        Loveletter virus, 19–20
        Morris worm, 18
        Nimda worm, 20–22
        replacement login, 17
        SQL Slammer worm, 21
    of effective defense-in-depth, 72
        external attack against corporate
            database, 72–77
        internal attacks against management
            servers, 77–79
exploits, 104

F

false negatives, 59
false positives, 59
finalizing CSA deployment, 198
firewalls, 6
flows, 164
form factor as sensor selection criteria,
    152–154
forwarding devices, 136
full CSA deployment, 197–198
future of IPS, intrinsic IPS, 80–81

G-H

generating alerts, 141
goals of IPS deployment
    defining, 213–216

HIDS (host-based intrusion detection
    systems), 25
hierarchical management model, 127
HIPS (host-based intrusion prevention
    systems), 89, 101
    benefits of
        acceptable use policy enforcement,
            95–96
        attack prevention, 92

internal attack propagation prevention, 93
patch relief, 92–93
policy enforcement, 94–95
endpoint agents, 101
access control process, 101–124
limitations of, acceptable use policy enforcement, 96–97
management infrastructure, 125
management center, 127–129
management interface, 129
required capabilities, 90–92
role in layered defense, 79
security policies
anomaly-based, 120
atomic-rule based, 121
behavioral, 122–123
home office IPS deployment, 250
HIPS implementation, 251–252
limiting factors, 251
NIPS implementation, 252
security policy goals, 251
Host IPS
deploying, 53–55
role in layered defense, 77
signature tuning, 59–60
host-based signatures
atomic, 35
stateful, 36
triggering mechanisms, 39
host-level attack mitigation, 23
antivirus, 23–24
HIDS, 25
personal firewalls, 24
hosts, classifying, 185–187
hubs, 158
hybrid IPS/IDS systems, 140, 145

I

IDSM-2 sensors, 207
impact of attack, 16
incident response plans, 66
individual management method, 65
information theft, 12
inline mode sensor operation, 208
capturing network traffic, 155, 157
sensor failure, 62

inline on a stick, 152
inline prevention, 26
insecure management protocol, 67
installing
IPS MC, 222
sensors, 221–222
integrated IPS software, 154
interfaces as sensor selection criteria, 151–152
Internet as security threat, 9
Internet perimeter firewall, role in layered defense, 74
Internet perimeter router, role in layered defense, 73
intrinsic IPS, 80–81
IP blocking, 143–146
IP logging, 142
IP spoofing, 144
IPSs
hosts, classifying, 185–187
integrated software, 154
network management options, 209–211
network traffic, capturing, 154–158
phases of deployment, 204
finalizing the project, 225
predeployment planning, 212–220
sensor deployment, 221–222
tuning, 222–224
understanding the product, 205–211
response methods
alerting actions, 166
blocking actions, 167
dropping actions, 167
logging actions, 167
sensors
Cisco Catalyst 6500 series IDSM-2, 206–207
Cisco IDS Network Module, 207
Cisco IOS IPS sensors, 208
Cisco IPS 4200 series appliance sensors, 206
Cisco product availability, 205
large deployments, 169
selecting location for placement, 216–218
small deployments, 168
signature updates, 212
IPS MC (IPS Management Center), installing, 222

K-L

kernel, 109
  modification, 111
  modules, 108

large enterprise IPS deployment, 229–230
  HIPS implementation, 231–233
  limiting factors, 231
  NIPS implementation, 233, 236
  security policy goals, 231
  sensor deployment, 169
layered defense. *See also* **defense-in-depth**
  against corporate database attacks,
    72–77
  against management server attacks,
    77–79
least privilege, 124
lifecycle of attacks, 103
  application execution, 107
  file resources, 108
  memory resources, 105, 107
  network resources, 104–105
  persistence process, 107, 109
limitations
  of IPS, 138–140, 145
  of HIPS, acceptable use policy enforcement,
    96–97
line cards, 153–154
location state conditions, 116
log response, 61
log signature action, 47
logging
  attacker traffic, 142
  traffic between attacker and victim, 143
  victim traffic, 142
Loveletter virus, 19–20

M

MAC (mandatory access control), 124
mainframes, 7
malicious mobile code, 103
malware, 232
management communication
  device-to-device, securing, 68
  OOB, securing, 67
  securing, 66
management console failure, 63–64

management infrastructure, 125
  management center, 125–129
  management interface, 129
management method, selecting, 65
manager-of-managers, 127
McAfee Entercept, 122
**medium educational institution IPS
  deployment, 243**
  HIPS implementation, 245–246
  limiting factors, 244
  NIPS implementation, 246–247
  security policy goals, 245
**medium financial enterprise IPS
  deployment, 240**
  HIPS implementation, 241–242
  limiting factors, 241
  NIPS implementation, 242–243
  security goals, 241
Microsoft Component Object Model, 109
mirroring traffic, 158
mitigating attacks
  at host level, 23
    antivirus, 23–24
    HIDS, 25
    personal firewalls, 24
  at network level, 25
    inline prevention, 26
    promiscuous monitoring, 25
    system log analysis, 25
mobile computing as security threat, 10–11
modems, 13
monitoring IPS activities, 64
Morris worm, 16, 18
Morris, Robert, 16

N

NetFlow, role in layered defense, 76
network adapters, 94
network flows, 164
network IPS
  deploying, 55
    determining factors, 56–58
  role in layered defense, 75, 78
  signature tuning, 59–60
network taps, 159

network traffic
    analyzing, 114
        via anomaly operations, 165
        via atomic operations, 164
        via normalizing operations, 165–166
        via protocol decode operations, 165
        via stateful operations, 164–165
    capturing, 154
        devices for, 158–161
        with inline mode IPS, 155–157
        with promiscuous mode IPS, 157–158
        with RSPAN, 162
        with SPAN, 162
        with VACLs, 164
network-based signatures
    atomic signatures, 35
    stateful signatures, 37
    triggering mechanisms, 39
network-level attack mitigation, 25
    inline prevention, 26
    promiscuous monitoring, 25
    system log analysis, 25
Nimda worm, 20–22
NIPS, selecting management architecture, 218–220
normalizing traffic, 138, 165–166
NTP (Network Time Protocol), 65

O

Off mode (software bypass), 63
On mode (software bypass), 63
OOB (out-of-band) management communication, securing, 67
operating systems
    events, 109
    kernel, 109–111
organizational units (CSA MC), 190–191
OSI reference model, 26
OTPs (one-time passwords), 79

P

parent processes, 107
passwords, OTPs, 79
pattern detection, 40–41
pattern matching, regular expressions, 40
pattern-based security policies, 122

PCs, zombies, 12
peer-to-peer networks, 9
permissive systems, 186
persistence process
    application execution, 107
    file modification, 108
    system configuration, 108
personal firewalls, 24
phases of deployment, 177
    for CSA
        conducting pilot tests, 194–196
        finalizing the project, 198
        full deployment, 197–198
        implementing management, 189–194
        predeployment planning, 180–184
        selection and classification of target
           hosts, 184–188
        tuning, 196
        understanding the product, 178–179
    for IPS, 204
        finalizing the project, 225
        predeployment planning, 212–218, 220
        sensor deployment, 221–222
        tuning, 222–224
        understanding the product, 205–211
pilot test, conducting, 194, 196
placing IPS sensors in network, 216–218
policy groups
    configuring, 191–193
    secondary groups, 192–193
port security, 78
PortMapper, 45
predeployment planning phase of IPS deployment, 212–220
processing capacity as sensor selection criteria, 150–151
promiscuous mode sensor operation, 25, 246
    capturing network traffic, 157–158
protocol decodes, 38, 165
Pull model (management console), 64
Push model (management console), 64

R

RBAC (role-based access control) matrix, 124
regular expressions, 40
regulatory compliance, 27

remote delivery mechanisms, 14

replacement login, example of, 17

required HIPS capabilities, 90–92

reset signature action, 47

resetting TCP connections, 143

responses to suspicious activity

    alerting actions, 166

    blocking actions, 167

    dropping actions, 167

    logging actions, 167

restrictive systems, 186

reviewing corporate security policies, 212

RFI (Request for Information), sample
    questions, 261–269

rootkit, 109, 119

RPC (Remote Procedure Call), 45

RRs (risk ratings), 223

RSPAN (Remote Switch Port Analyzer),
    capturing network traffic, 162

rule modules, 190

S

sample RFI questions, 261–269

sandbox, 113

scenarios for IPS deployment

    at branch offices, 236–240

    at home office, 250–252

    at large enterprises, 229–233, 236

    at medium educational institutions,
        243–247

    at medium financial enterprises, 240–243

    at small offices, 247–250

secondary policy groups, configuring,
    192–193

securing management communication, 66

    device-to-device, 68

    OOB, 67

security policies

    anomaly-based, 120

    atomic rule-based, 121–122

    behavioral, 122–123

    pattern-based, 122

selecting

    location for IPS sensor placement, 216–218

    management method, 65

    NIPS management architecture,
        218–220

sensors, criteria

    form factor, 152–154

    interfaces, 151–152

    processing capacity, 150–151

sensors

    alerts, risk ratings, 223

    Cisco Catalyst 6500 series IDSM-2,
        206–207

    Cisco IDS Network Module, 207

    Cisco IOS IPS sensors, 208

    Cisco IPS 4200 series appliance
        sensors, 206

    Cisco product availability, 205

    configuring, 221

    inline mode

        failure of, 62

        functionality, 208

    installing, 221–222

    large deployments, 169

    promiscuous mode, 246

    selection criteria

        form factor, 152–154

        interfaces, 151–152

        processing capacity, 150–151

    small deployments, 168

shared IPS/IDS capabilities, 145

    alert generation, 141

    initiating IP blocking, 143–144

    IP logging, 142

    logging attacker traffic, 142

    logging traffic between
        attacker and victim, 143

    logging victim traffic, 142

    resetting TCP connections, 143

shims, 111

signature updates, 212

signatures, 33

    alerts, 45

    allow signature action, 47

    atomic signatures, 34–35

        host-based, 35

        network-based, 35

    block signature action, 47

    cabling, 221

    characteristics of, 34

    drop signature action, 46

    event horizon, 36

    event responses, 61

    log signature action, 47

reset signature action, 47
stateful, 36
    host-based, 36
    network-based, 37
    with anomaly-based triggering
        mechanism, 43
triggering mechanisms, 37–39
    anomaly-based detection, 42–43
    behavior-based detection, 44
    pattern detection, 40–41
tuning, 59–60
single packets, dropping, 136
single-server management model, 127
small IPS sensor deployments, 168
small office IPS deployment, 247
    HIPS implementation, 248–249
    limiting factors, 248
    NIPS implementation, 250
    security policy goals, 248
social engineering, 105
software bypass, 63
software updates, 61
source IP addresses
    dropping all packets from, 137
    spoofing, 144
Spacefiller, 19
spam, 14
SPAN (Switch Port Analyzer), capturing
    network traffic, 162
spyware, 248
SQL Slammer worm, 230
stack memory, 106
standalone appliance sensors, 153
stateful operation method of network traffic
    analysis, 164–165
stateful signatures, 36
    host-based, 36
    network-based, 37
summary alerts, 46
suspicious activity, IPS response methods
    alerting actions, 166
    blocking actions, 167
    dropping actions, 167
    logging actions, 167
switch ports, role in layered defense, 78
switches, 136
    capturing network traffic, 160
symbolic links, 110
system call interception, 111–113

system log analysis, 25
system state conditions, 118–119

T

TCP connections
    resetting, 143
    three-way handshake, 74
TCP Reset interface, 207
TCP/IP, 10
threats to security, evolution of, 6
    client-server computing, 7, 9
    Internet, 9
    mobile computing, 10–11
    wireless connnectivity, 10
three-way handshake, 74
tiered management model, 127
traffic mirroring, 158
traffic flows, 164
traffic normalization, 138
triggers, 37–39
    anomaly-based detection, 42–43
    behavior-based detection, 44
    pattern detection, 40–41
Trojan horses, 19
    rootkits, 119
true negatives, 60
true positives, 60
tuning phase of CSA deployment, 196

U

uRPF (unicast reverse path forwarding), 73
user state conditions, 117

V

VACLs (VLAN access control lists), capturing
    network traffic, 164
virtual operating systems, 113
viruses, 18
    CIH virus, characteristics of, 19
    Loveletter virus, characteristics of, 19–20
vulnerabilities, 93, 104

W-X-Y-Z

war-dialers, 13
wireless connnectivity as security threat, 10
wireless network adapters, 94
worms, 19
     Nimda, characteristics of, 20–22
     SQL Slammer, characteristics of, 21

zombies, 12

THIS BOOK IS SAFARI ENABLED

INCLUDES FREE 45-DAY ACCESS TO THE ONLINE EDITION

The Safari® Enabled icon on the cover of your favorite technology book means the book is available through Safari Bookshelf. When you buy this book, you get free access to the online edition for 45 days.

Safari Bookshelf is an electronic reference library that lets you easily search thousands of technical books, find code samples, download chapters, and access technical information whenever and wherever you need it.

TO GAIN 45-DAY SAFARI ENABLED ACCESS TO THIS BOOK:

- Go to **http://www.ciscopress.com/safarienabled**

- Enter the ISBN of this book (shown on the back cover, above the bar code)

- Log in or Sign up (site membership is required to register your book)

- Enter the coupon code found in the front of this book before the "Contents at a Glance" page

If you have difficulty registering on Safari Bookshelf or accessing the online edition, please e-mail customer-service@safaribooksonline.com.

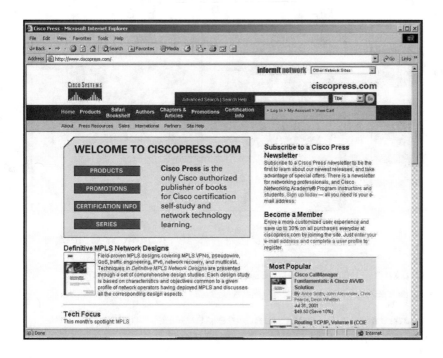
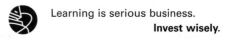

Cisco Press

3 STEPS TO LEARNING

STEP 1

First-Step

STEP 2

Fundamentals

STEP 3

**Networking
Technology Guides**

STEP 1   **First-Step**—Benefit from easy-to-grasp explanations.
No experience required!

STEP 2   **Fundamentals**—Understand the purpose, application,
and management of technology.

STEP 3   **Networking Technology Guides**—Gain the knowledge
to master the challenge of the network.

NETWORK BUSINESS SERIES

The Network Business series helps professionals tackle the
business issues surrounding the network. Whether you are a
seasoned IT professional or a business manager with minimal
technical expertise, this series will help you understand the
business case for technologies.

Justify Your Network Investment.

Look for Cisco Press titles at your favorite bookseller today.

Visit **www.ciscopress.com/series** for details on each of these book series.